The Philosophy of Hegel

Continental European Philosophy

This series provides accessible and stimulating introductions to the ideas of continental thinkers who have shaped the fundamentals of European philosophical thought. Powerful and radical, the ideas of these philosophers have often been contested, but they remain key to understanding current philosophical thinking as well as the current direction of disciplines such as political science, literary theory, social theory, art history, and cultural studies. Each book seeks to combine clarity with depth, introducing fresh insights and wider perspectives while also providing a comprehensive survey of each thinker's philosophical ideas.

Published titles

The Philosophy of Derrida
Mark Dooley and Liam Kavanagh

The Philosophy of Foucault
Todd May

The Philosophy of Gadamer
Jean Grondin

The Philosophy of Habermas
Andrew Edgar

The Philosophy of Hegel
Allen Speight

The Philosophy of Kierkegaard
George Pattison

The Philosophy of Merleau-Ponty
Eric Matthews

The Philosophy of Nietzsche
Rex Welshon

The Philosophy of Schopenhauer
Dale Jacquette

Forthcoming titles include

The Philosophy of Husserl
Burt Hopkins

The Philosophy of Kant
James O'Shea

The Philosophy of Sartre
Anthony Hatzimoysis

The Philosophy of Hegel

Allen Speight

McGill-Queen's University Press
Montreal & Kingston • Ithaca

ISBN 978-0-7735-3407-0 (bound)
ISBN 978-0-7735-3408-7 (pbk)

Legal deposit second quarter 2008
Bibliothèque nationale du Québec

Published simultaneously in the United Kingdom by Acumen Publishing Limited and in North America by McGill-Queen's University Press

Library and Archives Canada Cataloguing in Publication

Speight, Allen
The philosophy of Hegel / Allen Speight.

(Continental European philosophy)
Includes bibliographical references and index.
ISBN 978-0-7735-3407-0 (bound).—ISBN 978-0-7735-3408-7 (pbk.)

1. Hegel, Georg Wilhelm Friedrich, 1770–1831. I. Title. II. Series.

B2948.S64 2008 193 C2007-906829-4

Typeset by Graphicraft Limited, Hong Kong.
Printed and bound by Biddles Limited, King's Lynn.

Contents

Acknowledgements

For conversations that enriched this book, I am indebted to many friends and colleagues who share a philosophical interest in Hegel. I am grateful to Steven Gerrard for his encouragement of the project and to two anonymous readers for Acumen Publishing who offered helpful suggestions for improving both the style and content of the manuscript itself. I wish also to thank Margot Stevenson and Sarah Farkas, for their bibliographical and editorial assistance, and Hallie Speight, whose love and support I cannot sufficiently thank in print.

Abbreviations

Full bibliographical details of the works listed here are given in the Bibliography.

Aesthetics	*Aesthetics: Lectures on Fine Art*
Enc	*The Encyclopedia Logic*
LPEG	*Lectures on the Proof of the Existence of God*
LPR	*Lectures on the Philosophy of Religion*
PhS	*Phenomenology of Spirit*
PR	*Philosophy of Right*
PWH	*Lectures on the Philosophy of World History*
SL	*Science of Logic*

Introduction

Hegel is the first great philosopher to make *modernity* – in all its historical, cultural and philosophical complexity – his subject.[1] And on whatever lines that modernity is to be explored by our own present generation – as a project that has failed, is discernible only in traces, or that has come to fruition in some ways crucial for our practices and commitments – the Hegelian construal of it remains essential for coming to terms with how we understand ourselves, as agents in and contemplators of a world with a number of characteristics that Hegel was either the first or the most articulate in calling attention to. The sort of characteristics I have in mind are some rather resilient facets of a world that can be said to embrace both Hegel's day and our own, a world where the self and its awareness of its freedom is construed as an achievement, where the modern religious sense of a "death of God" has left a not entirely complete secularism and a seemingly irreducible plurality of religious perspectives in its wake, where the development of ethical and political institutions that "we" can in some sense be aware of "making" are nonetheless also subject to historical shifts and constraints, and where the realm of artistic expression has taken bold and inherently self-referential turns.

The account of modernity that Hegel opens up in these areas is, so I shall make the case, neither a triumphalist recognition and extension of Enlightenment values into the present time nor a philosophical act of mourning for the contradictions of a world that is in decline. Hegel's perspective – whether one looks at his ethics, politics, art, religion or philosophy – is one that is resolutely embracing of modernity *in* its oppositions, a stance that makes him neither Romantic, Enlightenment rationalist nor (I shall claim) any merely hybrid combination of the two.

To cast an introduction to Hegel's thought in terms of his interest in the problem of modernity is not immediately to take sides on what remains a contentious point at the moment among his most skilled and creative contemporary expositors. As will be discussed below, a long debate about whether Hegel should ultimately be construed as pushing forward an essentially Kantian intervention in modern philosophy or as rather closer in spirit to his earlier and more metaphysically minded predecessors such as Aristotle and Spinoza appears to be still very much alive. By focusing on Hegel as a philosopher of modernity, I do not mean to oppose the view of what I call below "traditionalist" readers, but only to emphasize that, even if Hegel's project is ultimately construed in important ways *as* metaphysical, this metaphysics cannot simply be a move *back* to a pre-critical stance, as though the Kantian revolution in thought never occurred. The question of precisely what sort of post-Kantian metaphysics Hegel might be engaged in, if he is, will no doubt be a point of focus in the years to come among Hegelian scholars. But even the most ardent traditionalist readers of Hegel's works will have to acknowledge that the stance Hegel takes more broadly towards the politics and culture of the world between 1807 and 1831 is one that (however metaphysically or non-metaphysically grounded) never allows the possibility that the modern world can *look back* in ethical and political, aesthetic or religious thought.

Hegel and Hegelianism

There is no dearth of books on Hegel, but the task of opening up his thought to a wider readership has perhaps never been more important than it is at the present moment. In the academic world, there has been much recent interest in the philosophical project associated with Hegel – and, at the same time, there are a number of notable attempts under way to reconstrue and even revise the meaning of Hegel's philosophical achievement. It is striking – particularly for a philosopher for whom history and philosophy have such crucial importance for one another – that the reawakened interest in work on Hegel represents one of the most seminal moments in the reappropriation of Hegel since his death in 1831. Put simply in world-historical terms, Hegel has seemed to be unusually of interest during large shifts in the tectonic plate of Western self-awareness.

Although Hegel has had significant interpreters quite consistently over the century and three-quarters since his death, there have been several previous moments in post-Hegelian history that have made distinctive philosophical contributions in their own right, going beyond the mere construal of Hegel to shape an intellectual *ethos* of a new and different sort. In the years between Hegel's death and the revolution of 1848, Hegel's immediate left- and right-wing followers (D. F. Strauss, Ludwig Feuerbach,

Bruno Bauer, Arnold Ruge) hotly disputed the meaning of his religious and political philosophy, setting the basis for a new generation of social theorists to emerge under Marx and Engels. A group of idealistically minded British thinkers (F. H. Bradley, T. H. Green, Bernard Bosanquet, William Wallace and others) took up Hegel in the later nineteenth century, establishing a philosophical environment that in many ways was the dialectical turning-point for the development of an opposing trend in twentieth-century analytic philosophy under Russell, Moore and others. In the ferment of the prewar Paris of the 1930s, a now-famous set of seminars by Alexandre Kojève drew a who's who of twentieth-century French intellectuals (Jacques Lacan, Maurice Merleau-Ponty, Georges Bataille, Raymond Aron) to the study of Hegel, setting up what was to be a distinctly critical stance towards Hegel in general in postwar French philosophy. Likewise, members of the Frankfurt School of critical social theorists (Theodor Adorno, Herbert Marcuse and Jürgen Habermas) were among many thinkers attempting to see what resources there were in Marx's great predecessor for making sense of the emerging cold war world. In a quite different vein, there was a sudden appeal (by Francis Fukuyama and others) in the years during and after the collapse of the Soviet empire to Hegel's notion of the "end of history". Although few serious scholars of Hegel today would endorse anything quite like Fukuyama's view of a Hegelian "end" of history, the importance of Hegel for any effort to reconstrue the scrambled conception of the political and "spiritual" world that lies in the shadow of the events of 1989 and 2001 cannot be overestimated.

Hegel in contemporary philosophy

In the contemporary philosophical context, there has been on the one hand an unusually active re-engagement on the part of scholars in the history of philosophy with the milieu from which Hegel's philosophy arose. The period that gave birth to German Idealism has been the subject of a wide range of new studies that have made it important to revise the conventional account of the developmental story of the crucial decade of the 1790s and in particular of the relation between German Idealism and early German Romanticism.[2] On the other hand, analytic philosophers have taken renewed interest in Hegel as a precursor of more recent projects: thus Hegel's criticism of the notion of "immediacy" in perception has been linked to Wilfrid Sellars's attempt to avoid the problems associated with the "myth of the given", while his holistic philosophical stance has been linked to the appeal made by Richard Rorty and others to pragmatism.

What has made possible this unusually auspicious moment for the re-envisioning of the Hegelian project is a surprising shift in two large conflictual standpoints that have until recently framed the philosophical landscape. The first of these conflicts – the division between the so-called "continental" and "analytic" approaches to philosophy – has in many ways dominated philosophical endeavour on both sides of the Atlantic for much of the last century but has started (by most accounts) to blur at the edges and even (by at least some accounts) to disappear in the wake of substantial philosophical interests that span the two traditions. The second conflict – that within Hegelian studies between "metaphysical" and "non-metaphysical" approaches – has also started to undergo a reconfiguration, as philosophers on both sides of this dispute have wrestled with the question of the meaning and status of metaphysics in the wake of Kant.

A generation ago, it was still possible for an academic to write that all that was left of Hegel as far as contemporary philosophy should be concerned was his "poetry". On the view of many in analytic philosophy, Hegel was to be read only by those fuzzy-headed enough to be also tempted by figures such as Josiah Royce or F. H. Bradley. But as many have come to question the usefulness of the distinction between "analytic" and "continental" philosophy – particularly as leading exponents of the analytic tradition have acknowledged the significance of wider corners of the history of philosophy than were previously admitted – so have the restrictions changed on how Hegel ought to be regarded. As John McDowell put it recently: "The very idea of an analytic reading of . . . Hegel would once have seemed something like contradictory, and now we are close to taking it in our stride."[3] McDowell's own recent work – with the claim that his *Mind and World* serves as a sort of "prolegomenon" to the *Phenomenology of Spirit* – nods significantly back to Sellars's perhaps puckish claim that his essay "Empiricism and the Philosophy of Mind" could be read as "incipient *Méditations hégéliennes*".[4] Likewise, the work of philosophers such as Charles Taylor, Robert Brandom, Robert Pippin and Terry Pinkard has paved the way for a "new" Hegel with significant contributions to the contemporary discussion of such topics as normativity, agency and sociality.

One question concerning the "new" approach to Hegel, of course, is what happens to the "spirit of Hegel" if that spirit becomes "bound in the fetters of Carnap" (as Rorty once suggested might present a difficulty for Sellars).[5] What does it mean, as Richard J. Bernstein has asked, to have a "domesticated" Hegel in the sense of the "minimal empiricism" or "naturalized Platonism" that McDowell has proposed?[6] That question has a bearing as well on the more localized dispute, that between "metaphysical" and "non-metaphysical" readers of Hegel, which has been of primary concern among Hegelian scholars for the last generation. Against older readings which had construed Hegel to be engaged in some traditional form of metaphysics, the "non-metaphysical" interpreters of Hegel, such as Klaus Hartmann, with whom the term is perhaps most associated, saw Hegel instead as primarily offering a metaphysically neutral analysis of concepts, or a category theory.[7] But this dispute, too, has undergone a significant shift in the last several years – in fact, some have recently suggested that the very terms of that dispute be given a different characterization that can incorporate the somewhat wider range of views that cohere on either side of the most prominent split in the current debate in Hegel studies.[8] Loosely put, contemporary Hegelianism tends at the moment to divide between readers who see Hegel as most inspired by the task of continuing the Kantian critical project in some way and readers who take Hegel to be pursuing a line of thought that brings him ultimately closer to something like Spinozistic monism. The philosophical grounds of this dispute are, of course, not merely a matter of whether Hegel is construed in terms of Kant *or* Spinoza (since many on both sides recognize that Hegel is philosophically engaged in a serious way with both thinkers), but it is a helpful way to begin seeing the difference in the kinds of philosophical questions each project focuses upon. Readers of the first sort, for example (such as Robert Pippin, Terry Pinkard and Robert Brandom) see Hegel as interested in "completing" the critical project in a way that holds on to the most central Kantian insights concerning the spontaneity underlying our experience, but in doing so without certain of Kant's own assumptions that Hegel thought belied those central insights: most prominently, Kant's famous commitments to the thing-in-itself and to the notion that concepts and intuitions are separable elements of our perception and agency. The Hegelian project that emerges on this reading is one that is both holistic and social, with its focus on the sort of *normative* commitments that one makes in experiencing the world and acting within it. By contrast, readers of the second type either see Hegel as committed to some sort of substance monism that can incorporate his new stress on the subject (this is Charles Taylor's view, of Hegel as positing a sort of cosmic spirit) or instead (like Rolf-Peter Horstmann) see Hegel as engaged in an ontological project of accounting for the structures that can explain our experience as parts of a systematic whole.

Although there have been significant developments in the articulation of these two approaches over the last generation, they still tend to stress different facets of Hegel's work and even different works within his corpus itself – the former, for example, often more the project of the *Phenomenology of Spirit* and the latter more the mature systematic form of the *Science of Logic*. Yet for all the opposition between these approaches, there do seem to be within the current conversation a number of possible grounds for the pursuit of interesting new perspectives on Hegel that transcend the usual lines of the old debate.

An approach to reading Hegel

For anyone trying, for the first time, to make sense of Hegel's philosophy, the iconic anecdotes are likely to be those that stress difficulty of comprehension. There is, of course, the famous story of Goethe's daughter, baffled and uncomprehending after lunch with her father's philosopher friend; there is Heinrich Heine's imagined portrait of the philosopher who died saying that only one other man had understood him in his life and that he had been mistaken.[9]

There are also a number of well-known but deceptive initial formulations alleged to be epitomes of Hegelian philosophy – "thesis, antithesis, synthesis", to take the most prominent example – that professional Hegelians make it a point to bracket as not from the original source.[10] One's choice as first-time student of Hegel seems often, then, to be determined either as a resort to the misleadingly formulaic or as a gesture towards giving up on the effort altogether in favour of caricature.

What might lie as a successful path in between is a route less frequently travelled, and one that has a number of pitfalls all its own. The geometer Euclid is said to have told King Ptolemy that "there is no royal road to geometry"; this remark would seem to be true of the road to Hegel, as well. The issues facing a reader of Hegel are extraordinary, even for the philosophically well trained and the hermeneutically astute: there are vocabulary and style issues, disagreement about what the project is, and the relation of his corpus to the history of philosophy and within itself to settle.

Existing English-language books that introduce Hegel to general readers have moreover tended in the past – despite their merits otherwise – either to be too brief (Peter Singer, at 92 pages) or too involved (Taylor, Inwood and Stace, each valuable in its own way but each weighing in at more than 500 pages) for many first-time readers. In the last couple of years, with the reawakened philosophical interest in matters Hegelian, there have been some quite welcome new introductions to Hegel in the middle page-range, more digestible for those encountering Hegel for the first time: Frederick Beiser's *Hegel*, which sets Hegel more firmly in the context of his idealist and especially Romantic contemporaries than previous introductions have;

and Stephen Houlgate's expanded *Introduction to Hegel*, which offers an unusually helpful path into aspects of Hegel's philosophy that do not often get sufficient treatment elsewhere (particularly Hegel's philosophy of nature). There are, as well, some helpful recent commentaries to specific Hegelian texts: Robert Stern's on the *Phenomenology of Spirit* and Dudley Knowles's on the *Philosophy of Right*, for example.

This volume is not intended to lay out a single line of interpretation but rather to open up Hegel's thought by examining crucial passages that have been central to the wide range of Hegel's interpreters, both contemporary and later. The book therefore attempts to provide for the first-time reader a tool for a middle path into Hegel's works as a whole, exploring them in an essentially chronological way – starting with his earliest philosophical sketches and moving towards the final lectures in Berlin. Central philosophical themes that weigh unusually heavily in the contemporary literature and that will be emphasized in what follows include: the nature of scepticism and its relation to philosophy; sense perception and the related notions of "immediacy" and "mediation"; systematicity and the related problems of openness and closure; agency and sociality; normativity, freedom and responsiveness to reasons (or what it is that makes us more than merely natural creatures).

The first chapter will begin to trace Hegel's philosophical approach from its emergence within its historical context in German Idealism. There has long been an "official" story about Hegel's place within German Idealism that even some of its proponents have questioned as insufficiently attentive to the philosophical complexities involved. On this received view, Hegel's place within German Idealism is the result of an interior logic that has a culmination within his systematic work: from Kant to Fichte's "subjective" idealism, from Fichte to Schelling's "objective" idealism and from Schelling to Hegel's "absolute" idealism. Hegel himself of course tells this story, but the story of German Idealism – and of Hegel's place within it – is far more complicated, as many have realized. Among the more engaging facets of contemporary research into German Idealism in the last several years has been the light shed on a number of figures whose importance to philosophical development has sometimes been underestimated: Jacobi, Reinhold, Schulze and Maimon, but also the Romantics Friedrich Schlegel and Novalis. For Hegel himself, as we shall see in Chapter 1, it was above all his poet friend Hölderlin who had a large influence on Hegel's early attitude towards Fichte and idealism. Following the first chapter's exploration of the development of the young Hegel from his earliest writings at Frankfurt and Jena, the second chapter takes up the emergence of Hegel's own philosophical stance in the *Phenomenology of Spirit*. Chapter 3 examines the systematic project of Hegel's *Science of Logic* and the *Encyclopedia*, which incorporates his wide-ranging thought on ethical and political philosophy (Chapter 4), history (Chapter 5), aesthetics (Chapter 6) and religion (Chapter 7).

CHAPTER ONE

German Idealism and the young Hegel

The story of the "young Hegel" – Hegel in the earliest years of his development before the writing of the *Phenomenology of Spirit* – is one that has been told from a number of different and not necessarily incompatible perspectives: some have read it as the story of a young man focused on political issues and the task of being a philosophical educator of some sort, while others have read it as the story of a former seminarian whose concern for essentially theological issues gave way to a critical stance on existing forms of religion and moved him to systematic philosophy. However partial these readings may be, they share a correct view: an exploration of the philosophical development of the young Hegel is a crucial point of departure for anyone trying to make sense of who Hegel became and what we can take Hegelianism to be as a result.

In this chapter, I shall take up the question of Hegel's philosophical development with two particular concerns in mind: (a) the general intellectual background of the post-Kantian world that is the common framework for German Idealism and early German Romanticism, and (b) Hegel's interest in the issues posed within that intellectual world. (The small German town of Jena turns out to be unusually important for both.) What will emerge at the end of this period is a Hegel whose philosophical views have been shaped importantly by a concern with the range of questions of interest to idealists and Romantics both, but whose individual contributions have begun to look distinctive against that general intellectual environment.

One general approach that has been taken to the young Hegel is to see his intellectual trajectory as linked, at least at its deepest point of origin, to a distinctly *Romantic* set of concerns – and by Romantic here is meant "early German Romantic", in the tradition of Friedrich Schlegel and Novalis. On this view of Romanticism, the most motivating concern is with what is often called being "at home" in the world: the Romantics looked somehow to emerge from the modern experience of division, alienation and oppression of nature to find themselves instead in a world that is experienced more as an organic whole. The Hegel who, on this reading, is moved by the Romantic concern with finding a home in the world comes to be the systematist that he does, however, because there is in his intellectual baggage as well an essentially Enlightenment commitment that is interested in giving a rational articulation of that organicist impulse.

This story is fine as far as it reaches, yet it will not be – for all that Hegel will be shown to share with the Romantics – the story told here. The Romantic impulse, after all, is frequently non-foundationalist and sceptical, rather than systematic in its aspiration (witness Novalis's famous comment that "philosophy is actually homesickness – the urge to be everywhere at home").[1] The point of departure I will suggest instead is one framed not by Schlegel and Novalis but first of all by the rather more tragic philosophical explorations of Hegel's friend Hölderlin. For it was Hölderlin who appears to have introduced Hegel to a line of criticism of the Fichtean approach to the post-Kantian philosophical project and to have suggested an essential rubric under which the relation between subject and object should be seen as a sort of initial separation emerging from a more primitive unity somehow "behind" all of our experience. It is this background image that Hegel seems to have had in mind as he started (in this case, along with his friend Schelling) to work out how it is essentially bound up with arriving at the correct "idealist" standpoint (and thus how infinity and finitude, subjective and objective could be united). But it would seem that Hegel (unlike Schelling) takes this question most to heart not merely in terms of the "stance" to be arrived at but – most importantly – the correct and rigorous journey that anyone could follow in order to get there. Thus it is that for the young Hegel the problem of *scepticism* retains an important hold – and one that in fact returns us indeed to some version of the problem of "being at home in the world", but with a different perspective, since the animating question for Hegel by the end of this period will be precisely how anyone could be *led* to the level of idealist philosophy's position, and so with the wider concern that the methodological project itself is somehow directly *social and political*.

In the present chapter, I shall chart this intellectual journey of Hegel's first by looking at his development within the context of the emergence of German Idealism itself during the years he spent at Berne and Frankfurt (1793–1800) following his graduation from the Tübingen seminary, and then by comparing four decisive early works from the Jena period (1801–6), which, taken together, offer an unusually rich and specific introduction to the set of questions that come to animate Hegel's ultimate philosophical stance.

Tendencies of a revolutionary age

Hegel's birth in 1770 (in the town of Stuttgart, capital of the German-speaking duchy of Württemberg) makes him a member of that generation which came of age just as the French Revolution was beginning – he was eighteen at the time of the storming of the Bastille. The romantic and revolutionary ferment of that era is often associated with the famous remark of Wordsworth, born the same year as Hegel: "Bliss was it in that dawn to be alive, but to be young was very heaven . . ." Yet the "age of revolution" is a notion that carried a somewhat different meaning in Germany than it did either in France or in Wordsworth's England.

To begin with, it is only a convenient contemporary fiction to say that Hegel was born in "Germany", since that was an entity that did not come to exist until decades after his death. Hegel's national identification was instead as a Swabian from Württemberg, one of the numerous duchies and principalities of the German-speaking world.[2] For the German-speaking generation that was born in or around Wordsworth's birth-year of 1770 and that came of age in the 1790s – a generation that included not only Hegel and his college classmates Hölderlin and Schelling, but also the Romantic figures Friedrich Schlegel and Novalis, as well as the composer Beethoven – the differences in how the "age of revolution" was viewed had a great deal to do with the intellectual and social character of German life at the time.

Perhaps the best place to begin an account of what made the German context of this era different is with the well-known fragment of Friedrich Schlegel (*Athenaeum Fragments* [no. 216]):

> The French Revolution, Fichte's philosophy, and Goethe's *Wilhelm Meister* are the greatest tendencies of the age. Whoever is offended by this juxtaposition, whoever cannot take any revolution seriously that isn't noisy and materialistic, hasn't yet achieved a lofty, broad perspective on the history of mankind.

There are a number of things worth noticing in Schlegel's juxtaposition. The first is something that becomes almost a commonplace in writing in and about the period – as Heine and Marx, among others, were later to stress: while the French revolutionary moment is one of political deeds, the corresponding German revolutionary contribution is philosophical and literary. No one perhaps has summed up better the move from the first tendency to the second – and the importance of their connection for the birth and developmental energy of German Idealism – than Schelling, who put it quite simply in one of his first publications: "the beginning and end of all philosophy is – *freedom*!"[3]

The events, distant and French though they were, mattered, of course, too. Hegel was a college student during the French Revolution; it is a probably apocryphal story that he and his two college friends, Schelling and Hölderlin, took time from their theological studies in Tübingen to plant a liberty tree, but there is no question about their initial fervour in relation to the ideals of the revolution. The story of how the three Tübingen students came to make contributions to this age of freedom is in the end much more dominated by Fichtean philosophy and the rise of the Romantic novel as a literary form, however: each of the three would in the end come to take an importantly different philosophical stance towards Fichte, and each would share in the aesthetic enthusiasm that surrounded the development of a distinctly modern form of narrative.

Fichte, Jena and the development of German Idealism

All of these currents in the German philosophical and literary world of the 1790s may be said to have had a remarkable geographical centre: the small university town of Jena (with 4,300 people and 800 students), on any account one of the most liberal and progressive university communities of its day in Germany or elsewhere. Drawn to its light in the mid- and late-1790s was a "who's who" of German intellectual culture: Friedrich and August Schlegel, along with their wives Caroline Schlegel Schelling and Dorothea Mendelssohn Veit, Novalis and Schleiermacher, with Goethe and Schiller close by in neighbouring Weimar. A leading edge of philosophical research stemming from Kant, it housed the important journal *Allgemeine Literatur-Zeitung* (*ALZ*), which had become an important organ of Kantian philosophical writing, and had attracted in succession Karl Reinhold in 1787 and Fichte in 1794.

The Jena of these years was thus, in Friedrich Schlegel's words, a "symphony of professors", but there was no one more central to the intellectual activity surrounding it than Fichte, whom Hölderlin called the "soul of Jena". Starting with his inaugural lecture on 23 May 1794, Fichte drew students widely, not only among aspiring philosophers but also among those whose interest and fame would prove to be more literary – Novalis, Friedrich Schlegel and Hölderlin, for example, were all drawn to make serious studies of Fichte's philosophy at one point or another in their own intellectual development.

Fichte's emerging philosophical stance in his Jena lectures presented to the public an important turn in the development of post-Kantian idealism. Reinhold had attempted to give what he thought was a necessary grounding to the Kantian project as a whole by beginning from a single first principle – what he called the "principle of consciousness", that "in consciousness the subject distinguishes the representation from the subject and object and relates it to both". But that attempt at grounding had quickly been called into question by G. E. Schulze in an essay named, after the ancient sceptic, *Aenesidemus*: Schulze argued, among other things, that if the "fact of consciousness" were the first principle of philosophy, it would be based on an infinite regress – since the subject needs to have a representation of itself, and there would need to be a representation of that, and so on.

The effect of Schulze's sceptical query to Reinhold was devastating for Reinhold's career, but Fichte (who reviewed the *Aenesidemus* essay for *ALZ*) not only picked up the difficulty but suggested a new way of proceeding: self-consciousness needed a different sort of account that was not representationalist, as Reinhold's attempt had been. What was needed was a point of departure not based in a *fact* (*Tatsache*) like the supposed "fact of consciousness" but rather was an *action* (*Tathandlung*). As Fichte came to state it in the course of his developing *Science of Knowledge* (*Wissenschaftslehre*, of which he wrote some sixteen versions), the proposition "I = I", which proclaims the necessary unity of self-consciousness, requires that there be some "not-I", but since that not-I can only be something *posited by* the I itself, the I must strive to overcome that not-I by showing that any possible other is what it is only by construction from the necessary conditions of the I itself. Our experience of objects of knowledge is thus something that we have by means of the self-grounding activity of the I.

Fichte's philosophical standpoint was still one that was rooted in the "I" as a single first principle. Among the listeners who began to raise questions about both the attempt at grounding philosophy on first principles (what Reinhold and Fichte shared) and the attempt to make that first principle the "I" was Hegel's old Tübingen friend Hölderlin, who had made it to Jena in November of 1794 (albeit with the task of looking after a rather difficult young student in his charge) and was now soaking up Fichte's lectures, both in public and in private.

Hegel and the 1790s: towards "Intervention in the Life of Men"

Hegel's own development during these heady years of Jena's golden era had been at some remove from the centre of philosophical and cultural activity, both geographically and philosophically. His post-graduation plans following Tübingen – serving as a house tutor to a wealthy family in the Swiss city of Berne – were, at least for the time being, decidedly less alluring than what either of his friends was up to. Hölderlin wrote to him from Jena in early 1795 with an account of how the Fichtean philosophy was developing, giving rapturous details also of his meeting with the illustrious Goethe ("Goethe and I have spoken. Brother! It is the most beautiful enjoyment of our life to find so much humanity among the great . . ."). Schelling, meanwhile, had already become something of a *Wunderkind*, with the publication of several important philosophical works (including *On the Possibility of a Form for All Philosophy*, *Of the "I" as Principle of Philosophy*, and *Philosophical Letters on Dogmatism and Criticism*) from 1794 on. (Still in Tübingen, Schelling wrote to Hegel only a few days after Hölderlin's letter about developments in Reinhold's philosophy and offered his old friend a remarkable confession stimulated by the new intellectual currents: "I have become a Spinozist . . .").

Hegel's intellectual progress in this time period, by contrast, seems to have been much more narrowly focused. Hegel had seemed to evince an interest from quite early in being a sort of philosophical "educator of the people" (a model he inherited in part from Lessing); his writing during this formative period is often said to be focused either on political issues (*The Young Hegel* in the title of Lukács's work) or on theological matters (*Early Theological Writings*, the title the Lutheran pastor Hermann Nohl gave to the collection of these juvenilia when they were first edited and published in the first decade of the twentieth century). The truth seems to be that both of these interests are present, although not yet connected to a systematic philosophical set of concerns.

At Tübingen Hegel had already written a "Life of Jesus" according to a Kantian moral template; while at Berne his religious and political interests focus particularly on what he calls (following Kant) the problem of "positivity" – of merely posited law or forms of obedience – and what would be the grounds instead for a "religion of freedom", for examples of which he looked particularly to the Greeks.

Perhaps the most decisive influence on the young Hegel, both practically and intellectually, was the move of his friend Hölderlin from Jena to Frankfurt – and his managing to arrange for Hegel to get a new house tutor's position in the same city. Around Hölderlin during this period there emerged a circle of friends, which included a number of notable figures, all interested in the connections between post-Kantian philosophy and the construal of the broader social world. Although much of what Hegel and Hölderlin shared in their conversations is a matter of some historical speculation, we do have some important windows in a couple of remarkable texts from this period.

The first of these texts is a short fragment that Hölderlin himself presumably wrote during his final months in Jena but never published. It is, however, no doubt reflective of a significant line of criticism of the Fichtean approach to philosophy which Hegel and Hölderlin must have discussed, for it retained a lifelong hold on Hegel, offering the promise of a new philosophical point of departure. In the fragment, which was given the title "Judgment and Being",[4] Hölderlin constructs an important play on words around the notion of "judgment", which in German is the word *Urteil* (in older German, *Urtheil*). Hölderlin takes the hidden meaning of this word to refer to an original (*Ur*) division (*Teilung*):

> *Judgment* [*Urtheil*], in the highest and strictest sense, is the original separation of object and subject which are most deeply united in intellectual intuition, that separation through which alone object and subject become possible, the original separation [*Ur-Theilung*]. In the concept of separation, there lies already the concept of the reciprocity of the object and subject and the necessary presupposition of the whole of which object and subject form the parts.

The second text, which has been given the title "Oldest System-Program of German Idealism", is of still disputed authorship, but was (unquestionably) written in Hegel's hand and (with all probability) had Hölderlin's (but perhaps also Schelling's) influence behind it. The "System-Program" is distinctive for its combination of aesthetic and political ideas, advocating a move to a politics that will not "treat free human beings like a mechanical set of wheels" and insisting that the "highest act of reason . . . is an aesthetic act" and that a mythology of reason is required to make ideas accessible to the people. This is, it should be added, the first document written in Hegel's hand that expresses, even if still only as an aspiration, some notion of *system*.

Most strikingly, as Henrich has argued, Hölderlin's influence gives Hegel a new concept of freedom. No longer will Hegel view freedom in terms of a Kantian or Fichtean overcoming of dependence – with the inherent fixity of oppositions implied – but rather as a *unification of opposites*. One version of such a "holistic" or unificatory view of freedom had already been articulated by Schiller in his 1795 aesthetic-cum-political *Letters on Aesthetic Education*, which suggest that beauty can give rise to freedom by bringing together the otherwise alienated Kantian moments of sense and form. At Frankfurt, with Hölderlin's influence, Hegel now begins to articulate his own account of such a connection between freedom and unity.

The fragments that Hegel wrote at Frankfurt (to which Nohl gave the evocative title "The Spirit of Christianity and its Fate") show not only the influence of the Hölderlinian "philosophy of unification" on Hegel's views but also what can be heard as a distinctively Hegelian inflection of that project: in some ways, Hegel's key issue remains the problem of positivity, but there is now a wider sense about what overcoming that must mean. Thus, in the underlying schema of the fragments there is a development from positivity to morality (which cannot entirely overcome the positivity issue), but then a move to love, preached by a figure – partly somehow Jesus, partly somehow Antigone – who embodies a more reconciliationist tendency than Kantian and Fichtean morality will allow. Yet this love and this preacher cannot adequately resolve all that is conflictual within the existing culture (and hence something like the category of "fate" is needed). But fate – and this is a distinctive Hegelian contribution, I believe – is not something an agent experiences in the way that an agent experiences punishment under a (moral or positive) law, but is more organically connected to the possibility of some sort of reconciliation. *In nuce*, there is something that has started to look like the Hegelian concern with spirit – although there is still a great distance to travel.

The question of when and how Hegel becomes Hegel has much to do with the period of his work that begins with his move from Frankfurt to Jena. Hegel was finally to make it to the important philosophical and cultural centre of Jena, but only in early 1801, two years after Fichte's departure over the dispute about his alleged atheism, months before Friedrich Schlegel would also have to decamp, coming to terms with his lack of immediate success as a university lecturer, and only a couple of years before his friend Schelling would escape the difficulties of having married August Schlegel's wife Caroline by heading off to the presumably friendlier confines of Bavaria.

The period in which Hegel moves from Frankfurt to Jena marks also the beginning of the pursuit of his developing concern with *systematic philosophy* and the relation of that to his longstanding interests in the social and political ideals of the French Revolution. One window on to the development of Hegel's thought in this regard can be found in a remarkable letter to his old Tübingen friend Schelling, whose public philosophical success Hegel says he has noted "with admiration and joy". In the letter, Hegel asks if Schelling might be of help in getting him a job – not necessarily in the midst of the "literary revel" at Jena, but anywhere there are "a few acquaintances and, for the sake of my physical condition, a good beer". But he also gives his friend a sense of his recent intellectual progress in what is often regarded as a sort of summary philosophical autobiography of Hegel at the age of thirty:

> In my scientific development, which started from [the] more sub-

> ordinate needs of man, I was inevitably driven toward science, and the ideal of [my] youth had to take the form of reflection and thus at once of a system. I now ask myself, while I am still occupied with it, what return to intervention in the life of men can be found . . .[5]

How Hegel comes to relate these two concerns – his long-term interest in the social and cultural "life of men" and his awakening interest in developing a genuinely systematic philosophical position from which human affairs could somehow be viewed – is a question that is widely debated in the scholarship.[6] Tracing out the twists and turns of Hegel's emerging philosophical system as it is visible in his published writings, lecture notes and the various outlines and sketches he undertook during his time at Jena is a complicated project. But it is possible, even for a reader just getting acquainted with Hegel, to get a sense of the animating project of Hegel during the crucial period when his philosophy comes to take real and effective shape as a systematic contribution within the larger project of German Idealism – precisely the six years he spent in Jena before the publication of the *Phenomenology of Spirit*. In the following section, I shall suggest a way of reading in a comparative way Hegel's major publications from this period that offers – together with some background about the unpublished material from this period – an immensely engaging portrait of a young philosopher.

Hegel at Jena (1801–6): four essays and the emergence of a philosophical project

In this section, we will consider what philosophical interests connect the four major works Hegel published at Jena before the *Phenomenology of Spirit*: the first philosophical book actually published under his name, *The Difference between Fichte's and Schelling's System of Philosophy* (published September 1801)[7] and – in rapid succession – the essays published in the *Critical Journal* (the literary project that he was at the time co-editing with Schelling) on *The Relationship of Skepticism to Philosophy* (March 1802), *Faith and Knowledge* (July 1802) and *The Scientific Ways of Treating Natural Law* (November/December 1802, with a second instalment in May/June 1803).[8] Comparing the framework of each of these important early writings gives us a sense of the driving forces behind Hegel's philosophical development during this period.

In particular, as we shall see, what underlies all of these works is a diagnosis of modernity and modern philosophy in terms of an inherent division or opposition that Hegel sees as stemming from *reflectivity*, or attachment to the *finite* standpoint of consciousness. In his diagnosis of the problem of division or opposition, Hegel of course has good company among Schiller, Schelling and the Romantics. But what begins to be evident in these four essays, taken together, is how Hegel is now thinking through that diagnosis in a way that will involve distinctive commitments of his own about the right way "out" of Kant, about philosophy's relation to scepticism, and about the relation between idealism and the conditions for modern political freedom.

(1) The *Difference* essay sets an early and distinctive Hegelian tone in its attack on what Hegel regards not merely as an academic problem but as reflective of a "need" in culture: the overcoming of basic division or dichotomy (*Entzweiung*) that characterizes the philosophical and cultural world of modernity. "Dichotomy is the source of the *need for philosophy*; and as the culture of the era, it is the unfree and given aspect of the whole configuration."[9]

The sort of "dichotomy" or division that Hegel has in mind can be found, he claims, in a range of characteristic modern divisions such as soul and body, subject and object, faith and intellect, freedom and necessity, reason and sensibility, and intelligence and nature. Hegel sees these divisions as the result of a historical and cultural development that philosophy must concern itself with: "the true peculiarity of a philosophy lies in the interesting individuality which is the organic shape that Reason has built for itself out of the material of a particular age" – and the age at present in which reason's activity can be seen is precisely an age of division.

It is the "sole interest of Reason" to suspend antitheses, Hegel claims, but reason is not thereby *opposed to* opposition and limitation, since

> the necessary dichotomy is One factor in life. Life eternally forms itself by setting up oppositions, and totality at the highest pitch of living energy is only possible through its own re-establishment out of the deepest fission. What Reason opposes, rather, is just the absolute fixity which the intellect gives to the dichotomy; and it does so all the more if the absolute opposites themselves originated in Reason.[10]

(Hegel is thus also already opposed here to figures such as Jacobi and Schleiermacher, who claim through immediacy – without mediating oppositions, that is – to connect to the Absolute.)

An important opposed pair of terms that emerges in the context of this essay's account of division is that of "speculation" versus "reflection": the former Hegel defines as the "activity of the one universal reason directed upon itself", an activity whose principle is the identity of subject and object (p. 80) and of reflection and intuition (p. 111); reflection is by contrast the "instrument of philosophizing" which Hegel takes to be the principle of modern philosophy (the tradition from Locke, who takes reflection to be "that notice which the mind takes of its own operations"). For Hegel, reflection carries implicit within it a dualism that "in isolation is the positing of opposites". (This opposition parallels the originally Kantian opposition that Hegel now develops in a distinctive way for his own purposes here between reason (*Vernunft*) as the suspender of antitheses and understanding (*Verstand*) or the "sound common sense", which Hegel regards as the capacity to set limits.)

What does all this say about Hegel's position on the "difference" between Fichte and Schelling? Hegel does seem to unite, together with Schelling and Hölderlin, in criticizing Fichte's notion of freedom as "fixed as negative freedom" rather than as "the suspension of opposites" (p. 133). The assumption of many readers of this essay was no doubt that Hegel, as a lesser-known collaborator of Schelling's, must be essentially taking a Schellingian position (Harris quotes a contemporary review by Böttinger that "Schelling has now fetched a stout warrior to Jena from his fatherland Württemberg, through whom he gives notice to the astonished public that even Fichte stands far below his own viewpoint"[11]). But if Hegel is more Schellingian than Fichtean in this essay, and the vocabulary that he employs is in general due to his friend, there is, however, something that is recognizably his own. Hegel stresses, for example, that reason might "raise itself to itself" in its identity with objects, a phrase that hints at something like the (unSchellingian) concern that the *Phenomenology* will have with tracing the insufficiencies of various finite forms of knowledge to the Absolute.[12] As we shall see, in the next essay, Hegel immediately linked this project of the destruction of finite forms of knowledge to the problem of scepticism and its relation to philosophy.

(2) *The Relationship of Skepticism to Philosophy: Presentation of its Different Modifications and Comparison of the Most Recent Skepticism with Ancient Skepticism.* Although Hegel until recently was not always regarded by the wider philosophical community as a rigorously informed methodological thinker, research in the last several years has started to emphasize this long-neglected aspect of his thought and the ways in which it was in fact central to his development as a philosopher. Among the most important pieces of evidence for Hegel's concern with philosophical method is the interest he takes in the problem of scepticism during the Jena period – and, quite remarkably, as this essay insists, in the great importance Hegel places on the tradition of ancient scepticism as practised by the Pyrrhonists.[13]

Hegel's essay is technically framed as a review of a recent book by G. E. Schulze, the author of *Aenesidemus*, which we have already seen to have a large historical significance for the development of German Idealism by raising a sceptical line of criticism of Reinhold's attempt to ground Kantian philosophy on the fact of consciousness. Following the *Aenesidemus*, Schulze had continued to pursue a line of critical attack on Kantian idealism, and Hegel's review takes on Schulze's more recent formulation of the relation between scepticism and philosophy in his *Critique of Theoretical Philosophy* (1801).

In so doing, Hegel draws a contrast between "modern" scepticism – the sort practised by Schulze and others in the wake of Hume – and the ancient scepticism associated with the Pyrrhonists. On the presentation of Sextus Empiricus, the Pyrrhonist sceptics viewed themselves as a middle between dogmatists and the so-called academic sceptics in that they claimed neither a position or dogma on the one hand nor the negative "academic" position that there cannot be knowledge on the other hand. Instead, the ancient sceptical claim is only a matter of what "appears" rather than truth or non-truth; the "modes" employed by ancient scepticism are thus designed instead to allow the sceptics a "check" (*epochē*) on taking a stance that involves actual belief regarding one claim or another – "neither this nor that", in Sextus Empiricus's phrase. The result of these modes allowed both sensual and rational claims to be opposed by claims of equal weight (the procedure known as *isostheneia* or equipollence). In the essay, Hegel contrasts these ancient sceptical modes with modern (Humean) scepticism which, he claims, relies on sense impressions in a way that would not be acceptable to the ancient Pyrrhonist.

In contrast with the ancient sceptic's stance, the particular form of scepticism that Schulze represents, Hegel argues, insists that there is an unalterable "in-itself" somehow "underneath" our sense perceptions which cannot be known: an epistemological stance that Hegel likens to the image of a mountain peak somehow always beneath the visible snow. At the same time, Schulze claims an undeniable certainty for immediate facts of consciousness.

From the perspective of the ancient sceptics, the focus of modern scepticism on the issue of mere "doubt" (*Zweifel*) is put in some relief: the issue for the ancient sceptics is not so much whether one can *doubt* this or that claim but rather "the *complete denial of all truth*" to finite (empirical) modes of cognition. In so far as scepticism fulfils this function, Hegel claims, it is not necessarily an enterprise *opposed to* or even separate from philosophy at all, but may indeed be taken as the "negative" side of what counts as "genuine" philosophizing. Hegel makes an appeal here to the philosopher who was in fact claimed by both dogmatists and sceptics in the ancient world as their predecessor – Plato:

> What more perfect and self-sustaining document and system of genuine skepticism could we find than the *Parmenides* in the Platonic philosophy? It embraces the whole domain of that knowledge through concepts of understanding, and destroys it. This Platonic skepticism is not concerned with doubting these truths of the understanding which cognizes things as manifold, as wholes consisting of parts, [etc.] . . . rather it is intent on the complete denial of all truth to this sort of cognition. This skepticism does not constitute a particular thing in a system, but it is itself the negative side of the cognition of the Absolute, and directly presupposes Reason as the positive side.[14]

Plato's *Parmenides* thus offers a picture of the relationship between a thoroughgoing scepticism and philosophy: "this skepticism that comes on the scene in its pure explicit shape in the *Parmenides* can . . . be found implicit in every genuine philosophical system, for it is the free side of every philosophy".

This discussion of the relationship between scepticism and "genuine" philosophy is linked with an account of what Hegel here calls the "proposition of Reason" [*vernünftiger Satz*] and elsewhere the "speculative proposition" [*spekulativer Satz*]. Examples of such propositions include Spinoza's "essence involving existence" or notion of an "immanent cause", where contradictory assertions are combined (in these cases, the contradictions arise from the fact that essence is usually conceived as involving abstraction from existence and cause is usually conceived as something that is distinct from effect). The "principle of scepticism" – Sextus's "against every argument there is an equal one on the other side" – is thus linked to Hegel's early questioning of the philosophical status of the principle of contradiction and to the "negative side" of "genuine philosophy": "Since every genuine philosophy has this negative side, or always sublates the principle of contradiction, anyone who has the urge can set this negative side in relief and set forth for himself a skepticism . . ." Hegel's stress here that the "negative side" of "genuine philosophy" embraces a self-cancelling proposition looks forward to what will become an essential aspect of his dialectic (although, at this point, there is not yet a movement forward of that cancellation, progressing, as the mature dialectic does, to a new and third thing).

(3) *Faith and Knowledge: or the Reflective Philosophy of Subjectivity in the Complete Range of its Forms as Kantian, Jacobian and Fichtean*

Philosophy. The subtitle of Hegel's essay on "faith and knowledge" points immediately back to the *Difference* essay's critique of the general philosophical culture of reflection. Here, the philosophical stances of Kant, Jacobi and Fichte are criticized as plagued by the reflective turn. Hegel sees these three figures as together expressing the singular form of the culture of reflection that has emerged in the contemporary world from the experience of Protestant individuality: "objectively" in the Kantian moral law, "subjectively" in Jacobi's appeal to intuition and feeling, and the "synthesis" of these two sides in the Fichtean notions of obligation and striving; together these three positions can be construed as representing the "idealism of the finite" – which means, in Hegel's view, not that the finite is "merely ideal" or nothing to them but that a *finite thinking subject* is the essential point of departure.

Philosophy is idealism, Hegel claims, "because it does not acknowledge either one of the opposites [infinite or finite] as existing for itself in its abstraction from the other". Kant's philosophy, for example, is an idealism because it shows that "intuition by itself is blind and the concept by itself is empty"; but Kant moves away from an idealist stance when he declares finite cognition to be all that is possible. Kant's notion of a synthetic unity needs to be seen not as something *produced* out of independently existing opposite terms but rather as an *original identity* of opposites, and in this connection Hegel prominently praises Kant's notion of the productive imagination and the "intuitive understanding" discussed in the *Critique of Judgment*, which, Hegel says, is "nothing else but the same idea of the transcendental imagination".

Hegel's appropriation of Kant in *Faith and Knowledge* has represented something of a watershed moment for interpreters of the early Jena writings, particularly with regard to the question of what sort of post-Kantian idealist – and what sort of metaphysician – the young Hegel should be taken to be. Most readers agree that Hegel takes himself, in his treatment of Kant's notion of the productive imagination, to be seizing upon a Kantian insight that represents "genuine idealism": as Hegel sees it, the Kantian claim in the B version of the transcendental deduction that the unity of intuition depends on a prior synthesis of the imagination poses fundamental questions for Kant's dual-source account of cognition, with its heterogeneous elements of sensible intuition on the one hand and concepts on the other.[15] Not all readers, of course, think that Hegel's interpretation of Kant here is correct; but if he is, it is clear that a revision of the dual-source account of cognition will require a move to something like what Hegel calls "speculation" – an idealism that does not recognize the grounds of finitude implicit in the dual-source model.

But how exactly to understand that speculative turn is more problematic, as is the question of how to read Hegel's construal of the notorious Kantian appeal to the "intuitive understanding" in paragraphs 76–77 of the *Critique of Judgment*. In those two paragraphs, which became something of a focal point for discussion among younger idealists and romantics, Kant had argued that, since we require the concept of purposiveness and cannot say that the world is actually purposive, we are led to the *regulative* idea of an intuitive understanding that – unlike our human understanding – is "not discursive but intuitive, and hence proceeds from the *synthetically universal* (the intuition of a whole as a whole) to the particular, i.e., from the whole to the parts". For such a teleologically judging understanding, if it could exist, there could be no distinction between the possibility and actuality of things.

Although Kant himself clearly denies the existence of such a "divine" form of understanding, Hegel makes a stronger claim for it by linking it directly to the earlier discussion of the transcendental imagination: "the *Idea* of this archetypal intuitive understanding is at bottom nothing else but the *same Idea* of the transcendental imagination that we considered above", Hegel says. On one side, some readers (Béatrice Longuenesse, Paul Franks) have interpreted Hegel to be moving here decisively away from the "finite" or human Kantian standpoint to an infinite view on which the divine and its intuition are (as Hegel was later to claim) the starting point of all philosophy. On the other side, readers such as Robert Pippin have insisted that Hegel cannot be construed to be interested in affirming what Kant denies, but that he is only introducing his own idea of a "progressively developing, collectively self-conscious subject".

Hegel's linking of the transcendental imagination and the intuitive understanding will have consequences for a number of facets of his developing system. Of particular interest for Hegel's views on aesthetics is his discussion of Kant's notion of reflective judgement ("the most interesting point in the Kantian system") and the experience of beauty (precisely the experience in which the "opposition between intuition and concept falls away").[16]

Hegel's assessment of the reflective philosophies of Kant, Jacobi and Fichte in *Faith and Knowledge* concludes in a way that makes clear (as he had in the *Difference* essay) that he does not think that reflective philosophy is simply a false philosophical start but rather (in language that looks back to the *Skepticism* essay) a mode of recognizing that "thinking is infinity, the negative side of the Absolute". Hegel now adds to this account, however, a religious overlay:

> out of this nothing, and pure night of infinity, as out of the secret abyss that is its birthplace, the truth lifts itself upward . . . Thereby

> it must re-establish for philosophy the Idea of absolute freedom and along with it the absolute Passion, the speculative Good Friday in place of the historic Good Friday.[17]

Hegel's reach for a tragic register in his account of the development of Protestantism and the philosophical expression of the culture of modern division will be heard again in several ways – most immediately, in the *Natural Law* essay's appropriation of tragic and courageous risk-taking, but more distantly in his later attempts to reconstrue the religious experience of modernity in light of his larger idealist project, evidence for which we will see in the Religion chapter of the *Phenomenology of Spirit* and in Hegel's later *Lectures on the Philosophy of Religion*.

(4) In the last of the four published Jena essays, Hegel now uses the philosophical framework developed in the previous three essays to give a more explicit articulation of the idea of freedom that had emerged initially at Frankfurt in the fragments on "The Spirit of Christianity and its Fate": the idea that freedom must involve a *unity of opposites*.[18]

The *Natural Law* essay is a remarkable window on to Hegel's emerging political thought. As the previous essays have attacked the reflective culture of modernity in general and unsuccessful modern attempts at scepticism, this essay undertakes a critique of "modern" modes of looking at natural law that are either (a) narrowly empirical, i.e., building upon just one empirical facet of political life to the exclusion of others (Hobbesian fear of death, for example) or (b) conceptual attempts to find a grounding in an *a priori* law that is in the end merely formalistic or dependent on a notion of an agent's internal compulsion to obey the law (Hegel here articulates an early version of his criticism of the emptiness of the Kantian moral law and of the internal divisions required in the moral and political philosophy of both Kant and Fichte). Hegel insists instead on (c) a holistic political view that can be found neither in restricted empiricism nor in *a priori* moral philosophizing. The view of the whole he seeks to articulate is termed here *Sittlichkeit* – the realm of "ethical life", as it is usually translated, defined by customs and practices (*Sitten*), rather than the narrower appeal to the explicitly *moral* sphere determined by the Kantian and Fichtean moral law (*Moralität*).

These three views – the empirical, the *a priori* and the holistic – are not simply alternative ways of looking at moral and political matters, but can be understood philosophically to have a necessary relation to each other. Hegel casts their relationship in terms of moments that should be familiar from the discussion in *Faith and Knowledge*: empirical and *a priori* political stances are related to one another as intuition (*Anschauung*) and concept (*Begriff*); the holistic view Hegel associates with their "indifference"

(*Indifferenz* – a term borrowed from Schelling's philosophical vocabulary). Concept, it appears here, holds a trump over intuition: any empirical claim that selects for a single feature of ethical or political life can be overcome by the claims of "inner infinite negativity" associated with Kantian/Fichtean morality – that is to say, the moral law can always negate the importance of any specific empirical claim. The problems of formalism and internal compulsion notwithstanding, there is an inner truth to the Kantian/Fichtean moral standpoint, and although Hegel is in the end arguing for something like an ancient notion of an ethical whole in his notion of *Sittlichkeit*, it is clear that he does not think such a standpoint can be reached without the conceptual means offered by the idealist standpoint.

The *Natural Law* essay is complicated by Hegel's linking of two associated problems with the appeal to the notion of an ethical whole as defended within ancient political philosophy: that of class division and economic activity – the former a problem because of ancient political philosophy's inability to allow slaves freedom, and the latter a problem because ancient political philosophy held private economic life a matter distinct from the specifically political concerns of the city or *polis* as a whole. Hegel's resolution of these issues at the time of the *Natural Law* essay – one might say, his mode of arguing for some sort of necessarily post-Kantian equivalent of the ancients' more organic political life – was clearly not satisfactory to him, but is nonetheless reflective of the creativity of his emerging philosophical approach.

Hegel frames the "absolute relation" here as one of both courage and tragedy, since resolving the political problem requires on his view both war and a warlike class as well as property and bourgeois life. The relation between the "organic" and "inorganic" sides of political life requires a "facing" or "intuiting" of this problem as a whole, and Hegel makes use here of an early notion of recognition, although not yet with a connection to an essentially historical dialectic. (As Pinkard points out, the concept of recognition already gives Hegel, at this point, a way, however to offer a "nondualistic yet also nonreductionist account" of the relation between spirit and nature as not two different substances but as different ways in which human beings regard themselves.[19])

*

If we connect these four essays together, we notice at least one prevalent common theme running through them: beginning with the *Difference* essay, Hegel offers a philosophical and cultural diagnosis of division and a contrasting notion of unity, but the notion of unity involved is on his view one that regards conflict and opposition as essential. This central question about the relation of division and unity becomes a *methodological* concern as well: how to move from the destruction of finite forms of knowledge to a speculative stance. And finally the concern with division connects to the important ethical and political concern with the notion of *freedom*, which Hegel has started to define in a distinctive way as involving the reconciliation of opposites rather than the negation or domination he takes to be characteristic of Kantian and Fichtean ethics.

These concerns of Hegel's most polished published writing during the Jena period compare interestingly to the serious efforts he was making in unpublished drafts projecting the organization of his evolving system. Two concerns in these unpublished writings – stemming from the very first lectures he gave while teaching at Jena – will come, in connection with the concerns we have already identified, to play a prominent role in the ultimate shape of the *Phenomenology of Spirit*: the concern with how to provide (if one could) an *introduction to philosophy* and the question of the *relation between logic and metaphysics*. Both of these issues raise the following problem: like Jacobi, Hegel was clear about the impossibility of moving from conditional knowledge to the unconditional. But – as the *Skepticism* essay evidences – Hegel also saw that there might be some possibility for a mode that thoroughly examined the insufficiencies of all subjective means of knowing. It will be to exactly such a thoroughgoing examination that Hegel now devotes his attention in the *Phenomenology of Spirit*.

CHAPTER TWO

The *Phenomenology of Spirit*

The *Phenomenology of Spirit* (*Phenomenology*; *PhS*) is at once one of the strangest and most fascinating of philosophical works. Its uniqueness has much to do with the union of two philosophical capabilities that do not always fall together in a single work or philosopher: a genuinely sympathetic philosophical imagination for what the experience of various "forms of life" – Hegel's word is "shapes of consciousness" – might be *like* (the "phenomenological" side of Hegel's project) and a speculative rigour concerned with what would be required for the enterprise of philosophy to become in a genuine way "science" (and hence for a critique of all the modes of finite knowledge that lead to what Hegel will call "absolute knowing").

The marriage of phenomenological and speculative philosophical abilities is part of what makes for the extraordinary relation between form and content that characterizes the work. Most strikingly for its narrative structure, there is a constant tension between two perspectives: the experience of any given shape and the "we" who is doing the narrating and knows how that experience will turn out. The progress of the whole is thus an essentially *re-enacted* or "recollected" engagement – one that has its own distinct shape but which emerges nonetheless from an encounter with important (historical, literary, religious and philosophical) forms of predecessor narrative.

But coming to understand what Hegel's project in the *Phenomenology* is, is not so easy. Finished (or so Hegel claimed) in the heat of the battle of Jena, as Napoleon crushed the Prussian army, it bears not a few scars of hasty completion. The book carries not just one but two apparent titles, has (at least) two competing organizational schemes at work in its table of contents and was, moreover, published without various important directional and structural clues Hegel had thought necessary for readers to pick up the plan of the whole.

Despite the peculiarity of its both highly abstract and yet deeply allusive style, Hegel clearly wrote the work with the intention that it serve as *the* way into his philosophical system. But is it *just* an introduction or is it also necessarily (as Hegel also claims) already the *first part* of that system? And, if it is both of these things, how does fulfilling the one task not presuppose the other?

It is no wonder, perhaps, that, just before his death, Hegel wrote the following about the forthcoming second edition of the *Phenomenology*: "idiosyncratic early work, not to be revised". Hegel's later comment has been interpreted by many as being something of a repudiation of the *Phenomenology*, but it can hardly be that, since he also contemporaneously wrote of its important justifying function for the mature system as a whole.[1] The *Phenomenology* in fact (so I shall argue) retained a crucial status for Hegel philosophically, but moreover – precisely for the reasons that Hegel looked to it to serve as an introduction to his system in the first place – remains an indispensable work (and point of departure) for those who want to understand Hegel's place within German Idealism.

So how to understand the project behind the *Phenomenology*? In this chapter, I shall address (i) the difficulties of its underlying aim and scope, (ii) its overall structure and problems of unity and (iii) its apparent method. I shall finally turn (iv) to a consideration of the *Phenomenology* as a whole, focusing particular attention on three crucial moments within its structure that have been – and remain so for the most vigorous of contemporary debates – at the centre of philosophical interest in Hegel: his treatments, respectively, of the putative "givenness" of sense experience, the master–slave dialectic and the evolution of spirit as an essential and distinctively Hegelian category. In examining these crucial moments, I will also look at how each of them has spawned various contemporary lines of (significant but often conflicting) interpretation.

Background, aim and scope of the *Phenomenology*: genesis, title and tasks

Many philosophical and literary works come to involve a certain myth of their own creation, but the completion of the *Phenomenology* is genuinely the stuff of legend. Hegel himself speaks about it as a dramatic moment both personally and historically. Personally, it was the book in which he came into his own philosophically (and was thus no longer merely a former theological student trying out various ideas or a mere protégé of Schelling): Hegel's student Michelet claimed that his teacher was in the habit of referring to the book as his "voyage of discovery" (*Entdeckungsreise*).

In the autumn of 1806, Hegel was, at the age of 36, the equivalent of an assistant professor who had until then only published a few shorter works (see Chapter 1), and who moreover was four months away from the expected birth of his illegitimate child by his landlord's wife, and not yet through with the manuscript of a book that was supposed to have been out at Easter. Hegel had been kindly rescued on the book deal by his friend Immanuel Niethammer, who renegotiated Hegel's contract and agreed to pay the printer if Hegel missed the new deadline of 18 October.

Hegel's personal travails are cast against the background of the significant historical events taking place quite literally around him as he struggled to make that deadline. In October 1806, Napoleon's drive against the Prussian army reached Jena ("I saw the emperor – this world-soul – riding through town on reconnaissance", Hegel wrote in a letter). The battle that ensued would leave the university closed and much of the town turned into soldiers' quarters. In the midst of the confusion, however, Hegel was nonetheless able to send off the two large remaining chunks of his manuscript through French lines.

Napoleon went on to Berlin and the *Phenomenology* itself was finally published in March 1807. The *Phenomenology* (whose preface brims with language about the dawn of a new era – "ours is a birth-time and a period of transition to a new era") thus represents a dramatic turn, both personally and politically. What sort of book emerged out of this dramatic and chaotic moment in Hegel's own life and the life of Germany? Scholars have disagreed about what the book is doing and even about whether it can be said to have a coherent unified philosophical project at all. In this section, we will look at the apparent shifts in Hegel's title for the work and at the problems in organizational structure that have suggested to some a change in plans while writing

What can we learn from the title of Hegel's work? On its title page, the first edition of the *Phenomenology*, which was finished in early 1807, is declared to be the "System of Science, First Part: Phenomenology of Spirit". Hegel's "self-announcement" of the *Phenomenology* (published in the newspaper he himself was editing in Bamberg at the time) indicates that this first part of the system will be followed by the remainder of his intended system: "a second volume will contain the system of logic as speculative philosophy and the two remaining parts of philosophy, the sciences of nature and spirit".

Hegel never followed exactly that plan, but there are even more difficult problems with the work's title that betray more than a year's worth of difficulty between Hegel and his printer. Philosophically, the issue of interest is this: between the preface (which Hegel wrote last) and the introduction (which apparently had been printed in early 1806) Hegel had originally intended for the subtitle "Science of the Experience of Consciousness" to appear, but apparently changed his mind and insisted instead that the subtitle "Science of the Phenomenology of Spirit" be inserted in place of the original subtitle. (The printer, whose frustration can only be imagined, did not exactly insist on quality control: there are copies of the initial printing of the *Phenomenology* with one or the other of these titles and copies which just kept both of them.)[2]

Did Hegel then change his conception of the project from that of a concern with the *experience of consciousness* to that of a *phenomenology of spirit*? And what might it mean if he came to emphasize the latter over the former? Despite his switch in the subtitle in favour of a "phenomenology", Hegel certainly did not abandon the notion of a science of the experience of consciousness (in the preface, which Hegel wrote last, he is still referring to the *Phenomenology* as the "science of experience, which comprises consciousness"). As Ludwig Siep has put it: "history of experience and phenomenology are rather two aspects of the same subject instead of two methods which characterize the different parts of the book" – in somewhat simplified terms, as Siep suggests, experience might be taken to be the perspective "from below" and phenomenology the perspective "from above".[3]

Structure and problems of unity

If just figuring out what Hegel intended as a *title* for this work involves such difficulty, can we get any sense of its structure and method from looking at the table of contents? Even a quick look reveals some immediate difficulties in getting a handle on Hegel's organizational scheme. There are three main sections of the *Phenomenology*, marked with capital letters: consciousness is the first section (A) and self-consciousness is the second (B), but with "C" we have already encountered a problem: this third major section of the *Phenomenology* has no general title, but is further subdivided into sections marked with double capital letters – Reason (AA), Spirit (BB), Religion (CC) and Absolute Knowing (DD). Meanwhile, Hegel appears to have imposed yet another level of organization on the whole, marking off individual chapters with Roman numerals: the first three of these represent subsections of the first part of the earlier division ("consciousness" is thus divided into "sense certainty", "perception" and "force and the understanding") but the remaining chapters (from "self-consciousness" forward) correlate directly with one alphabetical letter (or double-letter) section each. Clearly the chapter organization appears to have spun out of control, too, as a quick page count will show: in Miller's English translation, the first three chapters are 9 pages, 12 pages and 25 pages, respectively; by chapter 4 we are up to 35 pages, but then we get to Reason and it is suddenly 124 pages; Spirit and Religion are likewise huge in comparison with the earlier chapters.

How to make sense of the unity of a work whose organizational scheme in the table of contents suggests, much like the history of Hegel's title itself, a project that perhaps got away from its author in its execution? There are three disputed issues concerning unity in the *Phenomenology*; each of these has traditionally been an important element of the debate in the scholarly literature, but in recent years there have been important shifts in how those debates are represented.

Philosophical

The most famous statement of the problem of the book's unity was Rudolf Haym's, who claimed that the project he thought evident at the book's start (providing a "transcendental-psychological proof" of the reality of absolute cognition) was "confused" by a second order of proof involving a concern with concrete historical data. Readers of the *Phenomenology* have often been portrayed as being members of one of two camps: in the first camp, those who have been most concerned to work through the claims to systematic connection particularly implicit in the work's original title ("The Science of the Experience of Consciousness"), and in the second camp, those who have been drawn to the "anthropological" concerns of the text with history, social structure and religion. For many of the former, it has been Hegel's later system that must take priority over the *Phenomenology*'s explorations into the realm of the social; many of the latter have taken greatest interest in the *Phenomenology*'s wealth of anthropological detail (the master–slave dialectic, the account of religion's origins, etc.) because they understand it to be an element which pushes against the structures of the eventual system. As we shall see below, the representation of these two perspectives has changed somewhat in the last few years, with the emergence of a reading (perhaps most prominently defended by Robert Pippin, Terry Pinkard and Robert Brandom) that claims a unity to Hegel's project precisely in its sociality – i.e. that the turn to normativity and categories of the social is essential to Hegel's larger epistemological project, and not merely of "anthropological" interest in the old sense. But this more unified reading of Hegel's project has opposing readers of its own – as, for example, those who read the *Phenomenology* in terms of Hegel's systematic project as a deduction of an ontological monism (as Rolf-Peter Horstmann and Frederick Beiser do).

Philological/textual

On the textual level, there has been a similar split between readers of the *Phenomenology* who assume the unity of the published enterprise and those (like Haym, Theodor Haering, Otto Pöggeler and most recently Michael Forster) who have argued that the book is really a palimpsest (a text written over an erased and underlying older text) because Hegel encountered difficulty with one project and then attempted to revise the book as a result. The urgent circumstances of the book's completion – as we have noted, supposedly during the battle of Jena – have often in fact been appealed to as the explanation for its lack of coherence.

Stylistic/formal

Quite apart from these considerations of the overall philosophical or textual unity of the work, readers have never failed to find difficulty (or, depending on the case, amusement) at some admittedly peculiar elements of the *form* or style of the *Phenomenology*. The "shapes of consciousness" which the book presents often seem to involve allusions to works and figures that are not directly cited, or for which the reader is not particularly prepared. The "experience" of many of those shapes and the transitions from one to another often seem to be part of an underlying pattern of a sort which has suggested to many a connection with other literary modes. The developmental structure of the various moments has led some (Josiah Royce and many others) to characterize the *Phenomenology* as ultimately a sort of *Bildungsroman*. Hegel's stress in the book's preface on the "labor of the negative" and the self-destruction experienced in the various moments of the journey has led others to characterize it ultimately in terms of tragedy, while still others construe the brightness of the claims for "absolute knowing" that emerge from out of that tempestuous development as essentially comic. But this ground has shifted, as well, with recent attention to the carefulness with which Hegel undertook the distinctly literary side of his essentially narrative project in the *Phenomenology*.

Method: the *Phenomenology's* introduction

If the *Phenomenology* is about the exploration of the "experience" of "consciousness", then how should one begin that exploration? A good place to start is with the introduction's account of method. Hegel's introduction divides into two eight-paragraph sections: §§73–80, devoted to the general epistemological and sceptical issues involved with the question of how to make a beginning in the search for truth, and §§81–88, which sketch the resulting method that Hegel claims to be following in the remainder of the text. (A final paragraph, §89, transitions to the main text of the *Phenomenology*.)

The introduction's first half begins with a consideration of the claim – Hegel calls it a "natural assumption" – that, if knowledge is considered to be some sort of instrument (*Werkzeug*) or medium (*Mittel*), then we might proceed, if we want to get at the truth, by removing the effect of that instrument or medium and examining it on its own terms. As with most of the positions Hegel presents (or, in this case, caricatures) in the *Phenomenology*, it is not clear who actually holds the view that Hegel attributes to "natural consciousness". And it is not clear how one is to take Hegel's criticism of the caricatured view, either. If an examination of the instrument or medium of knowledge is impossible, does that mean we are justified philosophically to proceed without any scrutiny of the process of knowing? In *The Encyclopedia Logic* (*Enc*) Hegel makes fun of those who "seek to know before we venture to know" as being as "absurd as the wise resolution of Scholasticus, not to venture into the water until he had learned to swim" (*Enc*: §10). But certainly Hegel cannot be encouraging his reader to think that one can "dive right in" (whatever that would mean epistemologically – perhaps to proceed as if there is no difficulty about knowledge that could require us to engage in an examination of the means of knowing itself).

The point of this first discussion of Hegel's introduction is rather one that opens up the Hegelian notion of an immanent critique: there is no *external criterion* against which our claims about knowledge can be judged (*PhS*: §81); rather, if the examination of knowledge can only be carried out *by* an act of knowledge (as Hegel puts it in the discussion of Scholasticus), then "consciousness provides its own criterion from within itself" (*ibid.*: §82). Subject and object are not separated items that can be pulled apart from one another for the purposes of an initial epistemological investigation; rather, consciousness is an object that has a continual relation to a model of itself.

This continually evolving notion of the "object of experience" has aspects that may remind a reader of the difficulties associated with Heisenbergian uncertainty in physics: the object, in being known, is "altered for consciousness", Hegel says (*ibid.*: §86). Or, more precisely, for Hegel's purposes: "what first appeared as the object sinks for consciousness to the *level of its way of knowing it*" (*ibid.*: §88). Consciousness is often unaware of what is going on in this shift from initial object to an awareness of how that object is known: "It usually seems to be the case . . . that our experience of the untruth of our first notion comes by way of a second object which we come upon by chance and externally" (*ibid.*: §87). Thus there is a distinction between what happens *for* consciousness and what might be said to go on "behind its back", as it were – but visible to an observer of consciousness's experience. The distinction between consciousness's own perspective at any given moment and what "we" as phenomenological observers can notice (Hegel calls attention to this latter perspective always in terms of the first-person plural) remains one of the essential determining features of the *Phenomenology*'s progress as a whole. What emerges over the course of the experience of a given shape of consciousness may be clearly an experience of the conflicts inherent in that shape of consciousness itself, but how those conflicts lead to the transition to a *new* shape of consciousness is something that only "we" observers can discern.

Hegel terms this path of experience in the *Phenomenology* as a whole as one of "self-consummating scepticism" (*sich vollbringender Skeptizismus*) and further describes it as not just a "pathway of doubt" but as the "way of despair" (*ibid.*: §78) – a contrast which echoes the distinction of the Jena *Skepticism* essay between mere "doubt" and the "complete denial" of the claims of finite cognition. What does Hegel mean by this and what sort of relation between scepticism and philosophy does the *Phenomenology* suggest? Hegel contrasts "self-consummating scepticism" with two forms of scepticism that he thinks cannot be as thorough: a temporary strategy of doubting – a "shilly-shallying about this or that presumed truth, followed by a return to that truth again, after the doubt has been appropriately dispelled" (perhaps referring to something like Descartes's procedure in the *Meditations*) – and "the scepticism with which an earnest zeal for truth and Science fancies it has prepared and equipped in their service: the *resolve*, in Science, not to give oneself over to the thoughts of others, upon mere authority, but to examine everything for oneself and follow only one's own conviction, or better still, to produce everything oneself, and accept only one's own deed as what is true" (perhaps referring to something like Kant's praise of the Enlightenment as testing all claims that come from apparent authority). By contrast, "self-consummating scepticism" demands a rigour that can rest on no foundational claim or point of departure: it must involve instead the weighing of all knowledge claims, including the ultimate claim of Hegel's system itself, as claims that must count *as appearances* or phenomena, and the examination of what contradictions may be involved just on the terms of those claims themselves.

As he presents it, Hegel's notion of "self-consummating scepticism" has both negative and positive sides: it is at once a "pathway of doubt" that should better be called the "pathway of despair" but also the "education of consciousness to the standpoint of Science" (*PhS*: §78; Hegel's word for "education" is *Bildung*, which also means cultivation or formation). This positive or constructive side of the process to be undergone in the *Phenomenology* suggests that there is not only an *epistemological* task or concern connected with the work as "experience of consciousness" but also a *pedagogical* one. Thus the individual "has the right to demand that Science should at least provide him with the ladder to this standpoint, should show him this standpoint within himself" (*ibid.*: §26). Given what we have said, it should be clear that the *Phenomenology* does not simply *give* consciousness that ladder, but rather allows consciousness to follow the implications of its *own* standpoint up to the point of science.

Hegel's interest in the possibility of such an immanently arising ladder from consciousness to science highlights one of the distinctive differences between the approach to philosophy he takes in the *Phenomenology* and that of his friend Schelling. Unlike Schelling, who appealed in his "identity philosophy" to intuition as a starting-point, Hegel insists that philosophy cannot be esoteric. Among the remarks in the *Phenomenology*'s "Preface" which no doubt changed the friendship between Hegel and Schelling are Hegel's claim that the "coming to be" of science presented in the *Phenomenology* is not "like the rapturous enthusiasm which, like a shot from a pistol, begins straightaway with absolute knowledge, and makes short work of other standpoints by declaring that it takes no notice of them" (*ibid.*: §27).

The distinctly *exoteric* method of the *Phenomenology* outlined in the introduction is thus a form of "self-consummating scepticism", in which shapes of consciousness experience the negative side of the loss of what they initially took to be their objects, but there is nonetheless a formative or educative progression of shapes – visible to a phenomenological observer – stretching from ordinary consciousness to the standpoint of science. But does Hegel in fact apply this method? In the remainder of this chapter, I shall sketch the general progress of the *Phenomenology* with a stress on three moments that form essential points of junction within it and which have correspondingly come to be particularly crucial sites of contention within Hegel interpretation – each in its own way providing a sort of litmus test for the kind of reader of Hegel one is inclined to be. The first of these is the initial shape of consciousness taken up in the *Phenomenology*, that of "sense certainty", where the issues of givenness and knowledge are central; the section which effects the transition from "consciousness" to "self-consciousness", which involves the relation between master and slave and consequently the range of claims made for and against the notion of sociality in Hegel's work; and the introduction of spirit as a new essential explanatory term. In considering each of these moments, I shall examine significant lines of interpretation which turn particularly on a reading of the section in question.

Overview of the project: three crucial moments and leading strategies of their interpretation

Sense certainty

The first moment in the *Phenomenology*'s development is entitled "Sense Certainty: Or the 'This' and 'Meaning'". Sense certainty is the first of what Hegel terms "shapes of consciousness" – that range of figures that stretches from this first chapter to the concluding chapter on "Absolute Knowing" – but it is also the first of the three initial moments of the work that Hegel groups together under the notion of "consciousness" in a more specific sense: consciousness understood as a standpoint from which what is true for the subject is an *object* that is *other* than itself (*PhS*: §166). It is this more specific sense of consciousness that defines the first large organizational section of the *Phenomenology*, composed of the individual chapters entitled "Sense-Certainty", "Perception" and "Force and the Understanding".

In the simplest terms, sense certainty involves a claim of knowledge in sensual immediacy. Hegel begins the chapter with the claim that "the knowledge or knowing which is at the start or is immediately our object cannot be anything else but immediate knowledge itself, a knowledge of the immediate or of what simply *is*" (*PhS*: §90). While readers of the *Phenomenology* agree about the need to understand the essential *immediacy* of the claim of sense certainty, there is, however, a wide disagreement about *why* Hegel claims that "our" first object *cannot be anything but* such immediate knowledge. I shall first explore the claims of immediacy in sense certainty and then turn to the range of interpretations that have developed about why it is Hegel's point of departure in the *Phenomenology*. The claim of certainty about something sensually immediate is putatively one of *pure receptivity*, unmediated by conceptual effort on our part. This claim of pure receptivity is what is at issue in each of the three moments of sense certainty – concerning the "object" (the "this" sense certainty intends), the subject (the "I" in the experience of sensing) and the presumed unity of the two sides of sensation.

(1) The "object" that sense certainty initially claims connection to is an immediate "this". But what is "this"? If sense certainty is "asked", it can answer in terms of "here" and "now": "here is a tree" or "now is night".

But the certainty that attaches to what is "here" and "now" quickly disappears, as Hegel says, if we test this truth with a "simple experiment": "[if] I turn round, this truth ['here is a tree'] has vanished and is converted into its opposite: 'No tree is here, but a house instead.' 'Here' itself does not vanish; on the contrary, it abides constant in the vanishing of the house, the tree, etc., and is indifferently house or tree" (*PhS*: §98); similarly, with the claim "now is night", if we write down this truth and read it again tomorrow at noon, "the now does indeed preserve itself, but as something that is *not* night" (*ibid.*: §96).

The truth that Hegel says is "preserved" in the "now" or "here" is in the form not of a sensed particular but of a universal: this universal is "a simple thing . . . which *is* through negation, which is neither This nor That, a *not-This*, and is with equal indifference This as well as That" (*ibid.*). While the specific *referent* of sense certainty's "this" or "here" varies from moment to moment and place to place, the *sense* of its claim (what we *mean* by trying to indicate a "now" or "here") remains the same. There is, as Hegel puts it, a difference between what we *mean* and what we *say*, which indicates an important role for *language* that has not been initially imagined by sense certainty:

> Of course, we do not *imagine* (*vorstellen*) the universal This or Being in general, but we *utter* (*aussprechen*) the universal; in other words, we do not strictly say what in this sense-certainty we *mean* to say. But language, as we see, is the more truthful; in it, we ourselves directly refute what we *mean* to say, and since the universal is what is true of sense-certainty and language expresses what is true alone, it is just not possible for us ever to say, or express in words, a sensuous being that we *mean*. (*PhS*: §97)

(2) If sense certainty's object has disappeared, as it were, into a universal, what is left for it to insist upon is what it *meant* – something that *I* alone can claim to know. (Hegel plays here on the pun in German between the verb "to mean", *meinen* and what is "mine", *Mein*.) But again a similar problem arises if we "test" this second claim of sense certainty: "I, *this* 'I', see the tree and assert that 'here' is a tree; but another 'I' sees the house and maintains that 'here' is not a tree but a house instead" (*PhS*: §101). And it is again the universal which emerges as the "truth" of the individual attempts at trying to capture individual experience:

> What does not disappear in all this is the 'I' as *universal*, whose seeing is neither a seeing of the tree nor of this house, but is a simple seeing which, though mediated by the negation of this

> house, etc., is all the same simple and indifferent to whatever happens in it, to the house, the tree, etc. The 'I' is merely universal like 'now,' 'here,' or 'this' in general; I do indeed *mean* a single 'I,' but I can no more say what I *mean* in the case of 'I' than I can in the case of 'now' or 'here.' When I say 'this here,' 'this now,' or a 'single item,' I am saying all thises, heres nows, all single items. Similarly, when I say 'I,' this singular 'I,' I say in general all 'I's; everyone is what I say, everyone is 'I,' this singular 'I.' (*PhS*: §102)

(3) While sense certainty's experience both of "this" and "I" is that what it *meant* in either case has disappeared into the universal, its final attempt to grasp what it intended is in terms of the *sensing whole* – *this* I asserting *this* here-now as a tree: I thus become a "pure act of intuiting" (*reines Anschauen*) and "stick to the fact that the now is day or that here is a tree", without comparing here and now themselves with one another (*PhS*: §104). Given the insistence of this third moment on a unique relation between a sensing "I" and a sensed "this" at a given moment, its "testing" does not involve the immediate turn to language that we have seen in the first two moments. Hegel says that "this certainty will no longer come forth (*hertreten*) to *us*" when we direct its attention to a now or an I that is other and that we must consequently "let ourselves *point to it*" or "enter the same point of time or space, point them out to ourselves, i.e., make ourselves into the same singular 'I' which is the one who knows with certainty" (*ibid.*: §105). It is as though sense certainty in this third moment had followed the lead of the ancient Presocratic thinker Cratylus, who tried to one-up Heraclitus by insisting that one could not step through a river even once – and who thus refused to try to capture intended sense referents in speech but would only point at them. But, as Cratylus no doubt knew, the now that is pointed to "has already ceased to be in the act of pointing to it" (*ibid.*: §106). (Hegel makes this contrast with another pun: sense certainty has insisted on grasping the *essence* of what is, but what *has been* [*ist gewesen*] is not an *essence* that is [*ist kein Wesen*].) The truth of this third moment of sense certainty has emerged in a somewhat different way still to have a universal result: the pointing-out of the now is "itself the movement which expresses what the now is in truth, viz., a result, or a plurality of nows taken together" – in their relations of before, after, etc.; likewise, "here" involves a "manifold otherness" of above, below, right and left.

The dialectic of sense certainty in these three moments is, says Hegel, "nothing else but just this history (*Geschichte*) that has emerged" (*PhS*: §109) – a history that depends on the very conceptual move to the universal that sense certainty had wanted initially to deny. (This is the theoretical equivalent, says Hegel, of the practical "refutation" of merely passive experience: even animals "do not just stand idly in front of sensuous things as if these possessed intrinsic being, but . . . fall to without ceremony and eat them up" (*ibid.*: §109).)

As sketched here, Hegel's exploration of these three moments of sense certainty raises a number of important philosophical questions, both about how one is to construe the philosophical significance of specific moves within the chapter and about how one is to view the chapter itself in terms of the project of the *Phenomenology* as a whole. Perhaps because it is the first exemplar of Hegel's method within the *Phenomenology*, "sense certainty" has attracted a high level of attention from commentators. What can we learn from a reading of this chapter, then, about why Hegel begins here? Answering this question about beginnings will take us into the fiercely contested but philosophically rich territory of arguments concerned with construing what Hegel's strategy with the *Phenomenology* as a whole must be. Several prominent interpretive options stick out. Perhaps most prominently, one set of Hegel's interpreters has taken him to be engaging in some form of *transcendental argument*. This claim is denied by others, but since there is a rather wide range of meanings and functions associated with the notion of transcendental argumentation – from Kant to Wittgenstein and more contemporary uses – it is worthwhile examining what claims have been made on behalf of reading the *Phenomenology* in this light.[4]

One form of transcendental argument attributed to Hegel is that articulated by Charles Taylor, who understands as transcendental arguments those that "start from some putatively undeniable facet of our experience in order to conclude that this experience must have certain features or be of a certain type, for otherwise this undeniable facet could not be".[5] The most obvious difficulty with this form of transcendental argument is that it has Hegel resting his argument on the making of a *presupposition* – something that he had clearly ruled out as unrigorous. Given his epistemological intentions, there can be *no* background natural assumption with which Hegel can begin the *Phenomenology*.

Other readers inclined to see some form of a transcendental argument in the *Phenomenology* (Pippin and Pinkard are in this latter group) view it as presenting something of a large *reductio* argument for experience as the result of conceptual and intentional activity; the point of departure thus has to be a moment that is not at all conceptual but rather some (putative) immediate, direct apprehending. One important element of this approach can be seen in Pinkard's insistence that the moments of the *Phenomenology* *present themselves* as claims: the task of the Hegelian phenomenologist is not to make initial decisions about what is essential to self-consciousness but to explore what would be the case if certain claims (such as "pure apprehension") held. A criticism of this form of transcendental approach is that it results in only a negative procedure in so far as sense certainty's claims are concerned.[6]

Another approach (Horstmann's) denies that Hegel is using a transcendental argument but takes him to be employing a sort of negative or "reverse" form of transcendental argument, which he calls "transcendentalist", in this case one that supports what he sees as Hegel's larger strategy for arguing for a monistic ontology. This reading thus sees a certain Kantian element within a more metaphysically-grounded reading of Hegel's philosophical project overall. For Horstmann's reading of sense certainty, this leads to the conclusion that the object of genuine knowledge cannot be "merely present, uninterpreted data, something that is simply and immediately given", but rather must be "an object of reference already loaded with conceptual expectations of its 'actual' constitution".[7]

Obviously, how one reads sense certainty in light of Hegel's project as a whole has implications for whether one thinks the section itself gives us as a result, say, Hegel's views on empiricism. For readers such as Pippin and Pinkard, the sense certainty section itself is not the place to look for such conclusions, for it presents only the failure of an artificially sketched claim; but for other readings clearly there is more to be read out of it for a direct notion of empirical claims of knowledge.

Beyond the issue of Hegel's employment of a transcendental argument, there are a number of other important interpretive questions that sense certainty raises at the start and that may be particularly at issue for first-time readers of the *Phenomenology*:

(1) What, for example, is the role of language in sense certainty? Does Hegel somehow take "saying" to be criterial in Wittgenstein's sense that "to know is to be able to say"? (There is much dispute, but it may be that the role of language here is just to show that sense certainty is on its own terms unable to determine itself.) Does Hegel mean by sense certainty's move to the universal that indexicals function exactly like class concepts? (The answer appears to be no: they do refer, like class concepts, to many different things, but pick out unique referents on each occasion of use.)

(2) Does Hegel not assume the forms of spatial and temporal intuition in his presentation of what sense certainty can claim, since it can say what is "here" and "now"? (Yes, Hegel does later seem to admit this – see *Enc*: §418.)

(3) How has history been involved? Many possible points of reference within the history of philosophy have been plausibly suggested, but in its first section the argument of the *Phenomenology* is (most readers admit)

notoriously vague on what all agree to be explicit references to claims about foundationalism, empiricism or realism. Among recent interpreters, perhaps the strongest claim for the historical function of the chapter as a whole within a larger historical cycle has been made by Forster, who associates the stance with Hegel's view of the "religion of light" in Persian Zoroastrianism (see *PhS*: §684ff.). Yet Hegel clearly differentiates the historicality of the shapes and transitions in Spirit and Religion from those of earlier moments in the *Phenomenology*.

The move from what sense certainty *meant* to its *truth* – requiring the shift that we have seen from sensible particulars to a consideration of universal terms – marks therefore a transition to a further phase of consciousness's experience. What has emerged in the experience of sense certainty is not merely a claim about the certainty of a "this" or a "now", but a concern with what can be taken *as true*. Hegel again appeals to a German pun in heralding the transition to the second moment of consciousness, *perception* (*Wahrnehmung*, which he renders literally as the taking, *nehmen*, of what is true, *wahr*). What we take in perception is – unlike the initial claim of sense certainty – "no longer something that just happens to us" (*PhS*: §111), but requires the distinction of properties and things. This gives rise to a dialectic of one and many: things are what they are only because of properties, and vice versa.

Perception in its turn involves a transition to "force and the understanding" – a notoriously baroque and difficult chapter even for a book as baroque and difficult as the *Phenomenology*. Unlike "sense certainty" and "perception", however, whose descriptions, as we have seen, are sufficiently unspecific to have been construed by interpreters in light of a rather wide range of historically significant empirical and realist positions, the account of force and the understanding makes use of a number of terms ("solicitation", "porosity") that appear to link to specific accounts of the physical world in eighteenth-century science. The basic idea, however, is a move to a (non-"thing"-like) relation where the intelligibility of something is bound up with its manifestations. Force is something that has both a centre and radiating expression; understanding (*Verstand*) looks through the mediating play of forces to the true background of things in, say, stable laws, with the result that we have an "inversion" in accounts (on the one hand) that push toward the supersensible but make sense only in light of the sensible, and (on the other hand) empirical accounts that must rely on supersensible terms for explanation. The conclusion of this moment – as of the section on consciousness in general – is that consciousness of a thing is possible only *for* a self-consciousness (*PhS*: §164). The movement of the *Phenomenology* will shift from a concern with objects of cognition to the cognizer as agent, a transition that, as we shall see in the next section, will require a move from terms of eighteenth-century natural science to the balder terms of a life-and-death struggle.

Self-consciousness, recognition and the master–slave dialectic

The second crucial moment in the itinerary of the *Phenomenology* that we shall explore in detail is the transition from "consciousness" to "self-consciousness", a transition in which, as Hegel claims, we first reach the "native realm of truth" (*PhS*: §167) – where knowing no longer has an object other than itself but is its own object and certainty thus is "identical with truth". As with the initial shape of "sense certainty", so this moment has been fiercely contested among Hegel's interpreters. Most particularly at issue in this transition is the conflict between master and slave (or lord and bondsman, as Miller's translation has it).[8] Why is this conflict so central to the turn that Hegel's project takes toward *self*-consciousness? What do master and slave in fact represent? Are they distinct individuals facing one another in some form of primal struggle or does the dialectic as a whole have somehow to represent a more unified and "internal" process between two sides? Another way of asking these questions: how implicitly *social* or *recognitive* is Hegel's transition from consciousness to self-consciousness? Hegel famously describes spirit in the section on "self-consciousness" as an "I that is a we and a we that is an I" (*PhS*: §177), but is the sociality implicit in this ultimate destination of the *Phenomenology*'s movement something that enters with the master–slave struggle or only later on?

This turn to self-consciousness is another moment which has been revisited in the light of recent interest in Hegel. As we saw above, the interpretive dispute about this transition was often regarded in an earlier generation as one between the "anthropological" readers of the *Phenomenology* (Marcuse, and especially Kojève, for whom the conflict between master and slave became the crucial turning-point of the whole Hegelian philosophical project) and "logical" readers, but new claims about the *sociality* of the project of the *Phenomenology* have to some extent raised questions about the lines of this dispute.

There is much that makes Hegel's account of self-consciousness difficult to understand. Hegel brings into the start of self-consciousness a not especially clear set of terms and moves, introducing the roles of "life" and "desire" with a not easily unpacked transition to the lord–bondsman relation itself. But the general frame of Hegel's section on master and slave seems initially to be much clearer; from the outset, Hegel presents this struggle as centering on the question of *recognition* (*Anerkennung*): "[s]elf-consciousness exists in and for itself when, and by the fact that, it so exists for another; that is, it exists only in being acknowledged" (*PhS*: §178). Because recognition is involved, the relation between the two central figures in this passage is consistently dual: "the movement is . . . the double movement of the two self-consciousnesses. Each sees the *other* do the same as it does; each does itself what it demands of the other, and therefore also does what it does only in so far as the other does the same . . . what is to happen can only be brought about by both" (*ibid.*: §182).

While the figures in the master–slave dialectic may begin their relation in an apparent initial equality, what quickly results is a fundamental inequality: in their struggle, one of the two will be willing to stake itself and so fight to the death, but the other will not. But since "it is only through staking one's life that *freedom* is won", the individual who has not risked himself "may well be recognized as a *person*, but he has not attained to the truth of this recognition as an independent self-consciousness" (*PhS*: §187). Out of this struggle, then, emerge a "master", who has shown his independence of life and mere things, and a "slave", for whom life has mattered more (*ibid.*: §189).

But while it is a struggle for recognition that has resulted in the relation between master and slave, the recognition that is possible between these two figures will prove insufficient. The master, after all, cannot gain anything that would count as full recognition of himself from a mere slave – "for recognition proper the moment is lacking, that what the lord does to the other he also does to himself . . . the outcome is a recognition that is one-sided and unequal" (*ibid.*: §191).

The inequality and hence insufficiency of recognition is only the beginning of the story, however. While the master cannot find in the slave an adequate recognition of his independence – and thus things turn out for him quite oppositely from what he had sought initially in the struggle (*ibid.*: §193) – there is a curious but perhaps more important reversal in the slave's situation. The slave's experience is characterized by two aspects – the first his "fear of death as absolute Lord" (*ibid.*: §194) and the second the formative and shaping activity of his work for the lord or master as "desire held in check" (*ibid.*: §195) – which together allow him to gain something in the relationship that the lord or master does not: the slave "realizes that it is precisely in his work wherein he seemed to have only an alienated existence that he acquires a mind of his own" (*ibid.*: §196). While Hegel makes clear that this achievement on the part of the slave is not sufficient to count as real liberation for him – his will, says Hegel, is still a self-will and hence "enmeshed in servitude" (*ibid.*) – the larger picture suggests that what the slave has done will have a new significance for the dialectic of increasingly less inadequate recognitions that is to follow in Hegel's account.

How to interpret this scene of conflict and struggle and the importance of the formative activity that moves it forward towards other forms of recognition? According to the most prominent line of interpretation over the last several generations of Hegelians, the master–slave dialectic should be read as an encounter that is essentially *social*, involving an *inter*personal relationship: master and slave are on this reading to be understood as distinct and separate individuals, and their relation is one of genuine *otherness*. This line of interpretation is characteristic of a wide range of readers but was particularly important to the so-called "anthropological" interpreters of Hegel's *Phenomenology*. Perhaps most prominently, Alexandre Kojève's reading of the passage stressed the struggle for recognition as the driving force behind Hegel's account of politics and history. The very nature of *human*, as opposed to animal, desire, Kojève insisted, was bound up with its origin in the struggle for recognition in the desire *of others*: "it is human to desire what others desire, because they desire it. Thus, an object perfectly useless from the biological point of view (such as a medal, or the enemy's flag) can be desired because it is the object of other desires."[9] Even on its own terms as a political reading, however, this interpretive stress on the essential otherness involved in the struggle for recognition faced some minority opposition – G. A. Kelly, for example, argued that the struggle for recognition needed to be placed in the larger context of spirit's "return-to-self" and of the importance of the development of interior subjectivity to Hegel's account.[10]

Two more recent trends in the interpretation of this passage have been most striking: on the one hand, the social aspect of Hegel's account has been accepted (by readers such as Pinkard, Pippin and Brandom) as not part of a merely anthropological or political project on Hegel's part but as essential to the larger philosophical – especially epistemological – concerns involved. Rather, Hegel's project in the *Phenomenology* is seen as opening up a set of normative questions that involve an inherent sociality: the move to self-consciousness represented in the lord–bondsman dialectic is on this line of interpretation thus construed as a move from the consideration of objects of cognition to us as cognizers – how *we take* or construe objects to be such and such and the "social space" in which we describe, classify and explain those objects. The question of this section then becomes how an agent can come to determine what is to count as an authoritative reason and not just a given desire from the realm of "life" (Pinkard), or how some fundamental "like-mindedness" among agents can be achieved as the condition of knowledge (Pippin). This connection between the master–slave dialectic and the sociality of recent Hegel interpretation has also been challenged, on behalf of readings that see the question of the struggle involved at the level of self-consciousness – as distinct from that of the later account of "spirit" – as one that is better understood in terms of the internal relation between, say, the apperceptive "I" and the empirical self.[11]

However the struggle between master and slave is construed, Hegel is quite clear about its importance as a moment within the larger project of the *Phenomenology*, since the *concept* (*Begriff*) of spirit is, he insists, already present in the emergence of self-consciousness itself:

> it is in self-consciousness, in the Concept of Spirit, that consciousness first finds its turning-point, where it leaves behind it the colorful show of the sensuous here-and-now and the nightlike void of the supersensible beyond, and steps out into spiritual daylight of the present. (*PhS*: §177)

What still lies ahead, of course, is the *experience* of what spirit is (*ibid.*). The specific development undergone between the emergence of self-consciousness and the arrival of spirit involves the three further moments in the development of self-consciousness itself – Stoicism, Scepticism and the Unhappy Consciousness – and the ensuing (often unduly neglected) chapter that Hegel devotes to Reason in its theoretical and practical forms.

The three moments that conclude the chapter on self-consciousness raise a number of interesting questions, not the least of which is how the apparent specific historicality of those moments is to be construed. Both stoicism and scepticism seem clearly modelled on the specific ancient philosophical schools which bore those names, and the portrait of the unhappy consciousness is interwoven with numerous allusions to the development of Christianity in the centuries before the Enlightenment. However these historical allusions are to be read in light of Hegel's project as a whole, the progression of these three shapes can clearly be construed as internally emerging from self-consciousness's initial wrestling with the issue of freedom and independence. Hegel's account of stoicism is that of a stance which claims an ultimately masterful grasp based on the independence that the slave has worked up: the stoic can claim – whether (like the manumitted slave Epictetus) in chains or (like Marcus Aurelius) on the throne (*PhS*: §199) – to be free precisely *in* his thought as a free self-consciousness. The sceptic can be understood as a critic of that stoic attempt at being free – a slave's-eye view that it is not so masterful after all – but the sceptic as such is nonetheless unable to *have a life* as a contingent individual grounded in that criticism (*ibid.*: §205, a problem that more recent commentators on scepticism have also raised).[12] The unhappy consciousness, finally, can be understood as the taking-together of both sceptic critic and the life as contingent individual that he found impossible to lead. It takes the contingency and changeableness of life to be an essential feature of itself and the world – a view that develops in terms that correspond to moments within the history of Christianity: an unattainable "beyond" that has flown this world.

The move from self-consciousness to reason (*Vernunft*) is explicitly said to be one of idealism, for reason is "certain that it is itself reality, or that everything actual is nothing other than itself" (*PhS*: §232); after "losing the grave of its truth" in the unhappy consciousness, reason "discovers the world as *its* new real world". This discovery first takes the form of *observation*, from initial classification and description to experiment to logical and psychological laws. The turning-point from observing reason to *active* reason are the claims made by the pseudo-sciences of physiognomy and phrenology, which, as Hegel puts it, falsely take an "I" to be a "thing" (i.e. see a person's character as revealed in bumps on the head).

Active reason is clear that the "I" is present not in things but in *deeds* – but this only raises further the question about exactly *how* a deed is one's own, and Hegel's unusually literary presentation of these figures (from a Faustian agent who takes pleasure as his principle, to Schillerian and Quixotic agents who oppose the goodness of their "heart" or "virtue" against the "world") opens up the central notion of a realm of judgement in which agents are also always spectators as well. This final realm of reason ("individuality which takes itself to be real in and for itself") has likewise three moments: the "spiritual animal kingdom", "reason as lawgiver" and "reason as testing laws". The first a realm in which action "simply translates an initially implicit being into a being that is made explicit" (*PhS*: §401) – Hegel calls this realm the "spiritual animal kingdom" (and Hyppolite suggested he must have the academic world in mind, where "a consciousness that opens up a subject-matter soon learns that others hurry along like flies to freshly poured-out milk and want to busy themselves with it", *ibid.*: §418). But what the "spiritual animal kingdom" has at its root is "the category" – "being that is the 'I' or the 'I' that is being" – and that status offers us "reason as lawgiver", where no justification of laws can be asked for but reason "knows immediately what is right and good" (*ibid.*: §422). But the content of such laws, on examination, reveals – as in Hegel's criticism of the "emptiness" or "formalism" of the Kantian moral law – only universality or self-contradictoriness as a standard. From this emptiness of reason's laws the *Phenomenology* turns directly to the contentfulness of spirit and the "ethical order".

Spirit and the realm of the normative

We turn now to the third crucial moment of our exploration of the *Phenomenology*: the chapter on Spirit. This transition may seem perplexing for a number of reasons. First there is the question of what spirit *is* that takes us beyond the perspective of reason. Secondly, there is the surprising and apparently anachronistic shift of moving from the concluding section of the Reason chapter, where we had been considering what seemed to be an essentially Kantian moment of "reason testing laws", to the initial section in Spirit, "ethical order", a moment that, as we shall see, appears to be quite rooted in the cultural context of ancient Greece.

What does Hegel mean by spirit and how is it a transition from out of reason? Hegel's initial answer (*PhS*: §438) is that reason becomes spirit when it becomes "conscious of itself as its own *world* and of the world as itself". This suggests strongly that Hegel's most fully developed sense of the project of the *Phenomenology* understands spirit as a development *out of* reason, a point questioned by those readers who find Hegel's narrative disjointed at precisely moments of transition such as this. (Those readers who stress the disunity or palimpsest readings of the *Phenomenology* point, for example, to what appears to have been Hegel's earlier intention for the work to transition directly from reason to absolute knowing.) But while it may seem at first glance that the move to spirit is a move *back* historically or a move to something motivated by *another* view of Hegel's initial project, there are recent readings of the *Phenomenology* that see an important conceptual development between the Kantian moment in reason and the beginning in spirit. Terry Pinkard, for example, sees this move as representing a reconsideration of the claims of Greek ethical life as an "alternative" to the claims of rationalist modernity that have been under exploration in the Reason chapter, and hence as a move from the characteristically "impersonal" view of reason in the Reason chapter to the conception of rationality as a reflective social practice. Construing spirit in terms of a move to an explicit awareness of social practice is stressed also by Robert Brandom, who defines spirit as "the realm of the normative", a realm that is "produced and sustained by the processes of mutual recognition, which simultaneously institute self-conscious selves and their communities".[13]

Hegel announces the change in the historical and cultural specificity that the *Phenomenology*'s shapes of consciousness now have beginning with spirit: "these shapes [i.e. of spirit] . . . are distinguished from the previous ones by the fact that they are real Spirits, actualities in the strict meaning of the word, and instead of being shapes merely of consciousness, are shapes of a world" (*PhS*: §441).

Spirit's trajectory as a whole will be one of leaving behind the beauty of ethical life and passing through a series of shapes to knowledge of itself. In some ways this development is a reversal of the initial experience that we examined above in the move from sense *certainty* to its *truth* in perception: in this case, "true" spirit will be the beginning, and "self-certain" spirit will be the result.

Spirit's development is opened up by a deed – that of Antigone, who breaks the apparent harmony of the essentially Greek world of ethical life by exposing the existing but not yet explicitly colliding cultural forces in that world represented in Sophocles' play by the "divine" and "human" claims that Antigone and Creon focus upon (*PhS*: §464). The question on Hegel's mind here seems to be the move from an implicit social whole (think of Hegel applying in a somewhat different circumstance the rubric from Hölderlin's "Judgment and Being" fragment that was discussed in Chapter 1) to the individual taking-up or taking-on of normative roles within that whole – a move that would have disastrous consequences for ancient Greece, where the claims of individuality are not yet made explicit. The claim of the individual – in Sophocles' play, a claim that in the end only fits the dead for whom Antigone tries to act – becomes the essence of the world of Roman law, with its defence of atomistic personhood under a universal order.

The harmony of the Greek world and the succeeding Roman order give way to the middle moment of spirit's development, which Hegel explicitly terms one of *Bildung* – a formation that here as elsewhere involves both alienation and artifice. (Its representative figure, sketched in light of Diderot's *Rameau's Nephew*, is a character who can imitate all aspects of an entirely aritifical world.) Spirit's progress through the Enlightenment and the revolutionary experience of "absolute freedom and terror" is towards a final stage in which it is "certain of itself" – the "moral world-view" of Kant and Fichte, which breaks apart because of the dissemblance involved between the universal obligations on an agent and an agent's individuality.

The successor moment to Kantian morality is conscience – a view first articulated by Fichte and then by the Romantics, who give it the particular form of the "beautiful soul", a figure sketched in literary efforts by Goethe, Schiller, Jacobi and Schlegel, among others. On Hegel's treatment, the beautiful soul is either (a) a figure who leaves the world entirely (Hegel seems to be thinking of Novalis, who died of consumption), or (b) one of two competing possibilities: a judging figure who refuses to get his hands dirty by actually performing an action, or an ironic agent who is aware of acting on his own interests and standards. The culmination of spirit's development is a forgiveness between these two sides of agency – the individual agent and the judge – which allows a "reconciling yea, in which two I's let go their antithetical existence" and in so doing "manifest God in the midst of those who know themselves in the form of pure knowledge" (*PhS*: §671).

It is only religion's development – from naturalistic and imagistic views of God to a self-awareness about religious thought as a whole as bound to picture-thinking – that finally brings Hegel to the end-goal of the *Phenomenology*: absolute knowing. In the *Phenomenology*'s extremely compressed final paragraphs, Hegel stresses precisely the reconciliation offered by the beautiful soul in his recapitulatory account of spirit's coming to terms with itself: it is this moment that binds the others into itself (*PhS*: §793).

Hegel's transition from the beautiful soul's forgiveness at the end of spirit to religion as spirit's self-knowledge raises a number of questions about the status of religion in Hegel's philosophical project which we shall consider in Chapter 7. But two final questions that these last sections of the *Phenomenology* raise for our context here are important to address before turning to the systematic project Hegel took the *Phenomenology* to be introducing.

First, what sort of historical movement is involved in the *Phenomenology*? As we have seen, there is one curious transition which brings spirit on stage – Antigone appears in the next moment after the Kantian moment of "reason as testing laws" – and yet another that follows it, since the Romantic beautiful soul's forgiveness will be immediately followed by the beginning of another historical cycle, this one moving from Persian and Egyptian religion through the Greek gods to Christianity. Lukács (and more recently Forster) have argued that there are three historical "circles" within the development of the *Phenomenology*: (1) from consciousness to reason, with the individual rising to rationality by traversing all the phases of mankind's historical development; (2) spirit's development as a real history in its concrete social totality; and (3) religion's development as the attempts of human beings to comprehend that real history (in art, religion and philosophy). But Hegel himself underscores that only circles (2) and (3) are concretely historical – a fact that only confirms the difficulty readers have had in settling on the presumed historical references in consciousness, self-consciousness and reason.

Second, what is the relation between *Phenomenology* and the logic that is the basis of Hegel's developing system? Is the *Phenomenology* just a crucial window for Hegel's early project, or does it retain some importance for the ultimate shape of his philosophical system? It is to this question that we will turn in Chapter 3, which will explore the systematic range of Hegel's mature philosophical standpoint, beginning with the two versions of his logic, and continuing with the two further developed concrete aspects of that system, the philosophy of nature and of spirit.

CHAPTER THREE

The *Logic* and Hegel's system

As we saw in Chapter 2, the *Phenomenology of Spirit* is concerned with the ascent, through the various finite modes of consciousness, to the standpoint of Science – a standpoint which, says Hegel, "exists solely in the self-movement of the Concept" (*PhS*: §71). Hegel's prefatory and introductory remarks to the *Science of Logic* stress the purity and presuppositionlessness of this standpoint. "Pure Science presupposes liberation from the opposition of consciousness" – i.e. the very sort of opposition we have seen to be characteristic of the various moments of the *Phenomenology*; "it contains thought in so far as this is just as much the object in its own self, or the object in its own self in so far as it is equally pure thought" (*SL*: 49). The point of departure for such a science must be "an *absolute* . . . it *may not presuppose anything*, must not be mediated by anything nor have a ground; rather it is to be itself the ground of the entire science" (*ibid.*: 70).

These claims about the standpoint of the *Logic* raise many questions about the sort of philosophical undertaking in which it is engaged. What exactly does Hegel mean by a "presuppositionless" beginning? Can he really be justified in assuming that the *Logic* has one? What does Hegel mean when he says that "thought" and "object" are one and the same in the *Logic*? Do these claims concern a metaphysical or transcendental project, or both?

This chapter will examine, first, the emergence of Hegel's *Logic* in the light of his developing views on the question of what can count as a proper point of departure for science and will then turn to several distinctive elements of the resulting logic that have been continuing issues for readers of Hegel – the notions, for example, of dialectic, contradiction and infinity. It will turn in a final section to the question of how the science that Hegel understands logic to be is related to the other two major parts of his mature three-part system – the philosophies of nature and spirit.

The problem of beginnings

In discussing Hegel's system and the connection between it and the logic, I will be primarily referring to the so-called "greater logic", the 1812–16 *Science of Logic*, but I will also draw when needed on the comparatively briefer version of the logic that Hegel articulates in the first part of the *Encyclopedia* (the "lesser logic").[1] Both versions of Hegel's logic concern themselves significantly with the problem of beginnings.

"With What Must the Science Begin?" Hegel asks in the title of a preliminary section of the first volume of the *Science of Logic*. In no other science, he claims, is the need to begin with the subject matter itself, without preliminary reflections, felt more strongly than in the science of logic. Since in logic there can be no distinguishing between subject matter and method, there is no possibility of somehow stating beforehand what logic *is*; it must emerge within the exposition.

The claim to freedom implicit in this non-arbitrary, presupposition-free beginning is well captured in one of Hegel's boldest images about the idealist project: "When we think freely, voyaging on the open sea, with nothing under us and nothing over us, in solitude, alone by ourselves – then we are purely at home with ourselves" (*Enc*: §31A).

But what does Hegel mean by this, and is it clear that he has such a point of departure? The problem of beginnings in Hegel's *Logic* has spawned an extensive literature, from some of Hegel's earliest critics (Schelling and Feuerbach, for example) who claimed that the *Logic* actually presupposed what it was to prove, to more recent attempts both to criticize and to take seriously Hegel's aims.[2]

Those who take seriously Hegel's claim to "presuppositionlessness" do not necessarily hold that Hegel can eschew hermeneutic or historical presuppositions; as Houlgate points out, a certain interest and capacity on the part of the reader, for example, and perhaps even the development of a certain religious stance that puts aside claims to authority might be conditions for the appropriate beginning to the *Logic*.[3] On the historical side, Hegel makes clear that the prior work of the *Phenomenology of Spirit* is important, since its task was to demonstrate the standpoint of pure knowing as emerging from the series of standpoints of consciousness investigated over the course of its progress. Hegel acknowledges this task and the presumed achievement of the *Phenomenology* at the start of the *Logic* ("the Notion of pure science and its deduction is . . . presupposed in the present work in so far as the *Phenomenology of Spirit* is nothing other than the deduction of it").[4] But he also announces at the start of the *Logic* that he has rethought the relationship logic has to the *Phenomenology* and that the *Phenomenology* is no longer to be considered the "first part" of the science.[5] The difficulties do not end there, since Hegel also conceives a new role for a curtailed "phenomenology" *within* the new system itself (and not as an introductory appendage thereto),[6] but in the end it is clear that, while the *Phenomenology* may have been required for our reaching the level of science itself (as beings at some stage of consciousness and at some point in historical time), that science must itself in some sense be, within its own specifications and determinations, self-grounding.[7] As Hegel presents what is on the table at the beginning of the *Logic*: "all that is present is simply the *resolve*, which can also be regarded as arbitrary, that we propose to consider thought as such".[8]

The logic that will emerge is not a science that concerns itself with *things* (*Dinge*), Hegel says, but is rather a science concerned with their *import* (*die Sache*). Hegel's logic is not, however, simply concerned with the formal relationships of traditional propositional logic. Rather, logic on Hegel's view returns in some sense etymologically to what the Greeks called more broadly *logos* or reason – as Hegel puts it, "the absolute, self-subsistent subject matter . . . the reason of that which is"; the science of logic can thus only be the object, product and content *of thinking*.

But what sort of metaphysics is implied in this more expansive Hegelian notion of logic? Clearly, we will be concerned in the *Logic* with "thought's self-determination", but this claim is read in a number of different ways. Some have interpreted Hegel's task in the *Logic* as that of presenting a category theory (i.e. as concerned only with the relation of certain basic concepts to one another and not with any claims about what is).[9] Among those who take the *Logic* to be doing something more metaphysically, some read it as an inheritor of Kant's project in transcendental logic, understanding metaphysics not as the ancient consideration of "being *qua* being" but rather "being as *being thought*" – the concern with what *objects* there can be in our thought determinations.[10] In a more radical and perhaps ancient sense, however, are claims like that of Houlgate, who has a number of points in common with those who link Hegel to Kant's transcendental logic, but who sees the *Logic* as opening up rather more ontologically an engagement with "sheer immediate being".[11]

Being, Nothing and Becoming

The best way to consider the question of Hegel's beginning is to turn directly to the actual first moves in the *Logic*, where we can gain a clearer picture of the sort of science that Hegel is unable to write a useful preface for. The beginning of Hegel's treatment of "Being" is three paragraphs long: one paragraph each devoted to "Being", "Nothing" and "Becoming". The development of the three paragraphs runs as follows, to encapsulate it in the briefest terms:

(1) The paragraph on "Being" begins with the consideration of "pure being, without any further determination", in its immediacy "equal only to itself". But such unmediated purity cannot contain within itself any determination or content that could be distinguished within it. In other words, there is nothing that would allow "Being" to be distinguished from anything *else* – and hence there is "*nothing* to be intuited in it" and "Being, the indeterminate immediate, is in fact *nothing*".
(2) The paragraph on "Nothing" begins, exactly as the paragraph on "Being" does, with the consideration of "pure nothing" – emptiness or absence of all determination and content. But in so far as *nothing* – rather than *something* – is to be intuited or thought, nothing must itself have a meaning. "Nothing is therefore the same determination, or rather absence of determination, and thus altogether the same as, pure *being*".
(3) The third paragraph – subtitled "unity of being and nothing" – develops somewhat differently than the first two, building directly on the dual movement that has been experienced. If being has been shown to pass over into nothing and nothing into being, then "what is the truth is neither being nor nothing, but that being . . . has passed over into nothing, and nothing into being". The "truth" of being and nothing is thus their *movement*: becoming.

The three short paragraphs summarized here raise, all at once, a host of interpretive difficulties. Is the translation from "being" to "nothing" really just some form of wordplay if "being" is in the end "the same" as "nothing"? Or, if they are different, is it possible to understand this is a valid transition without implicitly presupposing in the apparent "immediacy" of the beginning some kind of "mediation" (i.e. without assuming some sort of theory of thinking)?[12] Hegel seems to rule out the first possibility when he insists that, while "being" and "nothing" are both "indeterminate immediacy", they are nonetheless "absolutely distinct".[13] The second question here goes to the heart of the worries about the "presuppositionless" start to the logic: for example, as some commentators have worried, do we have to assume something like the course of the whole logic in order to understand its very beginning? To some extent, as we shall see below in the discussion of immediacy and mediation, Hegel admits this latter charge, but the sort of problems this admission raises will depend upon the sort of reader of Hegel one is. Thus some readers of these paragraphs see Hegel as beginning with a claim about immediacy that is set up only to be refuted, while others take it as the beginning – even if as yet not fully determined – of the exploration of what being is.[14]

However these paragraphs are read, they open up a set of difficulties connected with well-known Hegelian terms of art. Let us see what we can already draw from these first paragraphs about several of the most famous terms associated with Hegel's thought: *Aufhebung*, thesis–antithesis–synthesis, dialectic, contradiction, philosophical history, immediacy and mediation, and abstraction and concretion.

Aufhebung

From these paragraphs, we already have a perspective on what is the most crucial term of art within Hegel's philosophical enterprise: *Aufhebung*, a German word which Hegel specifically made use of to refer to what happens in developments like that from being to becoming, and which has a range of meanings appropriate to the experience of negation and development we have seen. The term in German can mean on its negative side both "clear away" and "cancel", but also means in a more positive sense "preserve" (*Enc*: §96A). Sometimes translated by the Latinate term "sublate",[15] the term can often present something of a frustration for English-speaking Hegelians since no single English word can capture all the meanings of the German. What is important to notice is that what emerges from *Aufhebung* cannot be simply construed as a unity or even a "synthesis" (see below) in the sense often attributed to Hegel. Becoming is not a mere unity of being and nothing in the sense of a category that *abstracts* from them, but rather their *inward unrest*, Hegel says (*Enc*: §88), or *unseparatedness*: "in so far as being and nothing, each unseparated from its other, *is*, each *is not*. They *are* therefore in this unity but only as vanishing, sublated moments . . ." (*SL*: 105).

Thesis–antithesis–synthesis

Hegel's philosophical approach is often incorrectly summarized by these terms, which have their origin in a later popularizer of Hegel named Heinrich Moritz Chalybäus. Hegel himself never used them to describe his system or the development that occurs within it. The three paragraphs describing the development of being–nothing–becoming, however, point up the insufficiency of that construal. A *thesis* is literally a *positing*, and a *syn*thesis is usually taken to be a combination or unification of items, but the process involved in these first three paragraphs is one which we have noticed begins *within* the category of being and then moves, in an organic and *immanent* way, to something that is not a mere combination of categories but the result of their negative movement.

Dialectic

Part of what can be difficult to assess about the developments that occur in Hegel's philosophy is what it means for his thought to have a *dialectical* character. Hegel defines a moment as dialectical when "the universal . . . of its own accord determines itself out of itself to be the *other* of itself" (*SL*: 831), when "it is shown that there belongs to some subject matter or other, for example the world, motion, point, and so on, some determination or other . . . but further, that with equal necessity the opposite determination also belongs to the subject matter" (*ibid.*). Thus "the very nature of thinking *is* the dialectic" (*Enc*: §11), says Hegel, and *finite things* are inherently dialectical: for example, as Hegel's discussion of limit in geometry claims, "the point is this dialectic of its own self to become a line" (*SL*: 128). Dialectic is "one of those ancient sciences that have been most misunderstood in the metaphysics of the moderns", Hegel claims – he frequently nods in the direction of Plato when discussing the topic – but what is decisive about his own philosophy's appropriation of dialectic lies in the relation between the dialectical and the speculative. Just before the *Encyclopedia Logic*'s treatment of being, Hegel distinguishes in a section entitled "More Precise Conception and Division of the *Logic*" three essential moments or sides of the logical: that of the *abstract understanding*, the "*dialectical* or negatively rational side", and "the *speculative* or positively rational side". Hegel emphasizes that these are not to be considered as three *parts* of logic, but rather as three "moments of everything logically real; i.e. of every concept or of everything true in general". Hegel is thus not merely dismissive of the abstract formulations of the understanding or of the negative experience of the dialectic.

We might say that one of Hegel's essential claims here is that dialectic, for all its negative energy, in the end philosophically has a *positive result* – to return to the formulation of Hegel's earlier *Skepticism* essay, genuine philosophy "contains within it" the sceptical moment. The speculative is thus the positive side of the dialectic. (About Hegel's other term of art here: he acknowledges that the term "speculative", in his own day as well as our own, is most often applied to "very vague" enterprises – as he jokes, this seems to be most often a reference made in commercial or matrimonial contexts. But even such everyday references to what is "speculative" preserve two aspects that are present in the more philosophical notion that

Hegel has in mind: "first, that what is immediately at hand has to be passed and left behind; and secondly, that the subject-matter of such speculations, though in the first place only subjective, must not remain so, but be realized or translated into objectivity" (*Enc*: §82A).)

The law of contradiction and traditional logic

The first three paragraphs also raise a familiar question about how Hegel views the law of contradiction and the place of traditional Aristotelian logic. Aristotle's discussion of the law of contradiction – that "it is impossible for the same attribute at once to belong and not to belong to the same thing and in the same relation" (*Metaphysics* IV 1005b18) – insists that it is the "most certain of all principles", but one that because of its self-evidence cannot be proven like other axioms. Hegel is sometimes charged with "denying" the law of contradiction or ignoring its significance for logic in his claims about the fluidity of categories such as being and nothing.

In his discussion of contradiction in the treatment of "Essence" in the *Logic*, Hegel does claim that it is a fault of earlier logics that contradiction is not given a sufficient role:

> [I]t is one of the fundamental prejudices of logic as hitherto understood and of ordinary thinking, that contradiction is not so characteristically essential and immanent a determination as identity; but in fact, if it were a question of grading the two determinations and they had to be kept separate, then contradiction would have to be taken as the profounder determination and more characteristic of essence. For as against contradiction, identity is merely the determination of the simple immediate, of dead being; but contradiction is the root of all movement and vitality; it is only in so far as something has a contradiction within it that it moves, has an urge and activity.
>
> (*SL*: 439)

By contrast, Hegel turns the notion of *speculative* thinking around his own embrace of contradiction: "speculative thinking consists solely in the fact that thought holds fast contradiction, and in it, its own self, but does not allow itself to be *dominated* by it as in representational thinking, where its determinations are resolved by contradiction only into other determinations or into nothing" (*ibid.*).

But it is precisely such claims about "holding fast to contradiction" or Hegel's notion of there being an "identity in difference" that have been seized upon by those suspicious of the move to speculative thought. Does Hegel mean that we can assert, for example, both that "s is P" and that "s is not P"? Bertrand Russell, for one, thinks that Hegel's notion of contradiction must rest on a confusion:

> Hegel's argument . . . depends . . . upon confusing the "is" of predication, as in "Socrates is mortal," with the "is" of identity, as in "Socrates is the philosopher who drank the hemlock." Owing to this confusion, he thinks that "Socrates" and "mortal" must be identical . . . This is an example of how, for want of care at the start, vast and imposing systems of philosophy are built upon stupid and trivial confusions, which, but for the almost incredible fact that they are unintentional, one would be tempted to characterize as puns.[16]

Yet Hegel's notion of contradiction has been ably defended against Russell's charge.[17] Hegel does not simply confuse predication and identity claims, but is rather concerned with how *both* are at issue in any judgement that is to be both *essential* (i.e. one that tells us what something is and nothing else) and *informative* (i.e. one that is not simply a tautology).

Finally, although Hegel's interest in the move to a speculative logic makes clear the distance between his approach to contradiction and that of Aristotle's, it is not the case that traditional logic with its laws does not have *any* validity or a place in Hegel's system. In fact, it is precisely the role of the understanding within Hegel's system to give such laws a validity within their own sphere.

Logic and the history of philosophy

Hegel's own commentary to the first three paragraphs of the *Logic* immediately makes a claim that opens up a further rich vein of his thought. In the paragraph that directly follows the initial description of "becoming" ("Remark 1: The Opposition of Being and Nothing in Ordinary Thinking"), Hegel suggests that the thought of being and its tendency towards nothing is not simply an artificial construct of his own thinking but rather a stance that is found directly in the history of ancient philosophy – "it was the Eleatics, above all Parmenides, who first enunciated the simple thought of pure being as the absolute and sole truth . . . and in the surviving fragments of Parmenides this is enunciated with the pure enthusiasm of thought which has for the first time apprehended itself in its absolute abstraction" (*SL*: 83). In fact, Hegel claims, each of the moments involved in the first three paragraphs corresponds to a significant moment within the history of philosophy: as "Being" was a concern of Parmenides, "Nothing" or the void can be found expressed in various forms of Buddhism, and "Becoming" was embraced by Heraclitus (although not, according to Hegel, in a conceptual form). More broadly stated, on Hegel's view, the logic and the history of philosophy (at least according to his account of the history of philosophy) share the "same starting-point".

Immediacy and mediation

The opening moves of the *Logic* raise a particular question about the status of two terms that loom large in contemporary discussions of Hegel: immediacy and mediation. We have already seen something of Hegel's consideration of these terms at the beginning of the argument of the *Phenomenology*, but Hegel makes an aside which should be noted in light of that earlier conversation. The "logical beginning", says Hegel, makes it clear that "there is nothing, nothing in heaven or in nature or mind or anywhere else which does not equally contain both immediacy and mediation, so that these two determinations reveal themselves to be *unseparated* and inseparable and the opposition between them to be a nullity" (*SL*: 68).

Abstraction and concretion

Both being and nothing are abstract, Hegel points out, while the first *concrete* thought is that of becoming. This transition from abstract to concrete – another pair of terms of art within Hegel's philosophical system – is perhaps best understood, like most of Hegel's philosophical vocabulary, etymologically: to abstract is to "draw away" (*abstrahere*) while the concrete is what is "grown together" (*concrescere*). In his earlier years Hegel wrote an amusing short essay entitled "Who Thinks Abstractly?" which suggests that what we call "ordinary common sense" frequently involves a drawing away from the concrete through highly abstract thoughts and terms.[18]

The structure of the *Logic*

In moving from the initial moments of Hegel's *Logic* to the larger structure of the work itself, it is important to keep in mind his insistence on the organic experience that the *Logic* as a whole is. The headings and divisions that structure the work are inserted, he reminds us, primarily in order to facilitate the reader's grasp and are "only of historical value"; one should thus consider the *Logic* as a single movement without interruption.

Examining the structure of that larger movement, we notice that Hegel divides the text in two ways: there is the primary three-volume structure of Being (*Sein*), Essence (*Wesen*) and Concept (*Begriff*), and the overlaid two-part division between objective logic (including being and essence – the "relation" of being and concept – as a transition) and subjective logic (concept). Each of the main three moments of the work has a different logic attached to it: being involves "thought in its immediacy", essence involves thought in its reflection and mediation and the concept involves thought that has "returned to itself".

Being

As we noticed, Hegel regards "becoming" as the first concrete or *determinate* thought, and it is the notion of determinate being or *Dasein* that opens up the next cycle of development following the three paragraphs we have explored. The truth of the development from being and nothing to becoming is that we do not just assert "being" in its purity but *some determinate thing*, which comes to be and passes away. (Like Heidegger, Hegel unpacks the notion of *Dasein* with an appeal to its etymological parts as *Da-sein* – literally, a being *there*.) Like being, however, *Dasein* also involves an opposition: in its qualitative determinacy, *Dasein* involves a "something" that is alterable and finite, and so is *opposed to another*; this finitude is, on the other hand, precisely what is opposed in *negation*, which is infinite; the resolution of these two (the "becoming" of this further movement) is in an infinite that is free from opposition altogether – the *qualitative infinite*, which is the transition to what Hegel calls *being-for-self*. Being-for-self (*das Fürsichsein*) is thus the consummation of qualitative being, where the "difference between being and determinateness or negation on the other is posited and equalized" (*SL*: 157). (An example of the sort of for-self-being that Hegel has in mind is consciousness, which, as we recall from the *Phenomenology*, has the content of objects "within" itself but still maintains itself in this relationship – "we say that something is for itself in so far as it transcends otherness".)

The importance of infinity in this development from determinate being to being-for-self cannot be stressed too much. "The infinite in its simple Notion can, in the first place, be regarded as a fresh definition of the absolute" (*SL*: 137), Hegel says. A few pages later, in a remark entitled "Idealism", Hegel points out that infinity is in fact inherently connected to the notion of idealism: "The proposition that the finite is ideal constitutes idealism. The idealism of philosophy consists in nothing else than in recognizing that the finite has no veritable being. Every philosophy is essentially an idealism or at least has idealism for its principle" (*SL*: 154–5).

Hegel's discussion draws a distinction that he uses elsewhere in numerous contexts: that between the "spurious" and the "genuine" or "true" infinite. The untrue infinite always involves some *otherness* – the finite – to which it is opposed, but the true infinite "consists in being at home with itself in its other, or, if enunciated as a process, in coming to itself in its other" (*Enc*: §94A). The image of the former is the straight line, defining a limit that is never reached and always has a "beyond", but the image of the latter is a circle, "the line which has reached itself, which is closed and wholly present, without *beginning* and *end*" (*SL*: 148–9). (The importance of circularity and circular motion to Hegel's philosophy as a whole should be clear by now: philosophy in its systematic entirety on his view is said to be a "circle of circles", with each part a whole within a whole (*Enc*: §15).)

Hegel's insistence that with the genuine notion of infinity the territory of idealism itself has been reached is important. The upshot of the development from pure being to qualitative infinity involves an essential move to the ideal – something not encounterable in experience but an essential whole (as Pinkard puts it) within which judgements of being are made:

> True infinity taken . . . generally as determinate being which is posited as affirmative in contrast to the abstract negation, is *reality* in a higher sense than the former reality which was *simply* determinate; for here it has acquired a concrete content. (*SL*: 149)

> [t]he infinite *is*, and more intensively so [*in intensiverem Sinn*] than the first immediate being; it is the true being, the elevation above limitation. At the name of the infinite, the heart and the mind [*Gemüt und Geist*] light up, for in the infinite the spirit is not merely abstractly present to itself, but rises to its own self, to the light of its thinking, of its universality, of its freedom.
> (*Ibid.*: 137–8)

The movement we have so far explored – from being through *Dasein* to being-for-self – composes as a whole the development of *quality*, the first of the three moments into which the first volume of the *Logic* is divided. Quality is determinacy which is *identical with being* (what something *is* precisely a matter of what quality or qualities inhere within it), but the notion of quantity is different: it is a determinacy that can in fact be said to be *indifferent to being* (we can count and apply numerical considerations to things irrespective of their determinate qualities). Again, as with the original movement between being and nothing, so quality and quantity have each in their own turn become the other and their truth lies in a third moment, which Hegel calls *measure*. In measure, we have a "qualitative quantity" – an external determination (something that is more-or-less) that is at the same time reflected into itself. (In contrast with the measurelessness of Parmenides' Being, Hegel has in mind here something like the Greek sense of the importance of the measure, the avoidance of *hubris* or the notion of "nothing in excess" in life.) Measure likewise already implicitly involves a move to the next category, Essence, since it is a being self-identical in the immediacy of its determination.

Essence

Essence is the "truth" of being; it is thought in its reflection and mediation. Hegel himself acknowledges that Essence is the "most difficult" part of the *Logic* – it contains the categories of metaphysics and the sciences, both products of the understanding.[19] In comparison with being, it lacks presence or immediacy, and involves instead always *relation*. A pun helps make Hegel's point: Essence (*Wesen*) is being that *has gone by* (the German past participle *gewesen*).

The central opposition within the whole category of Essence is that between essence and its manifestation – a distinction between how the world *is* and how it appears. This opposition within Essence develops in three moments:[20] (1) essence as reflection within itself, which involves a relation to illusory being (or "showing", *Schein*) on the one hand and ground (*Grund*) on the other; (2) appearance (*Erscheinung*), which Hegel distinguishes from mere illusory being; and (3) actuality (*Wirklichkeit*), where essence is manifest (*offenbart*).

In the first section, as we see the development of the notion of ground, we see that there is nothing *behind* external reality, but that it rests on external reality as a system, and hence the notion of *Existenz*; a similar movement occurs in the second section, where the supposed difference between essence and manifestation is also overcome in favour of a relation that has an inner and outer; in the third section inner and outer are shown to be the same – and hence we move to actuality, a reality that manifests itself essentially (in Taylor's formulation). The final movements of the section as a whole concern the move to Concept; as substance became subject (*PhS*), so here we see, as substance develops into Concept, that necessity in its full development is freedom.

Concept

The Concept (as we shall translate *Begriff* here)[21] is "thought as it has returned to itself". Hegel again draws on an etymological connection to point up what is important in *Begriff* – the relation to *begreifen*, a verb which means "to grasp". The Concept thus offers a comprehensive grasp-as-a-whole – there is only *one* Concept, which makes it thus distinguished from our ordinary reference to the range of concepts (lower-case c) and ideas that may happen to occur to us. The Concept, developed into a concrete existence that is free, is the "I" ("true, I *have* concepts, but the 'I' is the pure Concept itself which, as Concept, has come into existence" – Hegel connects this with what he here underscores as the important achievement of Kantian philosophy in the "I think" or synthetic unity of apperception). The Concept must rise to the Idea (which Hegel defines as the unity of Concept and reality, or the adequate Concept – that which is objectively true) in the sense that it must be able to cognize the world in its subjectivity. The "subjective" side of the Concept develops in terms of the three moments of universality, particularity and individuality (the last, as the result of the first two, is distinguished by now being *determinate* or *self-related*) and Hegel's account of the forms of judgement (which he still associates with Hölderlin's "original division") and syllogism (which, unlike the "formal" structure of the traditional syllogism, does not hide in a "formal and boring" structure the importance of the unity of extremes which the syllogism achieves). On the objective side, as the *Logic* reaches its conclusion, Hegel takes up the explanatory concerns of mechanism, chemism and teleology; and finally turns to the Idea as "life" (here "logical life as pure idea", unlike life in nature, which presupposes inorganic nature and other conditions), cognition of the true and the good and finally the absolute Idea itself.

Logic, Nature, Spirit: relation of the *Logic* to the system

In considering the move from the *Logic* itself to the rest of the system, Hegel's favourite image is that of an immediacy that *outers* itself and then *returns to itself*. However that imagistic description of the movement of Hegelian logic is viewed, it is important to avoid one temptation that many readers of Hegel have experienced: the direct "application" of the categories and transitions within the *Logic* to the concrete parts of Hegel's system, as though it were possible simply to read off the movements in nature and spirit from the preceding logic. As much by his practice as anything else, Hegel makes clear that the aspects of each of these concrete parts of the system cannot be understood simply by referencing the moments of the *Logic*. Each of these is instead determined by a concrete idea that has emerged from the process itself. Thus, for example, while Hegel does make a number of explicit references back to moments and transitions within the *Logic* itself in his account of objective spirit, it is the *concept of the will* and the will's freedom that a reader has to take as most important for understanding the development of abstract right, morality and ethical life.

In explaining the relation between the *Logic* and the structures of the concrete system, Hegel also liked to make use of an analogy between logic and grammar: while it is possible for a youth as well as an experienced adult to make correct use of logic and of grammar, "the *value* of logic is only appreciated when it is preceded by experience of the sciences" (*SL*: preface). In what follows, then, it will be important to be alert to the concrete development in each case of the two parts of Hegel's system.

Philosophy of nature

Hegel's philosophy of nature has been the target of much criticism over the years. It has been regarded by some philosophers as almost beneath consideration as an outmoded philosophical approach to questions of the natural world and scientific discovery. Many of the criticisms directed at Hegel's philosophy of nature make false (or at least uninformed) assumptions about its intent, linking it to vitalistic excesses of the Romantic movement or insisting that it was Hegel's intention somehow to "deduce" particular empirical facts – perhaps most frequently cited in this last regard is Hegel's supposed argument to have proved on an *a priori* basis the orbits of the planets.[22]

It is true that Hegel's approach to questions of nature – precisely because of its non-reductivist yet empirically informed character – makes commitments that may not appeal to every contemporary philosophical mind. Yet since the criticisms directed against it are more often than not wide of the mark, it is thus important in starting to discuss the status of Hegel's philosophy of nature to understand precisely what Hegel thinks is the task of such a philosophy.

To begin with, the philosophy of nature, as Hegel sees it, is to be distinguished on the one hand from the empirical natural sciences, which have their own ends and criteria, and the philosophy of science more generally. It does not attempt to take over the role of the natural sciences by finding alternative natural explanations, but looks to the explanations that the sciences provide to see the rationality inherent in them.

What Hegel's philosophy of nature *is* concerned with is the *levels of organization* discernible in natural phenomena – matter, physics and life – and it seeks to understand those levels of organization in terms of increasingly appropriate *modes of explanation*. Hegel sees the philosophy of nature as a "system of stages" (*Enc*: §249), which do not unfold in a necessarily temporal order. As suggested above, Hegel's approach in general in the transition from logic to the concrete parts of the system is not somehow to make the logic "apply" or fit the realms of nature and spirit. In the *Philosophy of Nature*, Hegel begins instead with the notion of nature as the Idea in the form of otherness or externality, and thus with reason's externality *in space*.

Although nature is the Idea in externality (and thus in some relevant sense the "embodiment" of reason), it is also the Idea as "the *negative* of itself" (*Enc*: §247), so incorporates unreason or contingency. Hegel makes clear that he thinks it "pointless" to demand a construal or deduction of contingent products of nature (*ibid.*: §250R). Hegel's familiar example of the sort of contingencies that cannot be deduced (*SL*: 682) is that reason cannot explain why there are more than sixty species of parrot; this is part of what Hegel means by the notion of the "impotence of nature" (*Enc*: §250; *SL*: 607) – "this impotence in unconceptual (*begrifflos*) multiplicity, at which we can wonder, because wonderment is unreasoning and its object the irrational".

As Stephen Houlgate has pointed out, Hegel has a conception of the philosophy of nature's relation to the natural sciences which makes it dependent *historically* on the advances of the natural sciences (since it is unlikely that without Galileo or Kepler speculative philosophy of nature would have come up on its own with their laws of motion), but is independent *logically or structurally* of the empirical sciences (since Hegel takes it as his serious task to show how Galileo and Kepler's laws "accord with the determination of the Concept", *Enc*: §267R).[23] Hegel describes his general method in this regard as follows: "our procedure consists in first fixing the thought demanded by the necessity of the Concept and then in asking how this thought appears in our ordinary *Vorstellungen*" (*ibid.*: §254A).

A central question for any student of Hegel is the relation between nature and spirit. One place to begin with that question is with Hegel's claim in the initial discussion of "The Concept of Spirit": spirit is "the *truth* of nature and therefore its absolute *prius*" (*ibid.*: §381).[24] Clearly Hegel is not a reductivist or what would be termed today an emergence theorist, since the structures of nature point in the direction of spirit and spirit offers the more adequate explanatory categories for what is in nature. Hegel's classic example of this is the inadmissibility of causal explanations for both physico-organic and spiritual life:

> the reason is that that which acts on a living being is independently determined, changed and transmuted by it, because the living thing does not let the cause come to its effect, that is, it sublates it as cause. Thus it is inadmissible to say that food is the *cause* of blood, or certain dishes or chill and damp are the *causes* of fever, and so on; it is equally inadmissible to assign the climate of Ionia as the *cause* of the downfall of the republican constitution of Rome.
> (*SL*: 562)

But if Hegel is not a reductivist, neither is he ultimately a dualist. A window onto this question can be seen from Hegel's view of what is usually referred to by philosophers as the "mind–body problem". Hegel's take on this problem, which one can begin to examine from his discussion in *Enc*: §389, is that, if body and mind (or soul) are not regarded as separable *things* or substances, then it may be that there is no "problem" to "resolve". The approach Hegel will take instead bears more similarity to that of Aristotle's functionalist account of soul than to anything like the sort of "mentalism" he is often accused of.[25]

Philosophy of spirit

The question "What is spirit?" is one that has often been asked either with rigidly dogmatic answers in mind (as T. S. Eliot once wryly noted) or as a preface to not entirely illegitimate accusations of obfuscation (as Derrida and others have suggested). As we have seen, however, if Hegel is right about the holistic and normative demands that spirit brings into our explanatory practices, neither the dogmatist nor the obfuscator can claim to have grasped what spirit – at least for Hegel – is about.

As a part of the *Encyclopedia* system, Hegel's philosophy of spirit in its various facets is arguably one of the most accessible topics within Hegelian philosophy for contemporary readers. The remainder of this book's chapters will focus on the development of important aspects of Hegel's ultimate philosophy of spirit, particularly in the forms of objective and absolute spirit: Chapter 4 will focus on the core of Hegel's account of objective spirit, his ethical and political theory; Chapter 5 will concentrate on the importance of Hegel's philosophy of history to that account of objective spirit; and Chapters 6 and 7 will discuss the three aspects of Hegel's notion of absolute spirit (art in Chapter 6 and religion and philosophy in Chapter 7).

CHAPTER FOUR

Ethics and politics

Hegel's ethical and political philosophy has had more than its share of critics. Marx's early critique of Hegel's central political work, the *Philosophy of Right*, is perhaps the most famous point of attack in the German tradition, but others in that tradition, such as the scholar Rudolf Haym, have voiced unusually harsh criticisms of Hegel's supposed links to the most authoritarian currents within Prussian politics.[1] In the Anglophone world, the high point of suspicion towards Hegel's ethics and politics can be found especially in the immediate aftermath of World War II, with Bertrand Russell's notorious claim that Hegel's concept of freedom amounted to no more than the "right to obey the police" and with the attack unleashed by Karl Popper in *The Open Society and Its Enemies*.[2]

Much has changed since the heyday of this postwar "Hegel to Hitler" form of critique. The shift began to take place in the English-speaking world particularly with the publication of Herbert Marcuse's *Reason and Revolution* and the careful attempts of Shlomo Avineri and others to recover at least elements of Hegel's political doctrine for a more liberal tradition.[3]

As for Hegel's ethics, a sustained complaint from a number of quarters in the present century, both analytic and continental, was about whether Hegel in fact *had* an ethics – the charge that morality and conscience, especially, simply disappeared into the larger dialectical machine. If not everyone held *that* view, many in the Anglophone tradition certainly thought that Hegel's ethics must rest on some musty Bradleyan account of "my ethical station" that was hardly worth consideration in the contemporary social world.

But both suspicions about Hegelian ethics have been heard much less frequently in the last fifteen years or so, as well. Allen Wood's book *Hegel's Ethical Thought* (1990) and a series of essays by Robert Pippin in the decade following marked genuine watersheds in the Anglophone tradition's consideration of Hegelian ethics, and Hegel's notions of agency and freedom now have a place in the contemporary conversation alongside the perhaps still more mainstream "new" appoaches to Kant.[4]

This rehabilitation of Hegel's image has occurred at an unusually propitious moment within the broader conversation in contemporary philosophical ethics and political theory, since both disciplines had come to be dominated in the last couple of generations by overly binary forms of opposition: in ethics, between Kantians and utilitarians; and in political theory, between liberal theorists and communitarians. This sense of the need to push the conversation beyond an unusually restrictive set of dual opposing claims has made a number of "third" options – virtue theory in ethics, for example, and various hybrid forms of political theory – suddenly appealing.

Since it is at least the claim of Hegel's ethical and political theory to offer such a "third" perspective for getting beyond the duality of the contemporary opposition – a position that is neither simply liberal nor communitarian, and that is neither Kantian nor utilitarian, but that may offer resources of interest to both sides – it is important to examine what potential Hegel's approach might have for offering a new stance within that larger conversation. In pursuing that goal, two particular difficulties have emerged in some recent attempts to integrate Hegel's views in the current debate.

First, the attempt to place Hegel alongside the communitarian/liberal and Kantian/utilitarian positions has sometimes resulted in a Hegel who appears to share too much with either or both of those positions and whose own often much more distinctive (not to say idiosyncratic) full position has not always been seen to emerge. Hegel has been made safe for the liberal tradition, for example, and a happy part of the communitarian debate, and yet his own standpoint – harshly critical of certain presuppositions of both contractarians and communtarians alike – has sometimes failed to be made clear.

Secondly, there have been two large strands within the contemporary discussion of Hegelian ethical and political theory: one has attempted to argue for a Hegelian position in ethics or politics that has a plausibility within the current conversation but is free of larger systematic commitments; the other has insisted on the importance of re-examining the plausibility of Hegel's broader philosophical position in the current context.

If the pitfalls involved in both of these difficulties can be avoided, the Hegelian view of ethics and politics that could emerge in the contemporary debate in the years ahead may more thoroughly represent what is in itself a distinct and formidable position within the history of Western ethical and political thought. In this chapter, I shall attempt to further that larger goal by first articulating Hegel's ethical and political theory as it emerged from the wider tasks of the practical philosophy that developed within the project of German Idealism – loosely, what might be thought of as the working out of the Rousseauian commitments inherent in Kant's moral philosophy. I shall then sketch Hegel's distinctive conception of freedom and agency, turning then to the account of right, morality and the institutions of ethical life in the *Philosophy of Right*, before taking a concluding look at Hegel's politics.

Situating Hegel's ethical and political philosophy

Hegel's ethical and political philosophy – the task of his account of objective spirit – is spelled out most fully in the *Philosophy of Right* (*PR*), which stands both as one of the classics of ethical and political philosophy and as the culmination of certain aspirations within the ethical and political aims of the German Idealist tradition. In addition to the text of the *Philosophy of Right* itself, notes to the lectures Hegel gave on the philosophy of right open an important window on to his concrete political stance, given the crucial political developments that occurred both before and after the publication of the *Philosophy of Right*.[5] (Only one of the sets of notes from these series has as yet been translated into English, however.[6]) Further, Hegel's shorter journalistic and political writings – a collection that ranges from his very first to his very last publication on any topic – are brought together under the title of *Political Writings* and often provide a useful sense of how Hegel's political theory might have application to specific events.[7]

Hegel and the history of ethical and political thought: German Idealism and the task of a comprehensive ethics

We have seen in preceding chapters that the path of Hegel's own philosophical development involves a serious engagement with important figures from the history of ethical and political thought, as he moved (at Frankfurt and then Jena) from a Hölderlin-inspired critique of Kantian and Fichtean ethics through an Aristotelian phase and then back again to a Fichtean appropriation of the concept of recognition before he developed the historically inflected account of spirit that was finally to centre his own ethical and political thought. It is a commonly accepted view that the approach to ethics which emerges from this development is one that brings together an emphasis on the essentially Kantian claim that freedom is the ultimate value but places the account of what is necessary for agents to achieve such freedom in a more Aristotelian story of human actualization.[8] Hegel himself defines the crucial concept of "ethical life" in terms that stress the connection between freedom and the good: "Ethical life is the *Idea of freedom* as the living good which has its knowledge and volition in self-consciousness and its actuality through self-conscious action", he claims (*PR*: §142).

More specifically, however, the *Philosophy of Right* can be read as the culmination of the struggle of the German Idealists to articulate a *comprehensive* ethics and politics. How could the claims about practical reason and freedom essential to the practical side of the Kantian revolution be put together in a framework which also took seriously the claims of *right*, including not only specific property rights but also the state's power to *coerce* those who fail to acknowledge rights claims? In the wake of Kant's *Groundwork for the Metaphysics of Morals* and *Critique of Practical Reason*, all of the major idealist figures attempted to come to terms with the source of claims of both right and morality: even before Kant published his own two-part comprehensive ethics in the *Metaphysics of Morals*, Fichte and Schelling had attempted their own justifications of right within the scope of a broader picture of idealist ethics.[9]

Hegel, who came to the task of finding a ground for a comprehensive ethics somewhat later than Fichte and Schelling, introduces a third and integrating term into the task of finding a systematic grounding for both morality and right: the notion of "ethical life" or *Sittlichkeit*. Hegel contrasts this notion of ethical life directly with the "morality" (*Moralität*) characteristic of Kantian practical reason: although both terms are etymologically linked to *mores* (the German *Sitten* translates directly as "customs" or "morals"), Hegel differentiates between the larger social realm implied in *Sittlichkeit* versus the rather more narrowly individualistic claims of morality itself.

Hegel's readers have sometimes taken his notion of ethical life to involve a move perhaps to a more communitarian or unreflective set of values in the world, but Hegel's own account of *Sittlichkeit* insists on rationality and reflectiveness as an inherent part of the ethical world. How to understand this move to a social yet rational set of values? Among Hegel's recent commentators, Robert Pippin has offered perhaps the most thoroughgoing account of what "ethical reasons" for Hegel might mean: unlike "prudential" reasons, which involve the calculation of self-interest in any given action, and "moral" reasons of a Kantian sort, which are strictly universal, ethical reasons imply instead a commitment to specific institutions within an agent's world.[10] As will be seen, for Hegel the institutions most important for modern ethical life are those that involve family, economic activity and the state – all commitments in which an agent may see himself or herself "recognized" in acting on their behalf.

Hegel's ethics can thus be seen to rest on the notion of spirit and the socially recognitive world it involves, as discussed in Chapters 2 and 3. In the context of the *Philosophy of Right*, Hegel makes clear that "the basis [*Boden*] of right is the realm of spirit in general" (*PR*: §4) and that what is at issue in the system of right is "the world of spirit produced from within itself as a second nature" (*ibid.*).

It is important to notice the breadth of Hegel's appeal to the notion of *Recht* here. Grounded in his accounts of spirit and ethical life, the notion of right is not merely the narrow topic taken up by the earlier idealists in their considerations of property and the other claims of right involved in civil life: "when we speak here of right, we mean not merely civil right, which is what is usually understood by this term, but also morality, ethics, and world history" (*PR*: §33A). In its broadest contours, right means "any existence [*Dasein*] in general which is the *existence* of *free will*" (*ibid.*: §29).

From these considerations of spirit and right, the essentially *institutional* character of Hegel's ethics and politics has started to become clear. But how do those institutions – and the "ethical reasons" related to them – fit in Hegel's picture of freedom and agency? Among the first tasks of the *Philosophy of Right* is to outline how a Hegelian account of freedom and agency is situated within the notion of spirit and its institutional manifestations.

The *Philosophy of Right* and Hegel's concepts of freedom and agency

Perhaps the clearest and most succinct introduction to Hegel's account of freedom and agency can be found in the brief sketch of the will that Hegel sets out in the early paragraphs of the introduction to the *Philosophy of Right*. Hegel begins that sketch by discussing the close relation he finds obtaining between the will and *thought*: will is said to be "a particular way of thinking – thinking translating itself into existence" (*PR*: §4A); theoretical and practical are thus said to be "one and the same thing", both moments which "can be found in every activity, of thinking and willing alike". The importance of thought to will can be seen in a comparison of animal and human agency: animals, Hegel claims, can act by instinct, but human beings determine themselves by representing [*Vorstellen*] what they desire.

More broadly, the stance of a thinking agent represents a window on to the three crucial moments involved in the concept of the will, according to

Hegel: the will's ability to *universalize* or to *abstract from* any given content (*PR*: §5), the will's ability to *determine itself* or to *posit* a particular content (*ibid.*: §6), and the will's ability to *remain free* within its particular positing (*ibid.*: §7). Each of these three moments is evident in an agent's ordinary self-experience in attempting to act in the world:

(1) The first moment of the will is the moment of abstraction, universalization or "pure indeterminacy": "it is inherent in this element of the will that I am able to free myself from everything, to renounce all ends and to abstract from everything". This moment has a negative characteristic which Hegel sees evidenced in moments like the Reign of Terror during the French Revolution, in which, as he puts it, "all differences of talents and authority were supposed to be cancelled out".
(2) The second moment is a moment of "finitude or particularization": "I do not merely will – I will *something*" (*PR*: §6). The first and second moments together seem to involve the will in a sort of continual oscillation – between abstracting from any given content and willing any given content – that Hegel finds characteristic of the abstract and finite Kantian–Fichtean picture of the will.
(3) Overcoming such an oscillatory picture of the will, on Hegel's view, requires seeing what could be the basis of the "unity of both these moments": "what is properly called the will contains both the preceding moments . . . [T]he third moment is that 'I' is with itself in its limitation; as it determines itself, it nevertheless still remains with itself and does not cease to hold fast to the universal" (*PR*: §7A). The notion of *remaining with itself* – in German, *bei sich sein* – is central to what Hegel means by freedom. Freedom is neither the ability to abstract from any given content nor an arbitrary freedom of choice, but rather an ability to be who one is with respect to another that does not restrict that freedom. Hegel's favourite ethical example of freedom in this third sense is friendship or love: "[h]ere, we are not one-sidedly within ourselves, but willingly limit ourselves with reference to an other, even while knowing ourselves in this limitation as ourselves" (*ibid.*: §7A).

The picture of the will that emerges from taking together these three moments is reflective of the agent's sense of freedom both as *openness* and as *determination*. Hegel makes this point with an etymological aside:

> To resolve on something [*etwas beschließen* – literally, "to *close* something"] is to cancel [*aufheben*] that indeterminacy in which

> each and every content is initially no more than a possibility. But our language also contains the alternative expression *sich entschließen* ["to decide" – literally, "to *unclose* oneself"], which indicates that the indeterminacy of the will itself, as something neutral yet infinitely fruitful, the original seed of all existence [*Dasein*], contains its determinations and ends within itself, and merely brings them forth from within. (*PR*: §12)

Hegel contrasts this account of the will's freedom with what he acknowledges is "the commonest idea of freedom" (*ibid.*: §15): doing as you please. Why am I not *free* if I am able to do what I want? Hegel's response to this question is to ask how I know that what I want to do is not simply an *arbitrary* choice of mine (he distinguishes here the arbitrary will, *die Willkür*, from the actually free will, *der Wille*). What justification do my needs or wishes have that could make them grounds for my will as *free*? Hegel's claim is that it is not sufficient merely to reflect on my desires and ends, but that there must be something that counts as the *free content* of my will. Freedom cannot be freedom unless it takes an end or has an object that is in its content consistent with genuine freedom.

Hegel's distinction between genuine and arbitrary freedom is sometimes taken to implicate him on the wrong side of the distinction drawn by Isaiah Berlin between negative and positive liberty[11] – negative liberty understood as the absence of constraint or coercion (and hence a hallmark of the liberal political tradition) and positive liberty as identified with a specific course of action (and hence compatible with an agent's being compelled to act, as in Russell's famous "freedom to obey the police" remark). But Hegel makes clear that the arbitrary will – the agent's subjective ability to make a choice – is essentially part of *free* willing, as well: just as there is according to Hegel an *arbitrarily subjective* will, so there is an *unfree objective* will (as, for example, the wills of slaves or children: *PR*: §26).

On Hegel's account, the sense of the content of my freedom that would be involved in acting on behalf of a friend or family member – and thus having a sense of the concrete freedom he equates with "being oneself with another" – is something that can be experienced especially in friendship or love, where the connection is something evident in our *feelings*. But the presumably more impersonal and rational connections involved in other ethical institutions, such as those in economic and political life, are grounded as well in such a notion of freedom. Before turning to an account of such ethical institutions as they emerge in Hegel's *Philosophy of Right*, it will be important to say something more about the account Hegel's view of agency gives of the relationship between feeling and rationality.

Subjective and objective sides of agency

We have seen that Hegel's account of ethical life involves a claim about acting for reasons that imply a certain social embodiment in that they relate directly to persons and institutions that allow an agent to recognize himself as present in his activity on their behalf, even though they remain distinct "others". Reason, on Hegel's view, is not simply opposed to an agent's social commitments.

Nor is it, however, merely opposed to an agent's emotional life. If Hegel agrees with Kant on the issue of rational justification, it would appear that he disagrees when it comes to the issue of motivation:[12] does he not say clearly that "nothing great has been, nor can be accomplished without passion" (*Enc*: §474)?

Hegel in the end is not merely a compatibilist, but in Pippin's coinage, a *continualist* – that is to say, he holds that what starts out as a desire or drive must become in the end part of a "rational system of duties" (*PR*: §19). The process by which this occurs he calls variously the "purification", "education" or "cultivation" of the agent in his desires: I may have an emotional or desiring attraction to something, but to act in a way that counts as reasonable that content must have an ethical form or shape. The *Philosophy of Right*'s task, in some way, is to show how the range of motivating desires that are most often discussed in social life – familial bonds, desire for gain, desire for recognition – all have an ethical shape or form (in the rational duties associated, respectively, with the family, civil society and activity in the state, for example). Each moment within the *Philosophy of Right*, then, represents at once an emotional and rational centre of an agent's ethical life. (To return to Pippin's contrast between "ethical reasons" and "prudential" or "moral reasons": if I act on behalf of a family member, I do so out of an existing bond with that family member and not because I either calculate my rational advantage to do so or impersonally consider whether I can make my maxim to so act universalizable.[13])

Right, morality and ethical life

In this section, we shall explore the account of the three main sections of the *Philosophy of Right* – abstract right, morality and ethical life – that form the parts of Hegel's comprehensive ethics. Given the connection between subjective and objective sides of agency on Hegel's account, each of these objective or institutional moments corresponds with a particular kind of subject or agent: in the realm of right, the *person*; in morality, the *moral subject*; and in ethical life, the *individual ethical agent*. The central argumentative structure of the presentation of these moments is dialectical, since the "abstract" claims of the work – rights-claims on the one hand and morality-claims on the other – both result in conflicts that require the concrete notion of ethical life in order to be grounded.

Abstract right

Although, as we have seen, right in the broadest sense means the existence or embodiment of my will as free, the more specific assertion of rights-claims concerns a realm in which the central commandment is "be a person and respect others as persons" (*PR*: §36). Right as a consequence is usually concerned with permission or warrant, rather than the sort of specific positive set of duties one encounters in morality (*ibid.*: §38); rights are usually framed negatively, in terms of prohibitions.

Abstract right on Hegel's account involves three areas: property, contract and wrong. Hegel's argument for property is rooted in a fundamental claim about the need for property as a condition for the exercise of an agent's freedom: as Hegel puts it, the person must give himself an "external sphere of freedom" in order to have being as Idea (*PR*: §41). Having a sense of "me" requires that there be an external "mine". But why must that be *property*, in the conventional sense? Hegel's claims are partly developmental ("I give property my soul" (*ibid.*: §44) and thereby realize that I have a power as a *self* that can be externalized and attached to mere *things*) and partly social (property is a place where my will is *recognized*, publicly – I cannot just wish that something is mine; it requires another's recognition in a mutual system of recognition in order to count as such).

Hegel's argument for property here can be interestingly compared with those of Locke and Fichte. Hegel clearly follows Locke's stress that the "great foundation of property" lies in someone's "being master of himself and proprietor of his own person".[14] Likewise, Hegel can be seen as developing a fundamental insight of Fichte's in connecting the notion of the *will* inherently to right and seeing *recognition* as a key element of that story, but Hegel does not go as far as Fichte does in making an essentially transcendental argument that the concept of right must be a condition of self-consciousness; Hegel instead argues that the free will needs in something like property a *sphere for its realization*.[15]

There are a number of important questions raised by Hegel's argument concerning property and the will's freedom. Is it clear that the sphere of externalization required for property implies the establishment of *private* property? And what does Hegel have to say about the problems of inequality and poverty that result from private ownership? Hegel insists – against something like a Platonic argument for common ownership of goods – that common ownership exists inherently at the arbitrary whim of a community (*PR*: §46), and thus, if property is to be an externalization of *my* will, there is no possibility for that to occur except in some form of private ownership. This argument means that *everyone* should have property (*ibid.*: §49), on Hegel's view – which thus provides a certain baseline in any scheme of distribution – but Hegel seems to think that the question of *how much* property anyone has is a matter of contingency. Leaving some contingency to distribution means that Hegel's account of property does in the end fail to avoid the problem of inequality and poverty (a point that critics from Marx to the present day have pointed up).

Hegel's development of the notion of property involves a move from "taking possession" in the sense of mere physical seizure to possessing something by means of form or sign (branded cattle, for example) to mere temporary use of things to alienation (*Entäußerung*, an important Hegelian term) by means of wage-earning.

Contract furthers this development along the lines of the increasing *alienation* of the will – in contracting with someone, I in fact create a *common will* with them (*PR*: §75). But that common will is not yet a will that is "universal in and for itself", as Hegel puts it – i.e. it does not yet have the *authority* that the state will have, and so there is a potential conflict between the common will as inherent in contract and the particular will of individuals who may not at all moments maintain their sense of participation in that common will.

The final moment of abstract right thus concerns this conflict between common and particular will – the notion of *wrong* and the response to it in punishment. More deeply, Hegel holds, this is a tension within the very concept of right itself, which is both an inherent investment of my will and at the same time something that requires the recognition of others. Pursuing this development dialectically, Hegel claims that punishment as response to wrongdoing is not something *external* to wrong, but in fact is precisely the expression of the self-destroying concept that the wrong was (*PR*: §92, §93) – it is, in Hegel's terms, the *negation of a negation* (*ibid.*: §97, §97A).

Hegel's self-negating notion of wrong and punishment is regarded by most as underlying an essentially retributivist argument for punishment, but it is important to notice that it is in a number of ways distinct from other forms of retributivism, particularly Kant's.[16] Hegel's notion of retributive punishment makes the following claims: (1) that punishment is in some sense the criminal's own *right*; (2) that punishment is not merely retribution but in some relevant sense a *reconciliation* (*Versöhnung*) of the wrong, since it is not an alien force being brought to bear on the wrong-doer, but – assuming that the conditions of justice are maintained in a state – punishment can involve nothing but the *deed itself* of the agent returning to itself; (3) retributivism requires an attentiveness to changing social norms about what *amount* of punishment should count as appropriately retributive: in earlier societies, punishment had to be severe, but in the modern world the state can allow lighter forms of punishment. (Hegel, like Kant, was a defender of capital punishment, on the grounds that it "honoured" the criminal as a rational agent and that there could be no appropriate retribution for taking a life besides death, since no other form of retribution would be commensurate. Yet, if Hegel's argument about changing social norms of justice is correct, it suggests that there could conceivably be Hegelian grounds for revising that view – he does at least venture the comment that capital punishment has become less frequent and that that is a reasonable development, *PR*: §100A.)[17]

Morality

The demand for something like morality emerges within the consideration of punishment, since legitimate punishment (as opposed to revenge) requires "a will which as particular and subjective also wills the universal as such" – and this is precisely the sort of will that is at the root of morality (*PR*: §103). While abstract right was expressed in claims that were essentially prohibitions, morality opens up a set of determinations that are positive and that require a broader notion of agency than mere legal personhood. Or, we might say more accurately: we now *have* a notion of agency on the table only with the consideration of morality. For the moral subject, how *I* determine my will, in all its particularity, is now the crucial concern: in right and contract, it did not matter what my inner intentions were so long as I outwardly did what was in accordance with the recognition of right. And, correspondingly, what is *mine* in the world must now have a deeper determination than the existence of something as my personal property: I must have intentions, interests and concern for the good.

Hegel's treatment of morality involves three stages, an argument structured in each case with an "inner" moment on the side of the agent related immediately to an element of existence in the world: (i) the development of an initial notion of agency in the concepts of purpose (*Vorsatz*) and responsibility – the concern is with what is *mine* in the alterable and social world of action; (ii) the relation of particular willing to universal claims in the notions of intention (*Absicht*) and welfare – where the question is one of what my *interests* are and how they relate to the interests of all other agents; and (iii) the notion of conscience (*Gewissen*) and its relation to the good.

Hegel's account of morality in these three moments is clearly concerned to offer a critique of the specifically Kantian or Fichtean notion of the moral. While the section devoted to purpose and responsibility raises a question about whether morality can sufficiently cope with the problem of justification raised by moral luck,[18] the later treatments of moral intention and conscience examine a set of objections to Kantian morality that are now virtually identified with Hegel: the problem of *formalism* or emptiness in the moral law (whether the moral law as Kant presents it or the formula of universal law as Kant derives it has content or can adequately determine the set of duties required by everyday life), as well as the charges of *rigorism* (whether an agent can act simply and only for the sake of the moral law as opposed to having other ends) and inadequate *moral motivation* (the charge that Kant's account of moral reason simply abstracts from the desires).[19]

The criticisms of Kantian and Fichtean morality that develop out of this section raise a further and more general set of questions that many readers have found of concern in Hegel's ethics: is morality somehow an essential moment within ethical life as a whole, or is it merely superseded? Do the claims of conscience possess an essential force within Hegel's view of modern life, or must they give way to the norms and demands implicit in the essentially institutional structure of ethical life? What ground do individual moral concerns have, in the end, in Hegel's ethics? These underlying questions may be taken together in the well-posed framework of Ludwig Siep's concerning the *Aufhebung* of morality in ethical life: any useful answers must in the end reflect the duality of Hegel's concept of *Aufhebung*,[20] since Hegel offers both a critique of moral claims and a preservation of them within aspects of ethical life. Thus, on the one hand, the resiliently first-personal experience of conscience is one that is essential to our agency and asserts a claim that cannot be examined by others as such; on the other hand, the actions conscience attempts to justify cannot be put simply beyond all intersubjective criteria. The larger context for Hegel would seem to be that it is only within the institutional structures of ethical life that anything like the claims of morality can be pursued and realized. (Individual morality turns out, for example, to have an essential place within the structures of civil society that allow an importance to the right to an agent's self-realization in conscious actions aimed at his welfare (*PR*: §207) and Hegel makes clear that individual moral activity has plenty of work to do within the institutional world of ethical life (*ibid.*: §242).)

Ethical life

As we have seen, the move to ethical life involves a set of specific commitments to larger institutions that Hegel outlines as essential to modern agency – the family, civil society and the state. Before we turn to an account of these institutions themselves, it is important to notice how Hegel situates the position of the individual within ethical life more generally.

Being an individual ethical agent, as opposed to simply a legal person or moral subject, means having an identity that is bound up with institutional commitments: as an ethical agent, one is not just recognized within a structure of mutually acknowledged rights or taken to be a responsible agent whose intentions in the world matter, but one is a member of an institution in which one can see oneself and one's agency as present, an institution to which one holds a commitment that does not involve a "giving up" of what is most one's own in order to be a part of it. Hegel's most explicit spelling-out of the individual's relation to his or her commitments comes in *Philosophy of Right*, §147, where he traces an increasingly self-aware development in an agent's own sense of the rationality of his or her commitments. Ethical life in general, Hegel says in that paragraph, is something the subject "bears spiritual witness to . . . as to its own essence, in which it has its self-awareness and lives as in its element" – not so much even a relationship as a "relationless identity" (*PR*: §147). But with the emergence of reflection on an agent's part, that identity can come to be experienced as a kind of *faith or trust*, where an agent's awareness of identity is determined by a representation (*Vorstellung*) of what that connection is (this is the relationship most discernible in the family); or with the further development of reflection and insight (*Einsicht*) that does not just accept relationships on trust but searches for a grounding in particular ends and interests (this is the relationship most clearly experienced within civil society); and finally there is the "adequate cognition" (*adequäte Erkenntnis*) of the relationship in conceptual thought (*Begriff*, which corresponds to the comprehensive grasp of relationships in the state).

Another important perspective on the individual's relation to his or her ethical commitments can be seen in Hegel's claim that it is only in ethical life that "duty and right coincide" (*PR*: §155). In abstract right, others had duties to me in so far as *I* had a right, and in morality there is only an obligation that the right of my knowledge and welfare be united with my duties, but in ethical life, "a human being has rights insofar as he has duties, and duties insofar as he has rights". Stated otherwise, it is ethical life that allows the particular sides of an agent's commitments (the *satisfaction* of the particular ends that I have a right to) to be reciprocally connected with the universal obligations or duties involved: I have both a right *and* a duty as a family member to receive an education while I am being brought up, it is both a right *and* a duty of mine to support myself by work in the realm of civil society, etc.

The institutions of modern ethical life

Ethical identity is bound up, as we have seen, with three large sets of commitments that concern an agent's familial ties, economic livelihood and larger political and social identity.

The family

The inveterate bachelor Kant had famously claimed that marriage was a contract for the use of one's partner's sexual organs, but for Hegel – for whom ethical life, like love, is essentially a seeing of oneself freely in another – that sort of contractual account could not be sufficient to represent the essentially ethical bonds involved in marriage and family life (*PR*: §161A). In addition to criticizing the contractual account of marriage, Hegel also rules out biological and romantic accounts of the family. What he offers instead is an account of what he calls the "ethical love" that is the determining character of familial life – an ethical tie that is more immediate, because connected to natural connections and subjective instincts, than those that will be considered in civil society or the state. Within that account, Hegel emphasizes the functions of the family in providing resources and property for daily life and for giving an education to children so that they can be active and productive agents within the larger world of civil society and the state.

Much recent discussion of Hegel's account of the family has focused on the specific character of the view of family and marriage that he outlines – that is to say, a monogamous, heterosexual and child-producing marriage within the context of an essentially nuclear, bourgeois and patriarchal family. Feminist critics of Hegel's position have questioned the apparently leading role that the father plays within Hegel's conception of the household, and it has also been asked why the essentially recognitive story that Hegel tells about this most intimate of ethical relationships could not, on rational grounds, be extended to same-sex marriages.[21]

Perhaps because of these critiques, it has become in some ways clearer that Hegel's claims about the ethical importance of the notion of family within the larger context of the actualization of freedom are ones that may indeed have a continuing resonance, even in light of the substantial changes that have occurred in the Western notion of the family since 1820. To follow in part Neuhouser's discussion, we might emphasize the ethical importance of familial life in these ways: if it matters in the contemporary world that there be an educative basis in which individuals' capacities for personhood and subjectivity are brought to flourishing, or that individuals have a way to connect their most immediate commitments to collective goods, then Hegel's notion of familial ethical ties is one that ought to be a part of contemporary ethical conversation.

Civil society

The crucial "middle" of Hegel's account of modern ethical life is bound up with his claim that between essentially familial ties and explicitly political forms of organization there is a third ethical structure important for agency. Hegel's construal of this middle term as the realm of civil society – a realm that has a certain independence for economic and other social activities apart from the political – forms in the end one of the most creative of his contributions to social theory.

The focus of civil society is the *economic or social agent in his individuality* (as Hegel says, drawing on the ambiguity of the German term for the individual in this context: the *Bürger* understood not as *citoyen* but as *bourgeois*). The realm of social and economic agency within this bourgeois realm is defined by two poles: the concrete *particular person*, who as a totality of needs is his own end, and the *universality* involved in the satisfaction that each such person seeks (*PR*: §182). Stated in bluntest economic terms, agents in the modern world do not simply satisfy supposedly "natural" individual needs on their own but require whole industries to provide for daily items – and their needs, in turn, come to be defined by what those industries produce and the larger social world that takes them to be important to acquire. Dozens of varieties of coffee, cognac and newspapers – items produced by the larger economic world and not thought essential on an earlier view of human needs – suddenly become indispensable items for everyday life. ("What the English call 'comfortable' is something utterly inexhaustible", Hegel grumps (*ibid.*: §191).)

This multiplication of needs in the evolution of economic production and consumption, so well described in the work of classical economists such as Smith, Ricardo and Say, marks an important shift in the development of Western society – a shift in which *natural* needs are superseded by *artificial* ones. Hegel embraces this shift as an inherently *rational* development, for it is in the supposed artificiality of modern existence, he claims, that the human becomes human as such (*PR*: §190), no longer a merely animal existence, but a being defining itself in terms of needs that require the *recognition* of others and hence a mutuality of need and satisfaction. "I acquire my means of satisfaction from others and must accordingly accept their opinions. But at the same time, I am compelled to produce means whereby others can be satisfied" (*ibid.*: §192A).

Civil society as the producing and consuming of these needs, says Hegel, "affords a spectacle both of extravagance and misery as well as of the physical and ethical corruption common to both" (*PR*: §185). Great wealth and great poverty are both inherent in it, and the attempts to make sense of it – on the one hand, the political economists' theories (which are, on Hegel's views, theories of the understanding) and the appalled stance of the cynics – are also both inherent to the rationality involved in civil society: "To recognize, in the sphere of needs, this manifestation of rationality which is present in the thing and active within it has, on the one hand, a conciliatory effect; but conversely, this is also the field in which the understanding, with its subjective ends and moral opinions, gives vent to its discontent and moral irritation" (*ibid.*: §189R).

Given the inherent conflicts and excesses of civil society, it is little wonder that Hegel is on the lookout for elements that can make clear why he thinks it is not simply a realm governed by economic laws – even ones that exemplify human activity and choice as free of natural necessity – but also an inherently *ethical* realm.[22] Hegel's account of civil society involves not just the "system of needs" (this is the primarily economic part of Hegel's discussion), but also the administration of justice (this is the place in his account where the initial discussion of punishment in abstract right is finally linked to an established and universal judicial system), and "the police" and "corporations" (two important terms which, as we shall see, have quite different meanings than they did in Hegel's time).

The balance of this account shows that Hegel is anything but a *laissez-faire* economist. The "police" – which in early nineteenth-century Prussia meant not only the cop on the beat but also the primary mechanism of policing the realm of civil society to make sure standards of fairness and exchange are in place – are concerned with a range of matters that would also involve many contemporary governmental regulatory agencies: street-lighting, bridge-building, pricing of necessities, public health and – in as much as civil society is on Hegel's view a sort of "universal family" – education. Hegel's notion of the "corporation", which should be distinguished from the modern business corporation as well as from certain attempts in the previous century (such as Mussolini's institutional plan for Italy) that have been called "corporatist", is in fact a form of workers' organization that ultimately gives the economic classes important political representation in the legislative body of the state. Modern in the sense that medieval guilds were not, and tasked with the larger welfare of their members at a level beyond that associated with most industrial unions in the West (at least certainly in the United States), the corporation in Hegel's view is "a means of giving the isolated trade an ethical status, and of admitting it to a circle in which it gains strength and honor" (*PR*: §255A).

The state

The third form of ethical life, the state, is not just one more moment in addition to family and civil society, but really the "apex and source" of them. Hegel's images of the state suggest something that is its own *end*: Hegel goes so far as to call it the "hieroglyph of reason", and its presence (at least on one translation) represents it as "the march of God in the world" (*PR*: §258A), an "earthly deity" which we should "venerate" (*ibid.*: §272A).[23] With some justification, then, the critics of Hegel's view of the state claimed that he was simply a deifier of the state and its powers, or a reconciliationist and apologist for the contemporary Prussian regime under which he lived.

But if we put aside for a moment the more provocative images (and take at least a more reasonable translation of one of them), it is important to notice the singular function that Hegel does give to the state in his account of ethical life. The state offers, first and most importantly, a connection for the individual to the whole on the level of rational *law* and constitutional structure, not on the level of feeling. It is where ethical life becomes clear to itself in an explicit way (*PR*: §257). Secondly, precisely what is rational about the state for Hegel is its *separation of powers* – or their *articulation*, to use Hegel's preferred word. The state is, in other words, an *organic* whole, composed (like organic beings in Hegel's philosophy of nature) of parts that have distinct functions but fit into a larger systematic order.

This notion of the state as an essentially *rationally articulated* whole implies, first, that Hegel's political theory is neither communitarian nor contractarian. Because the state is a whole, Hegel is not a contractarian: he does not think there is any implicit or explicit contract which has determined an individual's ultimate relation and obligation to the state. Because that whole has a rational and universal organization, Hegel is not (despite many affinities) a communitarian: what he articulates is the concept of a *Rechtsstaat*, a state that is grounded in universal principles discernible apart from birth in a particular ethnic or geographic context.

But, to take matters further: the notion of the state as a rationally articulated whole means, as well, that Hegel is (also despite many affinities) not an Aristotelian, but is instead more of a modern in the end. Not only does

Hegel put his ultimate stress on the concept of freedom as the central end which the state must help actualize; the question animating ancient political philosophy – whether aristocracy, monarchy or the republic is the best regime – is, Hegel emphasizes, not the essential question for his political theory. In the modern world, each of these forms of government is somehow involved, but what is crucial is a *differentiation* and articulation of their powers (*PR*: §272). Thus Hegel's state involves a sovereign (a monarch whose even occasionally arbitrary will it is important for individual citizens to see), an executive (with a universal class of bureaucrats – one of the elements of his political theory for which Hegel is best known) and a legislative body organized by the various Estates. The constitution as a whole is essentially a system of mediation that allows each function its role.

On its external side, Hegel's political theory makes further claims that have also often left him open to critics. Unlike Kant, who anticipated in his essay *Eternal Peace* a world in which republican governments freely organized themselves into a federation of states that allowed greater "conditions of universal hospitality", Hegel insists that no federation ever existed without creating an *enemy* for itself (*PR*: §324A) and that war – far from being some sort of absolute evil to be avoided – has in fact a positive ethical value in preserving the courage and ethical vigour of nations (*ibid.*: §324). (Hegel's argument here runs back to an early appreciation for Gibbon's descriptions of the long period of Roman peace in which the empire became flaccid and unable to defend itself.)

Hegel and politics

Hegel's theory of the state, like the work of any political theorist, should be compared with his actual views of concrete political affairs. As we mentioned at the start of the chapter, although Hegel was in fact allied with a group of fairly distinguished reformers when he came to Berlin, the charge of accommodationism seemed to stick with him, not just during his life but especially in the period of much harsher Prussian government that followed his death.[24]

Hegel's political interests ranged from an initial enthusiasm (and then horror) at the French Revolution to a fairly steady interest in reform in German institutions during the post-Napoleonic period, including an attempt to support the new king of Württemberg in his attempt at drawing up a modern constitution and, after his Berlin arrival, to contribute to the reform of institutions there. One of his most bitter rivals, J. F. Fries, characterized Hegel's political positions as giving in to whatever regime was in power at the moment: "Hegel's metaphysical mushroom has sprouted indeed not in the garden of science but on the dungheap of servility. Until 1813, his metaphysics was French, then it became monarchically Württembergian and now it kisses the bull-whip of Herr von Kamptz . . ."[25]

One should not, of course, let one's bitterest rivals define one's contributions, politically or otherwise. And there is a more philosophically compelling way to view the development of Hegel's political views in the broader perspective. As Terry Pinkard has emphasized in his biography, Hegel came of age at a time when politics had a choice between new claims to rationality inspired by the universal goals of the French Revolution – the "great teacher of constitutional law", Hegel once said, was none other than Napoleon himself – and the existing, quite local established order that had held sway in the range of German duchies and principalities since the Middle Ages. Between these two poles of universal principle and hometown custom, Hegel may be said in many ways to have attempted a middle course: defending, as he did in the *Philosophy of Right*, a set of institutions that included many that were part of existing Prussian life but many others (the jury trial, for example) that would have to be considered reforms.

CHAPTER FIVE

Hegel and the narrative task of history

If there is anything for which Hegel is thought to be most philosophically guilty, it is for enmeshing philosophy more deeply than almost any of his predecessors in the problems and contingencies of history. We have seen in the preceding chapters the importance of history to Hegel's phenomenological and encyclopaedic projects in general, but we have noticed at the same time how contentiously the historical character of those projects is regarded. Thus, although almost all readers of the *Phenomenology of Spirit* acknowledge that the project is tied broadly – at least in its chapters on Spirit and Religion – to a narrative that traces the development of Western history and culture, there is no general consensus on the use Hegel makes of history either in those chapters or elsewhere in the *Phenomenology*. Likewise, we have seen that Hegel himself asserts that the moments of his *Science of Logic* correspond to actual shapes within the history of philosophy, beginning with the connection he draws between pure being and Eleatic monism.

Although he never published a book on history as a topic in itself, Hegel did lecture frequently on the topics of the philosophy of world history and the history of philosophy as a discipline. The lecture series on world history, particularly the introduction to those lectures ("Reason in History", as it is titled in one of the most widely read English translations) is frequently taught in survey and introductory courses, and of all Hegel's works in English translation is often found by students to be among the most initially accessible. In this chapter, we shall examine Hegel's account of history in those lectures, focusing in particular on the context of these questions: What is history on Hegel's view, and how does philosophy relate both to the course of actual historical events and to the writing of history? Can philosophy make sense of historical progression – is there, as some interpreters have strongly insisted, an *end* to history, according to Hegel, and what does that mean for how we should judge history in general and particularly the historical events of the two centuries after Hegel? What sort of "justification" is implicit in Hegel's notion of history and does his (infamous) insistence on an operative notion of *theodicy* in history have any justification?

What is history? Hegelian modes of historiography and the task of philosophical history

Hegel's topic in *Lectures on the Philosophy of World History* (*PWH*) is the "*philosophical* history of the world" – or, as he explains, "universal world history", not "general reflections abstracted from world history and illustrated by concrete historical examples" (*PWH*: 11). What *history* is, Hegel says, is something everyone would seem to know, but he nonetheless makes two important distinctions about our use of that term.

There is first of all the distinction frequently made between history as *what happens* and history as the *narrative* written *about* the events in history – but this is a distinction that Hegel acknowledges that we make about something which might instead have an inner unity:

> In our language, the word "history" [*Geschichte*, derived from the verb *geschehen*, to happen] combines both objective and subjective meanings, for it denotes the *historia rerum gestarum* as well as the *res gestae* themselves, the historical narrative and the actual happenings, deeds and events – which, in the stricter sense, are quite distinct from one another. But this conjunction of the two meanings should be recognized as belonging to a higher order than that of mere external contingency: we must in fact suppose that the writing of history and the actual deeds and events of history make their appearance simultaneously, and that they emerge together from a common source.
>
> (*PWH*: 135)

Hegel's suggestion that there may not be such a hard-and-fast distinction between the supposed "facts" of history and their narration may make his view of history sound initially like the constructivist view asserted by more recent advocates of "meta-history" in our own day: that there is not an independently existing set of historical events outside of what is constructed by the activity of narrative itself.[1] We shall want to see in this chapter the extent to which Hegel may both concur with and dispute this constructivist view, but it is important to notice already the *ground* on which Hegel finds the connection between narrative form and content in history: the question about the *initial emergence* of historical consciousness itself, the possibility of which will frame as well, it turns out, the second distinction Hegel takes up about our sense of the term history.

Hegel's second distinction explicitly concerns the various forms of narrative historical writing, among which he differentiates *original*, *reflective* and *philosophical* types of history. As Hegel has already suggested, the importance of understanding the problem of the simultaneous emergence of history as both succession of events and their narrative construal, it is worth focusing some initial attention on his analysis of these different modes of historical narrative. First, we should notice that it is with this discussion of historical narrative that Hegel chose to begin his series of lecture courses on world history (Hoffmeister calls the section in which this discussion occurs the "first draft" of the lectures).[2] And Hegel's mode of presentation of these narrative forms also makes clear that there is a philosophical reason for his beginning consideration of the topic of history in just this way: his treatment of the modes bears not a little similarity to the dialectical procedure he follows elsewhere (but particularly in the *Phenomenology*) in justifying his own narrative approach.[3]

(1) In the category of original history, Hegel places such ancient historians as Herodotus, Thucydides and Caesar, but also modern historical writers of the same vein (he mentions Frederick the Great and Cardinal de Retz), who lived through the events they narrate and in whose writings thus the "spirit of the writer and the spirit of actions he relates are one and the same" (much as in poetry in which the poet's own emotions are present as the material of a poem itself). Hegel differentiates the sort of history he is interested in here from legends, folk-songs and traditions in cases where a country's self-consciousness is obscure; what original historians can offer in their writing is the expression of the consciousness of a country's own ends and interests and the principles underlying them.

Although he makes clear the limitations of this form of writing in terms of the academic concerns of "learned" historians, Hegel nonetheless offers striking praise of this first form of historical writing – where, presumably, one could most easily come to terms with the issue of the simultaneous and original emergence of both historical self-consciousness and historical narrative:

> Anyone who seeks to study the substance of history, the spirit of nations, to live in it and with it, must immerse himself in such original historians and spend much time on them; indeed, it is

> impossible to spend too long on them. For the history of a nation or government as they relate it comes to us fresh, alive, and at first hand. (*PWH*: 14)

(2) Historians in the first category are so immersed in the events they have lived through that they are not necessarily *reflective* about them. "Reflective" history, by contrast, where there is a separation between the historian and his subject, includes four general types of historical writing: (a) complete surveys of a nation or world; (b) what Hegel calls "pragmatic" history – attempts to place the "totality" of a past age or life before the reader's imagination; (c) critical history, or the sort of "history of history" which evaluates narratives for their authenticity and credibility; and (d) specialized histories of a field or topic (e.g. art, law or religion), which although abstract provide a sort of transition to philosophical world history.

In his discussion of this second category of history, Hegel questions whether historical *reflection* – despite all the encomia to "learn" from history – can indeed offer useful instruction. The "lesson" of history in fact proves to be that no one does learn from history, but that

> [e]ach age and each nation finds itself in such peculiar circumstances, in such a unique situation, that it can and must make decisions with reference to itself alone (and only the great individual can decide what the right course is). Amid the pressure of great events, a general principle is of no help, and it is not enough to look back on similar situations [in the past], for pale recollections are powerless before the stress of the moment, and impotent before the life and freedom of the present. (*PWH*: 21)

Hegel's point about the difficulty of historical instruction is mostly critical, but he does have praise in this context for Montesquieu as a historian, "both thorough and profound", who recognizes the uniqueness of historical circumstances – praise that points back in some sense not only to the interest that Hegel took in "original" history but to the need he saw in his Jena years (with Montesquieu again on his mind) for a holistic and non-fixed form of empirical political science: "Only a thorough, open-minded, comprehensive view of historical situations and a profound sense for the Idea and its realization in history can endow such reflections with truth and interest" (*ibid.*).

(3) Philosophical world history, Hegel says, offers a perspective that is "not abstractly general but concrete and absolute present". It brings with itself only "the simple idea of reason – the idea that reason governs the world, and that world history is therefore a rational process" (*PWH*: 27). In

arguing for philosophical history's stance as one that seeks rationality (at least in Hegel's sense) in the course of world affairs, Hegel first takes up a challenge posed by reflective historians who criticize the reading of history in the light of imported criteria. His argument, which picks up the concerns we saw involved at the start of the *Phenomenology* with immediate givenness and pure receptivity, is that no historical research can in fact be undertaken without certain essential categories (for example, the notions of change and of importance and unimportance):

> We can . . . lay it down as our first condition that history must be *apprehended accurately* [*daß wir das Historische getreu auffassen*]. But general expressions such as *apprehend* and *accurately* are not without ambiguity. Even the ordinary, run-of-the-mill historian who believes and professes that his attitude is entirely receptive [*nur aufnehmend*], that he is dedicated to the data [literally, to what is given, *dem Gegebenen*], is by no means passive in his thinking [*Denken*]; he brings his categories with him, and they influence his vision of the data he has before him. The truth is not to be found on the superficial plane of the senses; for, especially in subjects which claim a scientific status, reason must always remain alert, and conscious deliberation is indispensable. Whoever looks at the world rationally will find that it in turn assumes a rational aspect; the two exist in a reciprocal relationship. (*PWH*: 29)

If Hegel's argument is correct that the historian inevitably requires certain categories, what exactly does this mean for our understanding of what the historian does? Is it possible to gain a historical *understanding* of agents or *explain* their actions within the context of causal events? And what role would such explanations play in assessing the *rationality* that the philosophical historian brings to his study of history? These questions require us to look further at Hegel's notions of historial explanation and agency.

Historical explanation and historical agency

As we saw in Chapter 3, Hegel argues in the *Science of Logic* against the "*inadmissible application* of the relation of causality to relations of physico-organic and spiritual life" (*SL*: 562). In attempting to understand biological events, for example, the ascription of effects to presumably independent causes was said to be invalid because "the living thing does not let the cause come to its effect, that is, it sublates it as cause" – in Hegel's example, a living creature devours and "sublates" its food. In social and cultural matters, it is the nature of an agent, "in a much higher sense than it is the character of the living thing in general", not to "let a cause continue itself into it but to break it off and transmute it". Thus whatever is adduced as a cause in historical matters – "the climate of Ionia as the *cause* of Homer's works, or Caesar's ambition as the *cause* of the downfall of the republican constitution of Rome" – cannot give us an adequate explanation.

What does this claim about causal explanation mean for doing history and for the philosophy of history more generally? A helpful window on to this question can be found in Alasdair MacIntyre's classic discussion of Hegel's *Phenomenology* treatment of supposed causal explanation in the pseudo-sciences of phrenology and physiognomy. MacIntyre claims that

> [a] particular historical situation cannot on Hegel's view be dissolved into a set of properties . . . to respond to a particular situation, event, or state of affairs is not to respond to any situation, event or state of affairs with the same or similar properties in some respect; it is to respond to *that* situation conceived by both the agents who respond to it and those whose actions constitute it as particular.[4]

The point is not that Hegel is defending either in his analysis of phrenology or in his account of history some notion of unanalysable particularity (along the lines, say, of Russell's logical atomism). Hegel's actual point is more modest, but he "does assert what we may call the ultimacy of concreteness . . . just as there are good conceptual reasons for holding that existence is not a property, so there are good conceptual reasons for holding that occurrence at some specific time and place is not a property". Thus, argues MacIntyre, it is not that there *are not causal explanations* of a given action or event, but that "in so far as someone did respond to presentations of properties with the degree of uniformity that would warrant the construction of causal generalizations, he would not be at all like characteristic human agents as we actually know them and they actually exist". By contrast, MacIntyre suggests, Hegel's view of the task of history must involve a concern with a narrative that has an *inherent retrospectivity* and non-predictability and is open to *rational revisability* as the failures of previous historical construals are made clear.

One particular set of issues with regard to historical agency and the explanation of historical actions which is perhaps most frequently associated with Hegel is that of the relation between the ultimate (and presumably justifying) "reason" that emerges only as the result of action and the (usually less noble) "passions" that animated actual individuals in what they undertook. The most familiar of Hegel's claims in this regard is that of the *cunning of reason*:

> [i]t is not the universal Idea which enters into opposition, conflict and danger; it keeps itself in the background, untouched and unharmed, and sends forth the particular interests of passion to fight and wear themselves out in its stead. It is what we may call the *cunning of reason* [*List der Vernunft*] that it sets the passions to work in its service, so that the agents by which it gives itself existence must pay the penalty and suffer the loss. (*PWH*: 89)

As thus stated, the cunning of reason is not simply (as it is sometimes considered to be) a thesis about the *contingency* of historical events (i.e. some version of the "moral luck" problem, that in historical action events do not often turn out as their doers anticipate), but is really a thesis that rests on Hegel's larger points in the philosophy of agency about the relation between desire and reason (see the discussion in Chapter 4). While much of that thesis stands or falls with one's assessment of Hegel's philosophy of agency more broadly, there is a significant twist that makes Hegel's analysis of *world-historical* actions different from that of everyday ethical agency. This difference involves Hegel's oft-quoted claims about the so-called "great men of history", whose own ends mesh with the will of the world spirit: world-historical individuals are "those who have willed and accomplished not just the ends of their own imagination or personal opinions, but only those which were appropriate and necessary. Such individuals know what is necessary and timely, and have an inner vision of what it is" (*PWH*: 83). Hegel is clear that this knowledge on the part of historical agents may not be a philosophical knowledge of how what they are achieving is a moment within the universal Idea, but such agents do, however, "know and will their own enterprise, because the time is ripe for it, and it is already inwardly present" (*ibid.*).

Hegel on the course of world history

Hegel's concrete account of the development of world history is organized around four central nodes, corresponding with what Hegel calls (i) the "Oriental world", including the civilizations of China, India, Persia and Egypt, (ii) the Greek world, (iii) the Roman world and (iv) the "German world" (Hegel's somewhat overarching term for the history of Western Europe from Charlemagne to Napoleon). Each of these civilizations represents in Hegel's view a distinct phase of the development of world history only because, he claims, there was a fundamental political order: Hegel insists that only *states* can enter into history in a completely organized way.[5]

Hegel's view is that each of these moments of national spirit captures a crucial phase of the development of the universal spirit as a whole, but that the universal spirit keeps moving, as it were, to the next phase of its history: "the national spirit is a natural individual, and as such, it blossoms, grows strong, then fades away and dies" (*PWH*: 58), but each specific national spirit "does not simply fade away naturally with the passage of time, but is preserved in the self-determining, self-conscious activity of the self-consciousness . . . the universal spirit as such does not die; it dies only in its capacity as a national spirit" (*ibid.*: 61). The course that these moments together compose is determined in general by the level of freedom available in each. Asian tyranny, Greek and Roman aristocracy and the modern European state thus represent a movement in which freedom is expanded from one person (the Persian king or the Egyptian pharaoh) to a few (freedmen, as opposed to Greek and Roman slaves) to (at least in concept) all human beings alike:

> The history of the world . . . represents the successive stages in the development of the principle whose substantial content is the consciousness of freedom . . . during the first and immediate stage in the process, the spirit . . . is still immersed in nature, in which it exists in a state of unfree particularity (only One is free). But during the second stage it emerges into an awareness of its own freedom. The first departure from nature is, however, only imperfect and partial – only Some are free – for it is derived indirectly from a state of nature, and is therefore related to it and still encumbered with it as one of its essential moments. The third stage witnesses the ascent of the spirit out of this as yet specific form of freedom into its purely universal form – man as such is free – in which the spiritual essence becomes conscious of itself and aware of its own nature.
>
> (*PWH*: 129–30)

Ethical and political questions about history: history as end, history as judgement, history and individual suffering

When he began in 1822 the first of what would ultimately be the five lecture series he would give in Berlin on the philosophy of world history, Hegel noted the fact that he did not have an existing textbook on this topic for his students. He referred them instead to the brief but dense paragraphs on the course of world history that stand at the end of the *Philosophy of Right*. But these paragraphs are important to Hegel's philosophical project with respect to history for a further reason, since they offer a move from the consideration of "objective" spirit in politics and ethics to the realm of "absolute" spirit and raise several significant questions about the Hegelian approach to history. In their context, these paragraphs connect to the remarks on history in the Preface of the *Philosophy of Right*, which remain some of Hegel's most frequently cited (and contentious) thoughts on the subject – the two general reflections on history in the context of Hegel's larger ethical and political project thus serving as bookends of sorts.

It is important to remember the extent to which Hegel frames his account of history around the discussion of ethical and political matters because that ethical and political discussion offers perhaps the best ground from which to consider three of the most prominent objections or queries that have been raised about Hegel's view of history. The first I shall call Arendt's question, following up on the sharp interest that Hannah Arendt took in the question of a possible Kantian alternative to Hegel's notion of political judgement. Bluntly stated, her question is this: does Hegel not simply leave ultimate judgement in human affairs to success? The second we might call Kojève's (or more recently Fukuyama's) question: does Hegel think that there is an end of history and how does that view bear on the way we should read events since 1807? The third is a question asked about Hegel's philosophy of history from a number of perspectives and which is related to both of the first two: what is the role of the individual and particularly of individual suffering, if history – as Hegel claimed – is some kind of theodicy?

Arendt's question

On the title page of her unfinished work on *Judging* (which was to have been the third volume of her *Life of the Mind*), Hannah Arendt had typed as the first epigraph a statement attributed to the Roman statesman Cato: *Victrix causa deis placuit, sed victa Catoni* ("the victorious cause pleased the gods, but the defeated one pleases Cato"). Cato's statement was intended to serve as a reminder about the costs of the notion of historical judgement that in the end takes as justified what eventually happens – a view that she appears to attribute to (Marx and) Hegel:

> Either we can say with Hegel: *die Weltgeschichte ist das Weltgericht* ("world history is the world court of judgment"), leaving the ultimate judgment to Success, or we can maintain with Kant the

> autonomy of the minds of men and their possible independence of things as they are or as they have come into being.[6]

In light of the experience of the world in the century and three-quarters since Hegel's death, Arendt's question is one that Hegel's view of history must come to terms with. What sort of response would Hegel offer?

While Hegel does make use of the (Schillerian) phrase *die Weltgeschichte ist das Weltgericht* in the *Philosophy of Right*'s concluding discussion of world history (*PR*: §§341–2), the context makes it quite clear that the meaning Hegel attributes to this formulation is distinct from the "success is whatever wins" doctrine that Arendt supposes. Two points are important to notice from this discussion: (i) Hegel appears to be drawn to the phrase not with the question of theodicy in mind but largely because of the question he is concerned with at the end of the *Philosophy of Right*: what is the relation between particular political entities and their universal significance? The relation of particular to universal is precisely a question of *judgement*, Hegel claims: "World history is a court of judgment because, in its *universality* which has being in and for itself, the *particular* – i.e. the Penates, civil society, and the spirits of nations in their multifarious actuality – is present only as *ideal*, and the movement of spirit within this element is the demonstration of this fact" (*PR*: §341). In other words, Hegel's interest in the question of judgement is precisely how particular political institutions and claims are those that in the end can come to be judged to have universal significance at all; his interest is not – at least in this context – with Arendt's worry about how particular *individuals* may be unable to retain a certain independence of history's larger sweep or with how we might substantiate a claim to legitimate right even when it has failed to succeed. (ii) In using this phrase, Hegel immediately makes it clear that, within the very terms of the notion of spirit, it is essential to distinguish between what has happened to succeed and what can count as a *rational justification*:

> it is not just the *power* of spirit which passes judgment in world history – i.e. it is not the abstract and irrational necessity of a blind fate. On the contrary, since spirit in and for itself is *reason*, and since the being-for-itself of reason in spirit is knowledge, world history is the necessary development, from the *concept* of the freedom of spirit alone, of the *moments* of reason and hence of spirit's self-consciousness and freedom. (*PR*: §342)

Thus, while he acknowledges that power and contingency are inseparable from the whole realm of the historical that is to be judged, rational human judgement nonetheless has an essentially conceptual basis rooted in the notion of freedom.

Beyond Hegel's use of this particular phrase, however, the question Arendt raises is still one that would seem to be problematic for Hegel, if indeed he is committed, as it seems he must be, to a view on which freedom's development is something that must occur within the realm of history, where brute force and happenstance are acknowledged elements. To his credit, Hegel does clearly envision the possibility of moments in spirit's historical experience when a cause that has right on its side has failed to win. He discusses this issue in his account of conscience in the *Philosophy of Right*, and points to Socrates and the Stoics, particularly, as historical examples of conscientious opposition to a bad political order:

> The self-consciousness which has managed to attain this absolute reflection into itself knows itself in this reflection as a consciousness which cannot and should not be compromised by any present and given determination. In the shapes which it more commonly assumes in history (as in the case of Socrates, the Stoics, etc.), the tendency to look *inwards* into the self and to know and determine from within the self what is right and good appears in epochs when what is recognized as right and good in actuality and custom is unable to satisfy the better will. When the existing world of freedom has become unfaithful to the better will, this will no longer finds itself in the duties recognized in this world and must seek to recover in ideal inwardness alone that harmony which it has lost in actuality. (*PR*: §138R)

Fukuyama's (Kojève's) question

In 1989, in the wake of the imminent disintegration of the former Soviet Union, Francis Fukuyama (at the time a member of the State Department's policy planning staff) proposed that current political developments – which he construed as the "triumph of the West" and the "total exhaustion of viable systematic alternatives to Western liberalism" – needed to be understood not as the end of the cold war or the postwar period, but rather as "the end of history as such": "the end point of mankind's ideological evolution and the universalization of Western liberal democracy as the final form of human government".[7]

The notion of an "end" of history Fukuyama attributed to Marx and ultimately to Hegel, but it was the particular interpretation of Hegel's reading of history by Alexandre Kojève to which he appealed in making his argument about the end of history and the fall of the Soviet Union. It was thus Kojève's notion of homogeneous Western Europe, rather than Hegel's defence of post-Napoleonic political structures in Prussia, that anchored Fukuyama's argument.[8]

Fukuyama's Kojèvian position was widely misunderstood to hold that historical events would simply stop now that the "end" of history had arrived. But the claim put forward was that what was at issue was not the end of historical experience but rather of the ideological struggle that had now culminated in Western liberal democracy. Hegel, Fukuyama claimed, had understood in his notion of recognition the essential historical "engine" behind that struggle, but once the logical conclusion of that struggle for recognition was reached in a form of government that honoured the notion of democratic freedom, humankind was living in a "post-historical" phase of its existence.

Political developments in the years since the fall of the Berlin Wall have of course brought a different perspective to the events of 1989 (particularly to claims about the absence of asserted political alternatives to Western liberal democracy), but the question Fukuyama (and Kojève) raised concerning Hegel – to what extent is there an *end* in history and what is the meaning of that end? – is one that remains important, even in a world in which September 2001 marks at least an equally important turning-point. Was Fukuyama right to attribute an "end of history" thesis to Hegel, then?

What Fukuyama got correct is that Hegel's commitments *do* require him to discern an end of some sort in the development of Western history toward the fuller embodiment of the concept of freedom. Such a claim we have already seen in Hegel's formulation that "one was free, some were free, all are free". But the relevant sense of "end" for Hegel in this context is not one of history's *cessation*, but rather of its *consummation*—in the sense of Aristotle's notion of *telos*, for example.[9] This is an important point, because neither Hegel nor Marx spoke explicitly in any way about the sort of distinction Fukuyama and Kojève make between the "historical" and the "post-historical".

Moreover, as we have already seen, Hegel himself seems to eschew a predictive role for philosophy in historical matters and gives it instead the retrospective task of discerning how spirit and rationality have come to be present in the concept of modern agents. There are also some passages in Hegel's writings about specific future developments in world affairs that seem to contradict the notion of the world having reached a "post-historical" state. One of the most quoted of such passages is from Hegel's discussion in the *Lectures on the Philosophy of World History* in which he not only suggests that there are aspects of the New World that could bring something novel to historical experience, but begs the general question of predicting the future:

> America is . . . the country of the future, and its world-historical importance has yet to be revealed in the ages which lie ahead – perhaps in a conflict between North and South America. It is a land of desire, for all those who are weary of the historical arsenal of old Europe. Napoleon is said to have remarked: *Cette vieille Europe m'ennuie*. It is up to America to abandon the ground on which world history has hitherto been enacted. What has taken place there up to now is but an echo of the Old World and the expression of an alien life; and as a country of the future, it is of no interest to us here, for prophecy is not the business of the philosopher.
>
> (*PWH*: 170–71)

Finally, it should be noted that, while the Fukuyama/Kojève thesis looks to Western liberal democracy as the end of a historical development of the concept of freedom, Hegel's own defence of the institutions that can claim to embody modern freedom most fully centres, as we have seen in Chapter 4, on the somewhat less specific notions of the *Rechtsstaat*, the state founded in a notion of right or law, and of *Sittlichkeit* or ethical life more generally.[10] This is a particularly important point because, among the Hegelian passages that bear in an interesting way on considerations of the end of history, there is a brief reference to the West with respect to Islam that is of interest. In this fragment, from Hegel's Jena period, we can gather first of all the extent to which Hegel sees internal division and opposition as the forces constituting what realities – movements, religions, political parties – can be said to emerge historically and have historical existence. The question it raises at the end, however, is perhaps the most fascinating one for those of us trying to make sense of his notion of the "end of history":

> A *faction* [*eine Partei*] exists when there is internal fragmentation. This is the case with Protestantism, whose differences now are supposed to be coming together in attempts at unification – a proof that it no longer constitutes a faction. For it's in fragmentation that inner difference constitutes itself as reality. At the origin of Protestantism all the schisms of Catholicism ended. – Now the truth of the Christian religion is continually proven, who knows for whom, since we don't have anything to do with the Turks.[11]

The question of theodicy and individual suffering

Hegel's view of history's course and meaning leads him to put individual human suffering in the context of the larger historical development of reason and freedom, and to make an oft-criticized use of the notion of theodicy. The imagery of the "Introduction" to the *Lectures on the Philosophy of World History* offers a number of provocative claims about the status of the individual: "Reason cannot stop to consider the injuries sustained by single individuals, for particular ends are submerged in the universal end" (*PWH*: 43); "we look upon history as an altar on which the happiness of nations, the wisdom of states and the virtue of individuals are slaughtered" (*ibid.*: 69); "the individual may well be treated unjustly; but this is a matter of indifference to world history, which uses individuals only as instruments to further its own progress" (*ibid.*: 65); "our investigation can be seen as a theodicy, a justification of the ways of God (such as Leibniz attempted in his own metaphysical manner, but using categories which were as yet abstract and indeterminate). It should enable us to comprehend all the ills of the world, including the existence of evil, so that the thinking spirit may be reconciled with the negative aspects of existence; and it is in world history that we encounter the sum total of concrete evil" (*ibid.*: 42–3).

Hegel's imagery in these passages and his appeal to the tradition of theodicy are certainly problematic, not least because contemporary readers judge them against the background of the rise of totalitarian regimes that has taken place in the post-Hegelian world. Many Hegelian scholars simply dismiss the claims of such passages, focusing instead on the stress Hegel places in the *Philosophy of World History* on the emergence of forms of government in the Western world that enable individual satisfaction and freedom: "nothing can happen, nothing can be accomplished unless the individuals concerned can also gain satisfaction for themselves as particular individuals" (*PWH*: 70); "a state will be well constituted and internally powerful if the private interest of its citizens coincides with the general end of the state, so that the one can be satisfied and realized through the other" (*ibid.*: 73). However Hegel employs the notion of theodicy within his account of historical explanation, the most important level of historical "reconciliation" (or even "transfiguration", as Hegel describes it) is one that can only be accomplished by philosophical self-construal, a topic we shall take up again in Chapter 7.

CHAPTER SIX

Art, aesthetics and literary theory

Among the most striking features of the cultural and intellectual world in which Hegel came of age was its new and often enthusiastic appetite for art, which, together with an increasing sense of art's philosophical importance, may be said to be a characteristic element of the immediate post-Kantian era as a whole. This renewed exploration of art can be traced in an arc running from Kant's *Critique of Judgment* and Schiller's *Letters on Aesthetic Education*, through the endless journals and projects of the Romantics, to what finally emerge as the most ambitious attempts to present a comprehensive philosophy of art – the enormously detailed and systematically structured lectures on aesthetics given by Schelling and Hegel.

The sheer range of literary and artistic figures who help shape this period is extraordinary – Goethe, Schiller, Jean Paul Richter, Tieck, the Schlegels, Novalis, Hölderlin – but even more extraordinary is the extent to which each of those figures appears to be in significant dialogue with some or more of the central philosophical figures of the time – Kant, Fichte, Jacobi, Reinhold, Schelling, and ultimately Hegel. Dieter Henrich, whose own stress on the "constellation" of figures involved in the birth of German Idealism has inspired much of the last generation's research in this regard, is certainly right to note that there has hardly been "any time in history, before or after, in which the connection between literature and philosophy was as direct and mutual" as in the period following 1781.[1]

The contributions of Hegel's thought to art and literary theory in this period are distinctive and worth considering both from the perspective of philosophy's more general concerns and from the perspective of what insight they might offer to more direct reflections on artistic and literary endeavours. In this chapter, I shall thus stress not only the systematic importance of art and aesthetics for Hegel – their general development and organizational scheme – but also explore how his philosophical interests led him to make important contributions to disciplines such as art history (which can in some sense regard him as one of its founders) and literary theory (where his engagement with the Romantics, for example, turns out to be far more philosophically aware than is often thought).

Among the issues that will be most central to the account sketched here is the role of art within Hegel's view of modernity. Although Hegel's account of artistic beauty looks significantly back to the world of ancient Greece, there is nonetheless more room in his account for the art of modernity than is sometimes thought (in particular, the famous "end of art" thesis that is often attributed to him proves to be quite different on examination). In the first section, I shall explore Hegel's concepts of beauty and the purpose of art, and in the ensuing section take up how those concepts inform his (not always easily understood) organization of philosophical aesthetics. I shall conclude with a brief exploration of the importance of Hegel's view of narrative in the context of literary theory and practice.

Beauty, the ideal and the purpose of art

Art held a crucial importance for Hegel from the very beginning of his philosophical development. Of particular concern in Hegel's earliest phase was the "religion of beauty" that characterized ancient Greece – an ideal first invoked in a comparative way against certain trends in Christianity and later, with the historical inflection his philosophical project picked up in the years preceding the *Phenomenology of Spirit*, as an unrecoverable past moment in the larger narrative of the West's cultural and philosophical self-awareness that Hegel comes to speak of in terms of "spirit".[2] As we saw in Chapter 1, the project of the "Earliest System-Program of Idealism", with its aestheticized view of the political challenges facing a new age, certainly involved Hegel in some way – at the very least, as its transcriber.

Hegel first started to lecture on aesthetics relatively late in his career. He gave five series of lectures on the philosophy of art, first at Heidelberg (1818) and then at the University of Berlin (four series between 1820 and 1829). Like the *Lectures on the Philosophy of World History*, the text that we have involves the work of Hegel's students – in this case, it was Hegel's student H. G. Hotho, who compiled Hegel's manuscripts and student notes (taken by Hotho and others) from the last three versions of the lecture series into what are now known as the *Lectures* (here *Aesthetics*).[3]

In Hegel's mature system, art, religion and philosophy are the three moments in which absolute spirit comprehends itself. What makes art distinctive among these three moments is that it requires an *immediate and sensual shape* for expression; religion, by comparison, is characterized as a form of representational consciousness (*das vorstellende Bewusstsein*) and philosophy a form of free thought itself (*das freie Denken*).[4] These three modes share the same *content*, but grasp it in different ways. Art is thus on Hegel's view "one way of bringing to our minds and expressing the *Divine*, the deepest interests of mankind, and the most comprehensive truths of the spirit [*das Göttliche, die tiefsten Interessen des Menschen, die umfassendsten Wahrheiten des Geistes*]".[5]

Like Schelling, Hegel prefers the term "philosophy of art" for his investigation rather than "aesthetics" (although, like Schelling, he does not avoid use of the term "aesthetics" in general contexts where the philosophy of art is discussed); for both, the very notion of an "aesthetics" suggested the narrower focus of an earlier discipline that had concerned itself primarily with issues of feeling and subjective response. The central concern for the philosophy of art, on Hegel's view, is the *realm of beauty*, defined in terms of the *ideal* – or "the Idea in a particular form". As so defined, beauty is thus a mediation between thought and the particular shape it may have in appearance or sense. What is beautiful involves thus a relation between content (the Idea) and form (its configuration [*Gestalt*] as a concrete reality).

Hegel makes clear from the start that his treatment of the realm of beauty will focus on beautiful *art* in particular – and therefore privilege, as we might perhaps expect, beautiful experience available in the world of spirit over that available in the world of nature. Since, as we have seen in Chapter 3, Hegel does not think of nature and spirit as *opposed* terms, but rather takes spirit as the *comprehending* term in that it grasps the "truth" of nature, it makes no sense on Hegel's view to try to construe art as any sort of "imitation of nature". In the *Critique of Judgment*, Kant had suggested that if someone who thought he was listening to a nightingale was made aware that he had instead been listening all along to someone imitating a nightingale, he would no longer find the sound charming ("in order for us to be able to take a direct *interest* in the beautiful as such, it must be nature or we must consider it so").[6] Hegel's discussion of this example is telling for what it reveals about his own sense of the different relation between beauty and nature: he points out that such imitation does not even count as *art* in any case – it is a mere trick:

> neither the free production of nature or a work of art, since from the free productive power of man we expect something quite different from such music which interests us only when, as is the case with the nightingale's warbling, it gushes forth purposeless from the bird's own life, like the voice of human feeling. In general this delight in imitative skill can always be but restricted,

> and it befits man better to take delight in what he produces out of himself. (*Aesthetics* I: 43)

Although Hegel does have occasional praise for natural beauty where it can be found – he favours natural gardens, for example, over formal ones (*ibid.*: 248) – it is a beauty within a realm that does not manifest self-awareness and so cannot address "the universal need for art" in "man's rational need to lift the inner and outer world into his spiritual consciousness as an object in which he *recognizes again his own self*" (*ibid.*: 33). The natural beauty of birds in the field does not thus offer a "call to the mind" (*ibid.*: 71).

If the "imitation of nature" is not the purpose of art, neither can it be anything that is defined in terms of an external standard ("art exists for *moral* reasons") or merely formal criteria (for example, a general aim such as the "representation of all things human"). Hegel's account of the purpose of art looks instead to a notion that is more concretely connected to the work of art itself as a particular *embodiment* of the ideal: the purpose of art, on Hegel's view, is "to *unveil* the truth in sensual form, to set forth the reconciled opposition just mentioned, and so to have its end and aim in itself, in this very setting forth and unveiling" (*Aesthetics* I: 55). Or, put another way, art is engaged in giving its viewers "the *sensual presentation* [*Darstellung*] of the absolute itself" (*ibid.*: 70).

Organizing the realm of art

Hegel's definition of the purpose of art in terms of an adequate embodiment of form in content shapes the first organizational scheme of the *Aesthetics*: the differentiation of the particular "forms of art" into symbolic, classical and romantic. When form and content are adequate to one another, as in Hegel's account of classical sculpture, the work of art's significance and form of expression are at one: it is "not a meaning *of* this or that but what means [*Bedeutende*] itself and therefore intimates [or 'interprets,' *Deutende*] itself".[7] More concretely, we might say that the classical sculpture of an anthropomorphic god represents or reveals the human body in its ideal shape.

By comparison, the symbolic and romantic art forms are ones in which content and form fall apart. In the symbolic form, which Hegel links to pre-classical art in Egypt and Asiatic religions, the as-yet-undetermined idea is still in a "search" for its true portrayal: a stone idol may represent the divine, but does not *embody* it in the sense of the classical form. The romantic form is defined against the "pinnacle" of connection between content and form which the classical has achieved: here, the defect, Hegel says, "is just art itself and the restrictedness of the sphere of art".[8]

Hegel's construal of these three particular forms of art and the relation among them – something visible in nascent form already in the organization of the Religion chapter of the *Phenomenology of Spirit*[9] – represents an interesting aspect of his approach to the philosophy of art that was in many ways novel. Whereas the contrast between "classical" and "romantic" had become a *topos* among Hegel's contemporaries – used notably, of course, by Schiller and Friedrich Schlegel to frame their arguments about the position of art in the contemporary age – the triplicity that Hegel opens up is (as Gadamer argued) a step beyond that "abstract" duality.[10] Drawing on the work of Creuzer and others who helped expand his cultural, aesthetic and religious horizons to include ancient sources that were not merely Greek, Hegel now draws the familiar distinction between classical and romantic into a more comprehensive genetic account of modes of artistic presentation.

There is another organizational structure at work in Hegel's aesthetics, however – one whose relation to the first structure has raised a number of questions for Hegel scholars over the years: in addition to the particular *forms* of art, Hegel also develops a differentiation of *individual arts* themselves. While the scheme for the particular arts, as we have seen, is a creative Hegelian expansion upon a distinction that had come to be important within the quite contemporary debate about the purposes of art in the modern age, the scheme for individual arts draws on a much earlier tradition, the notion of a system of five arts.[11] Hegel sketches the relation of these five arts as a development: from architecture to sculpture to painting, music and poetry.

Hegel considers an organization of these five arts based on the senses: ruling out the senses of taste and smell (which annihilate what they encounter, Hegel claims) and the sense of touch (which, Hegel asserts, can only encounter matter, not spirit), we are left with the following possible correlations: the sense of sight relates to the visual arts (architecture, sculpture and painting), the sense of hearing to music and the "inner" senses of imagination and perception to poetry. But this division, Hegel says, is based on an abstract beginning (and, we might add, also involves a number of assumptions about sensory experience and its relation to art that must count as presuppositions).

In order to put the five arts into a systematic relation, Hegel instead offers us the following development: first, architecture makes use of heavy materials that are shapeable in ways that resemble the organic and inorganic forms of nature; sculpture still makes use of heavy materials but puts them into more spiritual form (especially in representations of the human form); the remaining three arts, now grouped together – not entirely unproblematically, as we shall see – as the "romantic" arts, represent a further development, but in a way that retreats successively from the use of three-dimensional materials. Painting can in some sense be said to make use of light itself, as the three dimensions of the architectural and sculptural world collapse into the two-dimensional representational plane of a painting. Music may be regarded as sound releasing the Ideal from its entanglement with matter, so that what is heard is the expression of inner feeling or subjectivity. And poetry's proper sphere becomes the imagination itself, where a sort of "total" or "universal art of the spirit which has become free in itself" makes possible a recapitulation of the previous forms – the objective experience of the visual arts in epic, the internal experience of feeling in music, and finally the drama, where "the whole man presents, by reproducing it, the work of art produced by man" (*Aesthetics* II: 627). (As for other arts besides these – for example, gardening, dancing, etc. – Hegel claims that, while these may "provide much that is enjoyable, graceful and meritorious", they are hybrid forms which "cannot hold fast to the essential differences grounded in the thing itself" (*ibid.*: 628).)

Hegel's scheme of organization of the five arts may strike one as puzzling. Although we might claim that a general trend toward inwardization or abstraction in the development from architecture to poetry is discernible, the relation that Hegel seems to be suggesting instead is somewhat more complicated, resembling not so much a movement in a single direction as the insistence on a *central point of focus* – the relation between content and form in sculpture – which then becomes the standpoint from which the other arts are viewed, with architecture looking towards it in anticipation and the romantic arts as moving away from it. Why does Hegel represent the relation of the specific arts in this way? Let us look briefly at the details of his development of the non-literary arts, first, and the interrelation discernible from it, before turning to some general questions about that development and then to the specifically literary forms themselves.

Architecture

Hegel's discussion of the first of the five arts begins with a reflection about "the primary and original need of art" being "that an idea or thought generated by the spirit shall be produced by man as his own work and presented by him" (*Aesthetics* II: 635) – the painting of a lion thus shows not merely the shape of a lion but the idea of a lion as a human being conceives of it. In the section on architecture, this reflection is important because Hegel organizes his account around the distinction between the human need for building enclosures and buildings that stand, like works of sculpture, independently for themselves (what Hegel calls "purposeless independence"). Thus we have a relation between "independent" architecture and what Hegel calls, somewhat strikingly, "architecture proper, the kind that is subservient to some purpose"; the truth, he claims, is "in the unity of these principles".

With this distinction in mind, Hegel traces the development of architecture into types based on the three particular forms of art: symbolic, classical and romantic architecture. Symbolic architecture gives us buildings that stand on their own (starting with towers such as those of the Babylonians that were unable to house anything) and moves in the direction of works like the pyramids, which are at least imagined as forms of housing for the dead. Classical architecture, or "architecture proper", involves buildings that serve as the space or environment, the housing for spiritual meanings already realized and thus not immanent in the work of architecture itself. Finally, romantic architecture, while not precisely a fusion of earlier symbolic and classical Greek architectural forms, still combines the notion of a roof-with-a-purpose and free-standingness: Gothic cathedrals are God's houses, but "their real character lies precisely in the fact that they transcend any specific end" (*Aesthetics* II: 684).

Sculpture

With Hegel's account of sculpture, something of the more idiosyncratic picture of his systematic organization of the specific arts starts to come into view. Sculpture, on his view, is the "center of classical art", the art that "more than any other art always points particularly to the Ideal":

> in the middle here, the really solid center, is the presentation of the Absolute, of God himself as God in his independence, not yet developed to movement and difference, not yet proceeding to action and self-particularization, but self-enclosed in grand divine peace and tranquillity: the Ideal shaped in a way adequate to itself, remaining in its existence identical and correspondent with itself.
> (*Aesthetics* II: 623)

Because Hegel sees sculpture so powerfully as the adequate embodiment of the ideal, his organization of that art's development will prove quite different from what we saw in architecture: while Hegel makes clear how architecture's historical development was determined by the symbolic–classical–romantic triad (*ibid.*: 634), he insists that "sculpture is so much the center of the classical form of art that here we cannot accept, as we could in the case of architecture, the symbolic, classical and romantic as decisive differences and the basis of our division" (*ibid.*: 708).

Hegel's connection of sculpture to the classical ideal itself leads him to see ancient Greece as a culture essentially *plastic* and self-forming, all of its individual members as somehow artists. One of the most famous passages in this connection suggests Hegel's view of the Greek world as being shaped from the perspective of a kind of statuary hall:

> In its poets and orators, historians and philosophers, Greece is not to be understood at its heart unless we bring with us as a key to our comprehension an insight into the ideals of sculpture and unless we consider from the point of view of their plasticity not only the heroic figures in epic and drama but also the actual statesmen and philosophers. After all, in the beautiful days of Greece, men of action, like poets and thinkers, had this same plastic and universal yet individual character both inwardly and outwardly. They are great and free, grown independently on the soil of their own inherently substantial personality, self-made and developing into what they [essentially] were and wanted to be . . . all of them are out-and-out artists by nature, ideal artists shaping themselves, individuals of a single cast, works of art standing there like immortal and deathless images of the gods, in which there is nothing temporal and doomed. (*Aesthetics* II: 719–20)

Although Hegel claims not to make use of the symbolic–classical–romantic motif in structuring his account, there are developmental elements within his presentation of sculpture: there is a development within the account of the modes of sculpture that runs from single statues to groups to reliefs (*ibid.*: 765–71) and there is an account of "historical stages" of sculpture that runs from Egyptian artisans (*Handwerker*) to Greek artists (*Künstler*). The difference between the latter two lies in whether it is "mechanical forms and rules" that have shaped the work or whether the artist can see "his own individuality in his work as specifically his own creation" (*ibid.*: 781).

With Hegel's praise of sculpture as the embodiment of the Ideal, why does it not represent the completion of art? Hegel's account of the need for a transition to the romantic arts of painting, music and sculpture is that we do not have a representation in sculpture yet of "the complete, concrete human being" (*der volle, konkrete Mensch*), since there is lacking both what Hegel calls the principle of *absolute personality* in the awareness of human subjectivity as such and there is also lacking "what is so commonly called 'human'" – weakness, contingent character, passion, caprice. Both are elements of a fuller account of human subjectivity that cannot be represented in sculpture but that will be central to each of the three romantic arts.

Painting

By contrast with sculpture, the chief determinant of painting, Hegel says, is "subjectivity aware of itself": the painter can represent everything, just as the subject by entering any sphere of life knows himself as alive. The shift to two dimensions is thus not a "loss of reality"; strikingly, Hegel here uses again the image of an *unveiling*: "even sculpture was not a bare imitation of what was existent in nature or corporeally; on the contrary, it was a *reproduction* issuing from the spirit and therefore it *stripped away* from the figure all those features in natural existence which did not correspond with the specific matter to be portrayed" (*Aesthetics* II: 805, italics mine).

Painting is both a *Widerschein* (reflection) of spirit and one that, reduced to a surface, has a relation to the spectator (thus *perspective* matters): "instead of what painting in this connection cannot place before us in its actual distance, as sculpture can in a *real* way, it must substitute the pure *appearance* of the reality" (*ibid.*: 837). Hegel appropriates in his account of painting's use of light and shadow Goethe's theory of colour, which viewed colour as a synthesis of light and dark over the Newtonian view of white light as the compound of the spectrum. Within that account, there is a singular importance to the human flesh tone as uniting colours: "the summit of coloring is 'carnation,' the color tone of human flesh which unites all other colors marvelously in itself without giving independent emphasis to either one or the other" (*ibid.*: 846). Hegel quotes in this context Goethe's translation of Diderot's *Essay on Painting*: "The man who has got the feel of flesh has already gone far. Everything else is nothing in comparison" (*ibid.*: 847).

Hegel praises love – "inwardly satisfied" or reconciled love – as "the most perfect subject for painting". The object of the portrayal of such love "is not a purely spiritual 'beyond' but is present, so that we can love itself before us in what is loved" (*ibid.*: 824); Hegel's supreme example of this is the representation of the Madonna, which he contrasts with Schelling's praise of Niobe, also using the comparison to make a point about what he takes to be the superiority of painting over sculpture: while Schelling saw in the ancient sculptural rendering of Niobe the perfect portrayal of serenity (or "indifference") in the face of suffering, Hegel thinks that it is only appropriate that she be rendered in stone because we do not see the inner side of her individuality at all. By contrast, he claims,

> Mary's grief is of a totally different kind. She is emotional, she feels the thrust of the dagger into the center of her soul, her heart breaks, but she does not turn into stone. She did not only *have* love; on the contrary, her whole inner life *is* love, the free concrete spiritual depth of feeling which preserves the absolute essence of what she has lost, and even in the loss of the loved one she ever retains the peace of love. Her heart breaks; but the very substance and burden of her heart and mind which shines through her soul's suffering with a vividness never to be lost is something infinitely higher. This is the living beauty of *soul* in contrast to the abstract *substance* which, when its ideal existence in the body perishes, remains imperishable, but in stone. (*Ibid.*: 826)

Religious topics are not the only ones that show painting's ability to represent the human subject, however. Hegel emphasizes the importance of painting's stretch to quite mundane human themes, with Dutch still life as a favourite example:

> Painting is concerned not only with the subjective inner life as such but at the same time with the inner life as *particularized* within. Precisely because it is the particular which is the principle of this inner life, this life cannot stay with the absolute subject-matter of religion, nor can it take as its content from the external world the life of nature only and its specific character as landscape; on the contrary, it must proceed to anything and everything in which a man as an individual subject can take an interest or find satisfaction. (*Ibid.*: 832)

Music

Painting is less physical than sculpture but space still persists in it; for the real portrayal of subjective inwardness, a non-persisting medium is needed – i.e. time, which annihilates space. Music is "the art of the soul and is directly addressed to the soul" (*ibid.*: 891); in music, "recollection (*Erinnerung*) of the theme adopted is at the same time the artist's inner collection (*Er-innerung*) of *himself*, i.e. an inner conviction that he is the artist and can expatiate in the theme at will and move hither and thither in it" (*ibid.*: 897).

Music is importantly the realm of expression of *feeling* – it accompanies spiritual ideas with feeling, just as architecture is the surrounding of sculpture (*ibid.*: 894), Hegel says – but it also unites feeling to its opposite, mathematical laws. Hegel is dismissive, however, of instrumental music because it "scarcely appeals to the general human interest in art" (*ibid.*: 899; Hegel does say that he hears in Mozart symphonies a dramatic sort of "dialogue" among instruments, *ibid.*: 923). Just as human flesh tone was the ideal unity of colour, containing the rest of colours within it and being itself the perfect colour, so within the realm of music the human voice contains the ideal totality of sound (*ibid.*: 922). Moreover, the individual human presence in musical performance is important to Hegel's account:

> In painting and sculpture, we have the work of art before us as the objectively and independently existent *result* of artistic activity, but not this activity itself as produced and alive. The musical work of art, on the other hand, as we saw, is presented to us only by the action of an executant artist, just as, in dramatic poetry, the whole man comes on the stage, fully alive, and is himself made into an animated work of art. (*Ibid.*: 955)

Assessing Hegel's organizational scheme

How should we compare the relation between the series of art forms and the series of specific arts? According to Hotho's text, this relation is determined, as we have seen, by an underlying tripartite division that goes back to Hegel's *Logic*: universal (ideal of the beautiful), particular (art forms) and individual (specific arts). But this was not Hegel's only scheme for representing the relationship between art forms and arts – at least, in the 1823 lectures, he appears to have had only a two-part division, according to which the art forms are *universal* and the specific arts *particular*.[12] Moreover, as we have seen, Hegel clearly thinks some point-to-point connections between the symbolic–classical–romantic scheme and the architecture–sculpture–romantic arts scheme are more useful for explanatory purposes: thus architecture was unproblematically divided according to its symbolic, classical and romantic forms, but sculpture is too centrally a classical mode of art for such a scheme to bring out sufficiently all that needs to be seen in its development. While there are a number of ways of addressing this organizational difficulty, it may be that this is one of the inherent perplexities in Hegel's organizational scheme, given all that he wanted to incorporate in his aesthetics (for example, his wish to have present in his philosophy of art *both* his broadened version of the Romantically influenced distinction between the classical and other forms *and* the traditional five-art schema that dates back to Aristotle).

The "end of art"?

If classical art can be regarded as achieving the fullness of *beauty*, why is the romantic nonetheless a higher *form of art*? Hegel's short answer, which we have already glimpsed in the transition from sculpture to painting, is that

> classical art became a conceptually adequate representation of the Ideal, the consummation of the realm of beauty. Nothing can be or become more beautiful.
>
> Yet there is something higher than the beautiful appearance of spirit in its immediate sensuous shape, even if this shape be created by spirit as adequate to itself.[13]

This remark is worth bearing in mind in considering what is perhaps the most famous claim frequently but falsely attributed to Hegel's aesthetics: the so-called "end of art" thesis, which supposedly asserts that, after the sculptural experience of Greek beauty, nothing more significant in art can emerge. Yet the very grounds we have seen involved in Hegel's transition to the romantic – and the detailed attention he gives especially to the literary art of his own day – would seem to counter this claim.

What Hegel *does* assert about art's "end" has a somewhat different character. Let us consider the two most frequently cited claims about the "end of art" thesis. The first is Hegel's remark about the purpose of art in an age that has now become inherently more reflective and philosophical: "art, considered in its highest vocation, is and remains for us a thing of the past" (*Aesthetics* I: 11). The second, a little later in the lectures is this: "No matter how excellent we find the statues of the Greek gods, no matter how we see God the Father, Christ, and Mary so estimably and perfectly portrayed: it is no help; we bow the knee no longer" (*ibid.*: 103).

It should be emphasized that the first remark is not one about whether there *is* or *will continue to be* art, but rather about art's relation to the "highest vocation" – presumably what Hegel had in mind in the quotation cited earlier in this chapter about "the *Divine*, the deepest interests of mankind, and the most comprehensive truths of the spirit". The point, in other words, is that, while the Greeks – thanks to Homer and Hesiod – saw their gods precisely in the form in which art represented them, the iconoclastic tendency of Christianity has introduced a non-artistically bound notion of divinity. Art is now not our connection to the highest aspiration of spirit, but religion – and more reflectively, philosophy – is. Further, we should note that the second remark just cited is prefaced with an important qualification that is often neglected: "We may well hope that art will always rise higher and come to perfection".

What all this says about Hegel's attitude towards modern art – particularly toward the trends to abstract expressionist art and to contemporary modes in which the arts turn an inherently reflective attention to their own praxis – is a large and important question. Some readers of Hegel (in their different ways, Robert Pippin and Dieter Henrich) have championed the grounds within his account of romantic and post-romantic art for an interpretation at least of the high-modernist phase of post-Hegelian art, while others (Stephen Houlgate) have encouraged a return to Hegel's more classical orientation.[14] While there is no consensus on this issue, what *is* clear on both sides is that art retains an important function within Hegel's view of modern life – a point that will only be further emphasized in the discussion of Hegel's literary theory.

Philosophy and literature: Hegel's "farewell to the Romantics" and the origin of his narrative project

In the final section of this chapter, I will turn to Hegel's specific treatment of the literary forms of art – the realm of poetry. Poetry is a totality uniting the visual arts and music, the "universal art which belongs equally to all the art forms". It is also, with an eye to the larger trajectory in which art will be transcended by religion, a mean between visual arts and abstract universality of thought (*Aesthetics* II: 965). As we have already seen, the unity that concerns Hegel most – in poetry and throughout his account of art – is of course the human being: just as Hegel pointed to human flesh tone as a sort of ideal unity of colour in his account of painting and took the human voice to be the ideal totality of sound in his account of music, so his organization of the realm of poetry looks towards the emergence of a form of poetry in which "the whole human being comes on stage", an animated work of art in and of himself (*ibid.*: 955).

The account of the three poetic genres reflects this transition (*ibid.*: 627): epic is a form of objectivity, concerned with the representation of a world, but also carries with it the objectivity of speech in "constituting itself as language"; lyric is a form of subjective speech revealing the inner life and often summoning music to its aid; and finally dramatic art, as we have noted, is a unity of objective and subjective sides "in which the whole man presents, by reproducing it, the work of art produced by man".

It is not language but the *imagination* that is poetry's real material, according to Hegel: "it is the *universal* art which can shape in any way and express any subject-matter capable at all of entering the imagination, because its proper material is the imagination itself, that universal foundation of all the particular art-forms and the individual arts" (*Aesthetics* II: 967). Because of this freedom of imagination, Hegel claims, every work of poetry is "an inherently infinite [self-bounded] organism . . . a whole . . . which closes with itself into a perfect circle", not dependent on content or any sphere of life but "creating freely from its own resources" (*ibid.*: 996).

Within the presentation of Hegel's official genre theory in the *Aesthetics*, there is a movement (heralded in the position of "action" as a topic in the initial discussion of "the beauty of art or the Ideal") that puts particular stress on the emergence of more and more adequate representations of human agency. Thus epic requires a "universal world situation" that is the background of action, and the difference between "action" in epic and action in drama is that the former seems rooted in nature and connected to "event", whereas the latter is more fully spiritual, and hence what would properly be called genuine action. Epic fate, for example, is on Hegel's view a nemesis that clips off whatever grows too proud, whereas the dramatic interest of tragedy is with a fate that is more intimately connected to a character's own action.

Beyond the official genre theory of the *Aesthetics*, however, there is more to say about Hegel's distinctive contribution to the relationship between philosophy and literature. In Chapter 2, we noticed that the most literarily attentive of Hegel's works in a *formal* sense, the *Phenomenology of Spirit*, involves itself in an explicit way with the question of narrative form, tracing in the Spirit chapter a series of developments tied to the emergence of tragedy, comedy and the romantic novel, and in the Religion chapter taking on those genres themselves in a meta-level critique of representational form that leads to the distinctly narrative *philosophical* project that the *Phenomenology* itself is. I shall conclude this section with a consideration of the two quite interesting windows Hegel opens up to the issue of literary form within the *Phenomenology*.

The first moment, the concluding section of the *Phenomenology* Spirit chapter, is often read as Hegel's "farewell to the Romantics", since it quotes, cites and imitates figures from Goethe to Novalis to Schlegel in characterizing the general range of voices of conscientious self-expression among Hegel's contemporaries.[15] It may in many ways be considered Hegel's attempt at something like Plato's *Symposium*, which may be read as one of the more explicit Platonic reflections on the distinctive literary form he had created in the philosophical dialogue. In the *Symposium*, Plato imagines together in conversation leading writers of comedy (Aristophanes) and tragedy (Agathon) in order to further a reflection on a distinctive narrative form in which "the same man might be capable of writing both tragedy and comedy" – presumably something achieved by the writer of philosophical dialogues. Hegel is doing something similar in his presentation in the final section of the *Phenomenology* Spirit chapter, which is organized essentially as a contest of novelistic forms – Jacobian and Schlegelian, with a broader background of essentially Romantic figures. The chief question for Hegel – raised also by our consideration of the "end of art" – is what sort of narrative form is required as the successor to these explicitly literary forms, and that is precisely the self-reflective concern of the *Phenomenology*, a unique narrative if ever there were one.

Secondly, in the Religion chapter of the *Phenomenology*, where the "manifest" religion emerges from the critique of the picture-thinking at the root of the imagistic Greek conception of the divine, Hegel offers a central image – much noted by those in the hermeneutic tradition – about modernity's relation to the literary products of the ancient world:

> The works of the Muse now lack the power of the Spirit, for the Spirit has gained its certainty of itself from the crushing of gods and men. They have become what they are for us now – beautiful fruit already picked from the tree, which a friendly Fate has offered us, as a girl might set the fruit before us. It cannot give us the actual life in which they existed, not the tree that bore them, not the earth and the elements which constituted their substance, not the climate which gave them their peculiar character, nor the cycle of the changing seasons that governed the process of their growth. So Fate does not restore their world to us along with the works of antique art, it gives not the spring and summer of the ethical life in which they blossomed and ripened, but only the veiled recollection of that actual world. (*PhS*: §753)

Taken together, these two windows – Hegel's "farewell" to the Romantics in a sort of symposial conversation and the concluding image of Greek art as given to us reflective moderns in a "veiled recollection" of what was an actual world – suggest a far more engaged Hegelian stance within the ancient "quarrel between philosophy and poetry" than is sometimes thought. At the very least, it should encourage students of Hegel to reflect further on the relation of his aesthetics more generally to the subtleties with which he applies both his notion of narrative (see Chapters 2 and 5) and the critique of imagistic thinking (as will be suggested in Chapter 7).

CHAPTER SEVEN

Religion and philosophy

Perhaps no facet of the philosophical turn taken by modernity has been so essential to the self-construal of philosophy itself as the stance it has taken towards the traditional place of religion and theology. Certainly no element of the modern philosophical project proved to be as controversial as the philosophical demand for the autonomy of its own enterprise. The importance of Hegel's philosophy of religion as a consummate moment in that modern philosophical turn may be estimated both by its immediate impact on the philosophical world and by its continuing importance for the modern – and postmodern – construal of the question of religion.

First, in the history of the reception of Hegelian philosophy, it is clear that Hegel's philosophy of religion was in many ways the primary point of contention and self-identification among Hegel's immediate followers. As is well known, a large part of the division among "left", "centre" and "right" Hegelians concerned precisely the issue of how to interpret religion in the philosophical world after Hegel. (One of Hegel's students went so far, for example, as to claim that philosophical debate in the crucial decade after Hegel's death was focused *only* on the status of two issues in Hegel's philosophy of religion: the ideas of God's personality and the immortality of soul.[1])

But Hegel's philosophy of religion is not important merely for the task of reconstructing the intellectual history of his followers but also, in a more wide-ranging way philosophically, for the ongoing attempt to understand the place of religion and religious thought in modern life. Despite the immense differences in their approaches to the question of religion, Hegel, Kant and Schleiermacher can all be identified as initiators of a distinctively modern – liberal and post-Enlightenment – religious project. Each of these figures might be said to share a view of the importance of the task of unpacking some relevant philosophical significance of the religious culture they inherited – Protestant Christianity – and for articulating within the context of modernity's liberalism and secularism a continuing relevance for that religious perspective. For Kant, the great critic of the traditional theoretical proofs of God's existence, the only viable proof of God's existence is a *moral* proof, one that begins in the experience of freedom that characterizes practical reason; what is thus salvageable from positive historical *faiths* for the purposes of a true and *rational* religion is therefore what needs to be postulated for moral reasons. For Schleiermacher, the freedom possible within modern religion is one that begins not with moral experience, but rather with feeling or intuition itself.

On the philosophical view of religion that Hegel comes to adopt,[2] the real importance of Christianity as a *religion of freedom* can be discovered in a way that also involves a sifting for its genuine "inner" meaning, but without the sharp Kantian separation between historical and true religion, and without the Schleiermacherian separation between feeling and thought. More specifically, what Hegel bequeaths to the more general liberal religious project he shares with Kant and Schleiermacher is the awareness that the freedom opened up in Christian religion is a clarity about religion itself – in particular, its reliance on imagination. Hegel's project is thus often linked with the great tradition of liberal demythologization, since his working out of that project involved a close consideration of the importance of the notion of the "death of God" for Christianity's development years before Nietzsche's appropriation of that term.[3]

It is easy to misinterpret Hegel's position here. One form of criticism that usually associates Hegel with the general liberal theological project just mentioned has been widely criticized by figures as diverse as Karl Barth and (more recently) Mark Lilla, who claims that the liberal theological tradition that so dominated the nineteenth and early twentieth centuries produced only a notion of a "stillborn God", powerless in the face of the great evils that the last century introduced.[4] But Hegel's god, as I shall argue, should not be construed merely as the abstract god of progressive, human-centred liberal religiosity; indeed, it would be odd if it ran into the difficulties associated with the "stillborn" God, since Hegel placed continuing stress in his treatment of religion on what is "living" and not merely abstract in religious experience.

Further, as Emil Fackenheim has argued, Hegel is not so much a *de*mythologizer (although he *is* certainly that) as he is a *trans*mythologizer – a philosopher who claims to find an essential *relation* between philosophy and religion in which both have a view on truth. Hegel's remarks about this relation are both striking and problematic: religion and philosophy are not only both concerned with the *truth* (*Enc*: §1) but may be said to share as well the same *content* (*Gehalt*); there can be religion without philosophy, but no philosophy without religion; philosophy and religion are both to be considered the "service of God".[5]

These sentences suggest an unavoidable connection between religion and philosophy, on Hegel's view. But what is the content that philosophy and religion share? And how does Hegel account for the different modes in which philosophy and religion appropriate the truth? Here other, equally difficult Hegelian remarks may come to mind: religion is "the mode, the type of consciousness, in which the truth is present for all men, or for all levels of education", whereas scientific cognition is "a particular type of the consciousness of truth, and not everyone, indeed only a few men, undertake the labor of it".

Given the nature of these claims, it is not surprising that misunderstandings of the relation between philosophy and religion in Hegel are widespread. Although Hegel does say that religion is the "mode in which the truth is present for all men", religion is *not*, on his view, Hegelianism for the masses. Certainly the points of attack of Hegel's critics made clear that his religious project was not always well understood: Hegel was charged by some with being a pantheist and by others with being a humanist atheist – but neither (for reasons he makes quite explicit in his lectures) is a true representation of his views. Hegel himself presented his approach as one locatable *between* two somewhat louder religious voices of his own day: the so-called religion of feeling (as expressed by Jacobi and Schleiermacher but also by a number of figures popular at the time, such as J. F. Fries, who were for Hegel far less philosophically significant) and the watered-down claims of Enlightenment theology (*aufgeklärte Theologie*, which in Hegel's view could be quickly summarized as defending only the narrow claims of freedom of conscience and enquiry).

In this chapter, I shall argue that the chief philosophical interest that Hegel has in the historical development of religion as such – and more specifically in the construal of Christianity's role in the West – lies in the emergence of a religious mode in which a *reflective or critical stance with respect to religion itself* becomes possible. If *classical art* was for Hegel the locus of form meeting matter within the realm of aesthetics, Christianity represented for him the religious view that presented as religious *content* the distinct *form* of religious experience – as he sees it, Christianity is thus religious picture-thinking about the very nature of religious picture-thinking – and hence offers the possibility of a transition to philosophy as reflection on that form of thinking itself. This is, above all, the meaning for him of the truth of the crucifixion and resurrection in Christian thought (which he had been speculating about since the Jena description of the "speculative Good Friday"). Although Hegel comes to defend this view in ways that are quite distinctive to him – connecting it, among other things, with an understanding of the historicality of spirit, an analysis of the decisive mode of religious picture thought or *Vorstellung* and with one of the more philosophically creative interpretations of the ontological proof of God's existence – the view as such is one that has a number of other contemporary resonances. (Schleiermacher, for one, with a Romantic notion of levels of potency in mind, claimed a similar role for Christianity as a religion whose "basic intuition" allowed it to treat "religion itself *as material for religion*, and thus, is, as it were, raised to a higher power of religion".)[6]

In this chapter, I shall first locate Hegel's account of religion within the systematic concerns of his philosophy, and then examine four issues that give it a distinctiveness in comparison with other philosophical approaches to the study of religion. Each of these issues involves, in typically Hegelian fashion, both a critique and an appropriation: (1) the notion of *positivity* as it emerges from the context of post-Kantian considerations of religion; (2) the *modes of religious experience*, particularly the claims of faith or immediate certainty, feeling and representational thought (*Vorstellung*); (3) the attempt to grasp the "meaning" of liberal Protestant Christianity in terms of the importance of *revelation or self-explicitness* (*Offenbarung*); and (4) the status of the traditional *proofs of God's existence* in the context of a general account of the soul's elevation (*Erhebung*) to God in the various determinate moments of historically encountered religious practice. The final two sections of the chapter will consider (5) what place a Hegelian philosophy of religion might still have within a contemporary religious and philosophical environment quite different from that which characterized Hegel's own lifetime and (6) examine the role of philosophy itself as a discipline or practice within modern life that now has an autonomy of its own.

Textual sources for what follows include Hegel's *Early Theological Writings*, the Religion chapter of the *Phenomenology of Spirit*, the *Science of Logic* and the *Encyclopedia Logic* (the last has particularly pregnant prefaces concerning the relation between philosophy and religion, especially that to the 1827 edition), but above all the mature exposition of Hegel's philosophy of religion in his Berlin *Lectures on the Philosophy of Religion* (*LPR*) given four times between 1821 and 1831, and the separate lecture series during the Berlin period on the *Lectures on the Proofs of the Existence of God* (*LPEG*). For readers interested in becoming further acquainted with the rather wide range of significant recent scholarly work on the *Lectures* and Hegel's philosophy of religion, see the guide to further reading at the end of this book.

Locating religion: the place of religious experience in the Hegelian system

Perhaps the most important place to begin in examining Hegel's account of religion is with its most basic claim – "God is essentially rational" – and the systematic location of religious considerations: God *is* Spirit and is *for* Spirit. This relation between Spirit and God follows from the priority for Hegel of the spiritual and its form of explanation over the natural: "The relationship which grounds (*das Grundverhältnis*) all religion and all philosophy is first of all the relationship of spirit as such to nature and then, that of absolute Spirit to finite spirit".[7]

Since God is Spirit, the *knowledge* of God and *God's self-knowing* are both central to the account Hegel gives of religion. "Religion is . . . a relation of spirit to absolute Spirit" (*LPR* I: 197), but this does not mean a relation between two separated items: "religion is the idea of the spirit which relates itself to its own self – *the self-consciousness of absolute Spirit*" (*ibid.*: 197–8).

Although Hegel stresses the importance of knowledge in his account of God, the *sociality* involved in his notion of Spirit is essential here, too. Hegel discusses the practical side of spiritual formation in the philosophy of religion and devotes one of the main sections of his account of the "concept" of religion to the notion of the *cultus* in its various historical formations. The object of the lectures on the philosophy of religion is not just God, Hegel says, but God as present in his community (i.e. *religion*). Thus Hegel stresses consistently in his writing on religion from his early writings forward the importance of the notion of a "living" religion and not merely abstract ("dead") forms – as he puts it in the lectures, the cognitive aim of philosophy is "to know and comprehend the religion that already *exists*" (*LPR* I: 91).

Hegel's at once cognitive and social understanding of God leads to a further reflection on his part on the relation between this level of absolute spirit and the ethical and political claims of objective spirit. For one thing, Hegel is well known for his basic thought that the level of freedom in the political organization of a particular historical people is something clearly and inevitably reflected in the God-concept of the latter.

> There cannot be *two kinds of reason* and *two kinds of spirit*, not a divine reason and a human, not a divine Spirit and a human, which would be *absolutely different*. Human reason, the consciousness of one's essence is indeed reason; it is the divine in man, and spirit, insofar as it is the Spirit of God, is not a spirit beyond the stars, beyond the world. On the contrary, God is present, omnipresent, and as Spirit is present in all spirits.[8]

This view – that there can be no such thing as a "double truth", somehow split between human and divine – has consequences, of course, both for Hegel's view of the freedom to be accorded to conscience in the political realm and the freedom of reason to investigate truths of religion: "Human spirit in its innermost aspect, in its conviction about the nature of God, is not, in this most inward conscience, the sort of divided thing in which the two sides of a contradiction could subsist – faith [on one side and] reason on the other that had achieved results deviating from this teaching of positive religion" (*LPR* I: 134–5).

A final point about the place of religion in Hegel's philosophy more broadly: the discussion of the rootedness of Hegel's account of God in the realm of Spirit and more particularly the insistence on human and divine conscience as not being a divided thing gives a window onto a claim of Hegel's that may seem somewhat surprising – that Kant set up the correct point of departure for the modern possibility of theology in *practical* philosophy:

> As regards the starting-point of that elevation [of the Spirit to God], Kant has on the whole adopted the most correct, when he treats belief in God as proceeding from the practical Reason. For that starting-point contains the material or content which constitutes the content of the notion of God. But the true concrete material is neither Being . . . nor mere action by design . . . but the Spirit, the absolute characteristic and function of which is effective reason, i.e. the self-determining and self-realizing notion itself – Freedom. (*Enc*: §552)

The position of Hegel's treatment of religion in the *Phenomenology* suggests something like this claim about the indispensability of the moral or practical standpoint for post-Kantian theology, as well, inasmuch as the transition to "Religion" takes place as a development out of the "Conscience" section of "Morality". But it is important to notice that Hegel says that practical reason is the *starting-point*: unlike Kant, the God that practical reason leads to for Hegel is not a God merely *postulated* among the various claims essential to practical philosophy, and the Good that religion concerns is not something merely *to be achieved* but something that *is*, even if that "is" is something that emerges from the conscientious agent's own claims and practice. Moreover, as we shall see in a consideration of Hegel's version of the Kantian attack on the notion of positivity, the narrowly or strictly *moral* stance cannot help a philosophical stance towards religion to avoid the problem of positivity either.

Positivity and the post-Kantian task of philosophy concerning religion

The genesis of Hegel's view of the relation between spirit and religion stems from his earlier engagement in an attack on a notion that came in many ways to define post-Kantian discussions of religion: *positivity*. As we saw in Chapter 1, like many of the figures in the generation of the 1790s – "romantic" and "idealist" alike – Hegel wrestled in his own writings of the period with the implications of the new approach in philosophy for religion. Among the chief concerns of Hegel's writings from the 1790s is the need to sift out what is merely a "positive" element in religion. Hegel's earliest writing from that period defines the notion of the positive in distinctly Kantian terms, as what is "grounded in authority and puts man's worth not at all, or at least not wholly, in morals".[9] While Hegel in his earliest writings saw possibilities for an explicitly *moral* possibility for overcoming positivity, his writings from the Frankfurt years on makes clear that a resort to morality itself will not be sufficient. The Frankfurt essay's contrast between the experience of punishment under the (positive *or* moral) law and the experience of tragic fate – as something to which an agent has a more organic relationship – is indicative of this new direction in Hegel's view.

Faith, feeling and representation: Hegel's critique of the modes of religious experience

What is religious experience? What is the relation between what a believer feels and what philosophy can say or know about who or what God is? In the *Lectures on the Philosophy of Religion*, Hegel devoted substantial attention to the modes of religious experience and how philosophy should view them. His treatment focuses on three such modes: immediate knowledge (certainty or faith), feeling and representative thought (imagination or *Vorstellung*).

Immediate knowledge

Hegel begins his consideration of the modes of religious experience by considering a simple claim of the sort that is often made within religious experience: "God is". What sort of claim is this? Hegel analyses it in terms of an immediacy attached to the assertion "God is", but any experience of "immediate" revelation is also a mediated knowledge, since the assertion that "God is" is made within the context of some religious instruction or community (*LPR* I: 411). Hegel of course has in mind here Jacobi's notion of "faith", yet Hegel's attack is more specifically directed against the hardened polemical version of claims to immediate knowledge in so far as it holds itself in a fixed way *against* all rational claims. Hegel acknowledges, for example, that there is a mode of genuine confidence that links to the more mediated and thoughtful notion of "conviction" that is important for his own view of conscience. In Hegel's treatment of this first mode of religious experience, then, we see both a critique and an appropriation – something that will also be true for Hegel's examination of the importance of religious feeling and representation.

Feeling

If Jacobi was the point of attack in Hegel's discussion of immediate certainty or faith, the attack here (most famously) is on Schleiermacher, whose appeal to religion as rooted in a "feeling of dependence" Hegel ridiculed in a barbed prefatory remark to his student Hinrichs's work on religion and philosophy: if Schleiermacher were right, then a dog would be the best Christian, Hegel claimed.[10] Hegel's criticism of the grounding of religion in feeling is that any content can be *felt* but that no content *attaches* – what we have instead is how the thing connects to ourselves; thus no justification attaches to feeling: we cannot say of any feeling that it is either good (correct) or not good (false) (*LPR* I: 271, 273).

As we saw with Hegel's discussion of immediate knowledge, however, there is a side of feeling that has an important place in Hegel's account of religion: "It must be added, however, that not only can every content be in feeling, but also the true content *must* be in our feeling. It is quite right to say, as we do, that we must have God in our hearts, have ethical principles at heart" (*ibid.* I: 274). It is striking that Hegel's interpretation of the importance of "heart" to religion focuses on the notion of *ethical character*: "The heart is what I am, not merely what I am at this instant, but what I am in general . . . The form of feeling as universal denotes basic principles or habits of my being, the settled pattern of my ways of acting" (*ibid.*)

Representational thought (*Vorstellung*)

As we saw in Chapter 2, Hegel's critique of representational (or picture-) thought played an important part in one of his earliest philosophical engagements with religion, that in the *Phenomenology of Spirit*. According to that account, religion is a form of thinking that places an image *before* me (*vor-stellt*); religious practice, on Hegel's view, is thus limited by the particular images by which it represents the divine (God as anthropomorphic, for example). Within the *Phenomenology* account, however, there is also the development *within religious practice* of a form of critique of representational thinking: thus the Greeks' highly imagistic view of the gods gives way to a more conceptually apt – if also still representationally bound – notion of God in Christianity. Hegel's account of religion is thus centred on a notion of a gradual demythologization of the strictly imagistic elements of religious life – but in the course of that demythologization, the "truth" about God has nonetheless been presented in a representational and religious form (e.g. the notion of the trinity will turn out to capture the truth of God's relation to a world that can be distinguished from him and yet still reconciled to him).

Towards the religion of revelation (*Offenbarung*)

The itinerary of Hegel's treatments of religion, both in the *Phenomenology of Spirit* and in the *Lectures on the Philosophy of Religion*, thus has in each case a similar culmination: an appropriation of Christian religion as the final mode in which religion appears and from which the transition to philosophy will be undertaken. The *Phenomenology* begins with an account of natural religions and moves to the "art-religion" of the Greeks, culminating in what Hegel terms *die offenbare Religion* – literally, the "open" or "manifest" religion (as H. S. Harris is right to insist), the form of religion that has resulted from the process of demythologizing the Greek imagistic view of the divine. In the *Lectures*, where an initial discussion of the concept of religion is followed by the comparative presentation of "determinate" world religions (magic, Chinese religion, Buddhism, Hinduism, Persian religion, Egyptian religion, Greek religion, Judaism and Roman religion), the concluding third of the work is devoted to what Hegel now calls the "consummate" or "revealed" (now as past participle, *geoffenbarte*) religion – even the "absolute" – religion.

While Hegel's stance on the development of world religions is certainly quite different from that found within the discipline of comparative religions today, it is worth noticing some facets of Hegel's account that make it less monolithic or Christian-centric than it might on first presentation appear. For one thing (as the careful scholarly treatment of these lectures over the last generation has shown), Hegel seems to be continually revising the arrangement of the comparative part of his philosophy of religion over the course of the various series. To take an interesting example: in considering the relation between Judaism (the "religion of sublimity") and Greek religion (the "religion of beauty"), Hegel in the first two versions of his lecture series places Judaism first within his scheme, but in the third version switches the two and in the fourth moves back to his original position. This set of moves suggests that Hegel views neither as a more complete dialectical development within the history of religions than the other, but instead considers them as different sides of a dialectical tension that might be inescapable.

Further, as Jaeschke has pointed out, Christianity does not emerge as the "absolute" religion by means of a comparison with the preceding history of religions but rather in so far as it develops something central to the *concept* of religion that Hegel has sketched: the Christian religion has for its object what religion as such is. As I suggested above, such a view of the emergence and function of Christianity within the religious experience of the West is shared at least by Schleiermacher, who defines Christianity as the religion that makes *religion itself* its own material. (Schleiermacher and Hegel also seem to share a view of the inherent development of Protestantism toward a pluralism, almost cacophony, of religious perspectives – a point that Schleiermacher stresses rather more than Hegel, but which Hegel does acknowledge in his reference to the "polemical" and centrifugal forces within Christianity.)

Hegel's account of Christianity does appropriate in philosophical terms various doctrinal elements that appear within Christian thought in a representational or imagistic mode. Thus Hegel interprets the notion of creation in terms of the world's ultimate idealty and the notion of the divine trinity as expressing the notion of the freedom and letting-be that are important to the relation between the Idea and its embodiment in the world (*LPR* III: 293, 285).

The question always arises in considering such claims on Hegel's part about the truth of the "absolute" or "consummate" religion: what was Hegel's own stance toward Christianity? Karl Löwith once called Hegel the last Christian philosopher; Stephen Houlgate, who stresses the dialecticality and historicality implicit in Hegel's view of Christianity, has suggested that Hegel may in some ways be considered the first Christian philosopher. Hegel himself did, of course, famously insist that he was a Lutheran, although there are a number of ways we might construe this claim. For one thing, being a Lutheran was a matter of rather deep cultural but not necessarily religious self-identity during his administrative detour in the Bavarian school system (where he and his fellow Swabian Niethammer introduced a course of reforms that aroused some intense conservative Catholic reaction). It is in this sense that Hegel speaks of Protestantism in quite a broad way, as the development of a certain mode of *thinking* about the world: in the Protestant world, he claims at one point, "our universities are our churches".[11] Likewise, the speech that Hegel gave in Berlin commemorating the 300th anniversary of the Augsburg Confession stresses German Idealism as the logical development of Protestantism. But Hegel did insist, when challenged on the issue in his later years in Berlin, on what seems to be a distinctively religious commitment to his Lutheranism, even if he was not an entirely orthodox thinker in this regard. (Pinkard's sense that Hegel personally had a genuinely religious side does a better job of pulling these disparate perspectives together than the view that Hegel simply used religion as a mask or cover to hide – in an age when Fichte could lose his job on religious grounds – an essentially atheistic stance.)

"Elevation" and the proofs of God's existence

Hegel's philosophy of religion makes what may seem to be a remarkably surprising post-Kantian appeal to the traditional proofs of God's existence. While acknowledging the seemingly unanswerable criticisms that Kant (as well as Hume, Jacobi and others) directed against rational theology in general – and against the specific forms of ontological, cosmological and physico-theological proofs relied upon in such theology – Hegel nonetheless claims to find an important philosophical "truth" within these traditional forms of proof, especially in the ontological proof itself. What characterizes Hegel's appropriation of the proofs is a distinct philosophical creativity in construing that "truth" – one that makes him among the more creative figures in the tradition from Anselm to Hartshorne.

Hegel speaks of the explication of the proofs of God's existence as "the explication of religion itself" (*LPR* I: 416): on his view, they actually function not as *proofs*, but rather as forms of the "*elevation* (*Erhebung*) to God".[12] Hegel even thinks (at least on the earlier versions of the lecture series) that he can correlate each of the traditional metaphysical proofs with one of the basic forms of determinate religion: thus the three forms of the cosmological proof, on his view, correspond to nature religion, Greek religion and Judaism; the teleological proof corresponds to Roman religion and the ontological proof to Christianity.[13]

Although Hegel clearly recognizes the logical flaws in each of these traditional forms of proof, his interest, as he puts it, is not in the issue of logical *form* but rather in what sort of *content* the proofs present in the sort of *Erhebung* they express. The central claim is this:

> Humanity rises from the finite to the infinite, rises above the singular and raises itself to the universal to being-in-and-for-self. Thus religion consists in this, that human beings have before them in their consciousness the nothingness of the finite, are aware of their dependence, and seek the ground of this nothingness, of this dependence – in a word, that they find no peace of mind until they set up the infinite before themselves.
>
> (*LPR* II: 254)

Or, as he put it succinctly in the series of lectures on the proofs themselves: "elevation *is* the fact of religion" (*LPEG*: 229).

And the transition that elevation represents, Hegel says, is "not just a factual episode in the history of religion, but is necessitated by the concept" (*LPR* II: 255) – a point echoed in his emphasis on the proofs as expressions of thought (if not logically valid in themselves): "The elevation [*Erhebung*] of thinking above the sensible, its *going out* above the finite to the infinite, the *leap* that is made into the supersensible when the sequences of the sensible are broken off, *all this is thinking itself*; this transition [*Übergehen*] is *only thinking*. To say this passage ought not to take place means that there is to be no thinking" (*Enc*: §50, italics mine).

What is logically deficient from the perspective of *Hegel*'s logic in the metaphysical proofs, however, is that they "do not express [*ausdrücken*], or rather they do not bring out [*herausheben*] the moment of *negation* that is contained in this elevation" (*ibid.*); "while this elevation is a passage and mediation [*Übergang und Vermittlung*], it is also the *Aufheben* of the passage and mediation, since that through which God could seem to be mediated, i.e. the world, is, on the contrary, shown up as what is null and void" (*ibid.*).

We might see what Hegel means here by considering his criticism of the nature religion "version" of the cosmological proof, for example. The proof runs as follows:

> The finite presupposes the infinite
> But the finite is, this particular entity exists
> Therefore the infinite is also

About this version of the cosmological proof, Hegel remarks: "What is amiss in the syllogism is that the finite is expressed as affirmative and its relation to the infinite is expressed as positive, whereas it is essentially a negative relation, and this dialectical element in the finite cannot be confined within the form of a syllogism of the understanding" (*LPR* II: 264). In other words, the traditional syllogistic form cannot capture the motion and negativity implicit in Hegel's interpretation of the proof's *meaning*.

Hegel develops perhaps most fully his account of the significance of the ontological proof, responding to Kant's criticism that "being" is not a predicate and that hence "that than which nothing greater can be conceived" (or the "sum total of realities") is a concept that does not include being or reality (just as the mere concept of $100 cannot make it an existing $100). This proof is the "only genuine" proof among the metaphysical proofs, Hegel claims, because it begins not with (finite) being in order to move to the concept of the infinite, but rather starts with the concept of infinity itself (*LPR* III: 352). As the editors of the English translation of the lecture series put it: "The insight of the ontological proof is that the 'elevation' to God is not an autonomous self-elevation of finite spirit into what could only be a spurious infinite, but, speculatively expressed, the return of true and infinite spirit into itself. The only genuine proof of the reality of God is God's self-proof".[14]

In his interpretation of the ontological proof, Hegel can be credited with discerning that Anselm's real achievement in articulating the proof was not one of logical validity in regard to its form but rather one of conceptual distinction in getting clear about what is meant by the concept "God": the importance of the ontological proof is that God is, on Anselm's and Hegel's view, not like any other object (say Kant's $100), but is "that which can only be thought *as* existing" (*Enc*: §51).

In assessing Hegel's appropriation of the proofs of God's existence, one might suggest seeing it as part of a general strategy Hegel employed – increasingly, it seems, in his later years – with respect to the relation between religion and philosophy: a strategy of linking certain philosophical practices and outcomes directly with analogies from religious life. Perhaps most famous in this regard is Hegel's linking of the notion of the Trinity in Christian thought with various triplicities that occur in his own thinking, most basically in the movement of implicitness, outering and return that characterizes the relation of logic, nature and spirit. We might also think here of the way in which Hegel's later iterations of the *Encyclopedia Logic* stress that the three aspects of logical thinking according to Hegel (that of the abstract understanding, the negative dialectic and the positive speculative) as well as the three *parts* of the logic itself (being, essence and the concept) all represent in some sense an experience comprehensible in religious terms. Thus each of the three aspects of logical thought in Hegel's sense is correlated with one of the primary attributes of God (the understanding with God's goodness, dialectic with God's power and speculation with God's truth), and the movement from being through essence to concept is likewise connected with the relation between God and the world ("this same relationship of the three stages of the logical Idea is exhibited in a more real and concrete shape in the fact that we achieve cognition of God, who is truth, in this his truth, i.e. as absolute Spirit, only when we recognized that the world created by Him – nature and finite spirit – is not true in its distinction from God" [*Enc*: §83]).

It is important to caution that these do not seem to be *mere analogies* on Hegel's part or the Hegelian equivalent of the often-retailed story about Kant bringing his philosophical views in line with the catechism available in his old servant Lampe. Rather, they suggest more directly that, however we want to cast the Hegelian relationship between religion and philosophy in contemporary terms, he understood himself to be engaged in explicating a fundamental connection between two modes of grasping the same *content*.

From religion to philosophy: assessing Hegel's view of religion

How to characterize in the end the philosophical stance that Hegel takes towards religion? Philosophers have often tried to characterize Hegel's view of religion in terms of the traditional contrast between the revealed God of biblical faith ("Jerusalem") and the rational God of philosophical thought ("Athens") – or, as Pascal puts it, between the "God of the philosophers" and the "God of Abraham, Isaac and Jacob". Fackenheim has claimed that no philosopher ever stated the case more strongly for there being an essential *connection* between Athens and Jerusalem than Hegel. But it must be admitted that that "case" was one Hegel considered and reconsidered in strikingly different ways. He is more harshly critical of traditional Judeo-Christian views in his works up through the *Phenomenology of Spirit*, where, despite an entire long chapter devoted to the essential conceptual and historical development of "Religion", Hegel never mentions Judaism. (One might make an interesting *argumentum ab silencio* about the *Phenomenology*'s view of the relation between Athens and Jerusalem on just these grounds – although there are significant ways in which the absence of the God of Abraham "appears" in that work, for example, in the "fear of the Lord" that is essential to the initiation of the whole movement of self-consciousness.) As we saw in an earlier section, the mature Hegel never fully resolved the *systematic* relation between Jerusalem and Athens, either: while he insisted upon beauty and sublimity as the relevant *principles* in each case, he alternated in how these two central poles of Western religious experience should be placed in relation to one another. That he therefore regarded this as a matter of continuing dialectical tension seems clear.

Another contrast – that between "right" and "left" Hegelians – has also had an important bearing on assessments of Hegel's philosophy of religion over the years. Dickey has suggested that what happened to Hegel's philosophy of religion in the decade or so following his death can be understood ultimately in terms of a "fraying middle" – the disappearance of some consensual ground that came to be untenable in the midst of the increasing strife among partisans of the right and the left. But what is conflictual in that middle can already be seen in the strains of Hegel's own presentation: contrast, for example, Hegel's concluding presentation of the lectures on the philosophy of religion in his original manuscript (1821) with what he appears to have said in the last oral version he completed (1827). In the former, Hegel offers a comparison of the decadence of the modern age to that of Rome: "finitude [turned] in upon itself, arrogant barrenness and lack of content, the extremity of self-satisfied dis-enlightenment [*Ausklärung*]" (*LPR* III: 160). In the latter, he looks to modern *Sittlichkeit* as the logical development from pietism and the era in which the Church was dominant: in this modern realm, "the principle of freedom has penetrated into the worldly realm itself" and the institutions of ethical life are "divine institutions – not holy in the sense that celibacy is supposed to be holy by contrast with marriage or familial love" but instead in reconciling religion and actuality (*ibid.*: 341–2); in this last context, Hegel insists that "philosophy is to this extent theology" in that it shows that all otherness is "implicitly divine" (*ibid.:* 347).

The difficulty for the Hegelian view of religion and philosophy is *not* in any case the difficulty that has been associated with the supposed "powerlessness" of the God of liberal theology. On Hegel's view, the actuality of ("living") religious experience still matters and has its own authenticity. It is true that the philosophical stance of Hegelian philosophy, on Hegel's conception, was not something that could be taken on by more than a few within society at large. In *that* sense, Hegel is perhaps more like Spinoza or Aristotle than like Schleiermacher – not a prophet of a modern liberal religious concept of God that failed to catch hold, but a stance that takes over the concept of God from the perspective of the philosophers in a way that will remain under the perspective of the philosophers, even if it is essential to whatever reconciled view of modernity ordinary believers experience.

The task of philosophy in the modern world

Despite his extraordinarily careful methodological approach to philosophy – and the ongoing shifts over the years in how he views the relation between, for example, logic and metaphysics – Hegel never says a great deal explicitly about the role of philosophy *per se* or how moderns should think about the relation philosophy has to the cultural and political world.[15] Hegel acknowledges that philosophy has a different status in modernity than it did among the Greeks – "philosophy with us is not in any case practiced as a private art, as it was with the Greeks . . . but has a public existence, impinging upon the public, especially – or solely – in the service of the state" (*PR*: 17) – but it must be said that *something* of the problem of the "philosopher and the city", the problem as set out in the city in speech in Plato's *Republic*, remains for Hegel an essential problem as well. On the one hand, the developed modern *Rechtsstaat* requires explicitly philosophical discernment as to its practices; on the other hand, philosophy presupposes sociality – and philosophy *is* itself a *cultus*, as Hegel goes so far at one point as to say.

> If we consider only what it contains, and not how it contains it, the true reason-world, so far from being the exclusive property of philosophy, is the right of every human being on whatever grade of culture or mental growth he may stand; which would justify man's ancient title of rational being. The general mode by which experience first makes us aware of the reasonable order of things is by accepted and unreasoned belief; and the character of the rational . . . is to be unconditioned, self-contained and thus to be self-determining. In this sense man above all things becomes aware of the reasonable order when he knows of God, and knows him to be the completely self-determined. Similarly, the consciousness a citizen has of his country and its laws is a perception of the reason-world, so long as he looks up to them as unconditioned and likewise universal powers, to which he must subject his individual will. (*Enc*: §82A)

Hegel's claim here about the essentially "philosophical" view that ordinary believers and citizens can have in their regard to religion and political life does not mean of course that the systematic discernment of universals does not require the work of philosophers. But it is nonetheless an important vote of confidence in the possibility of modern life that is genuinely free and plural – exactly the question that animated Hegel in his religious, political and philosophical journey from the time of his crucial formation at Jena to the last of his lectures at Berlin.

Notes

Introduction

1. As Habermas observes: "Hegel is not the first philosopher to belong to the modern age, but he is the first for whom modernity became a problem" (Jürgen Habermas, *The Philosophical Discourse of Modernity: Twelve Lectures*, Frederick G. Lawrence (trans.) (Cambridge, MA: MIT Press, 1987), 43). Terry Pinkard's recent biography makes Hegel's concern with modernity as a philosophical problem a central thematic issue see *Hegel: A Biography* (Cambridge: Cambridge University Press, 2000).
2. Recent studies of German Idealism and the wider philosophical context of its development include Frederick Beiser, *The Fate of Reason: German Philosophy from Kant to Fichte* (Cambridge, MA: Harvard University Press, 1987); *German Idealism: The Struggle Against Subjectivism, 1781–1801* (Cambridge, MA: Harvard University Press, 2002); Karl Ameriks (ed.), *The Cambridge Companion to German Idealism* (Cambridge: Cambridge University Press, 2000); Paul W. Franks, *All or Nothing: Systematicity, Transcendental Arguments and Skepticism in German Idealism* (Cambridge, MA: Harvard University Press, 2005); Terry Pinkard, *German Philosophy, 1760–1860: The Legacy of Idealism* (Cambridge: Cambridge University Press, 2002). There has been a large new interest in the importance of early German Romanticism, both on its own terms and for an assessment of German Idealism: see especially Frederick Beiser, *The Romantic Imperative: The Concept of Early German Romanticism* (Cambridge, MA: Harvard University Press, 2003) and *The Early Political Writings of the German Romantics* (Cambridge: Cambridge University Press, 1996); Manfred Frank, *The Philosophical Foundations of Early German Romanticism*, Elizabeth Millán-Zaibert (trans.), (Albany, NY: SUNY Press, 2004); Dieter Henrich, *The Course of Remembrance and Other Essays on Hölderlin*, Eckart Förster (ed.) (Stanford, CA: Stanford University Press, 1997), and *Between Kant and Hegel: Lectures on German Idealism*, David S. Pacini (ed.) (Cambridge, MA: Harvard University Press, 2003).
3. "Real colour", Review of Willem A. deVries, *Wilfrid Sellars* (Chesham: Acumen, 2006), *Times Literary Supplement* (27 April 2007), 7.
4. John McDowell, *Mind and World* (Cambridge, MA: Harvard Univesity Press, 1994), ix; Wilfrid Sellars, *Empiricism and the Philosophy of Mind* (Cambridge, MA: Harvard University Press, 1997), §20.
5. Rorty claims he asked (an apparently not very amused) Sellars an adapted version of a question put by W. G. Pogson-Smith about Spinoza: "If a man choose to bind the spirit of Christ in the fetters of Euclid, how shall he find readers?" See *Empiricism and the Philosophy of Mind*, Introduction, 10.

6. Richard J. Bernstein, "McDowell's Domesticated Hegelianism", in *Reading McDowell: On "Mind and World"*, Nicholas H. Smith (ed.) (London: Routledge, 2002), 9–24.
7. Klaus Hartmann, "Hegel: A Non-Metaphysical View", in *Hegel: A Collection of Critical Essays*, Alasdair MacIntyre (ed.) (Garden City, NY: Anchor Books, 1972).
8. Some evidence of this shift can be seen in Terry Pinkard's preference for casting the "non-metaphysical" side of the debate instead in terms of a "post-Kantian" approach to Hegel (Pinkard, "Virtues, Morality and *Sittlichkeit*: From Maxims to Practices", in *European Journal of Philosophy* 7(2) (August 1999): 217–39). Jim Kreines has recently suggested that the more elastic terms "traditional" and "non-traditional" would better represent the current state of the debate than "metaphysical" and "non-metaphysical" ("Hegel's Metaphysics: Changing the Debate", *Philosophy Compass* 1(5), September 2006: 466–80).
9. The Heine story is probably invented, the Goethe story real. The latter runs as follows: Goethe invited Hegel, apparently without introducing him by name, for lunch with his daughter. After the meal had ended and Hegel had departed, Goethe asked his daughter: "How did you like the man?" "Strange," she replied, "I cannot tell whether he is brilliant or mad. He seems to me to be an unclear thinker." Goethe smiled ironically. "Well, well, we just ate with the most famous of modern philosophers – Georg Wilhelm Friedrich Hegel" (Günther Nicolin, *Hegel in Berichten seiner Zeitgenossen* (Hamburg: Meiner, 1970), 350–51).
10. A helpful discussion of this and the rather wide range of common misconceptions about Hegel can be found in the introduction to Pinkard, *Hegel*. See also the essays in Jon Stewart (ed.), *The Hegel Myths and Legends* (Evanston, IL: Northwestern University Press, 1996) and in particular Gustav E. Mueller, "The Hegel Legend of 'Thesis–Antithesis–Synthesis'," *The Journal of the History of Ideas* X (June 1958): 412–14.

Chapter 1: German Idealism and the young Hegel

1. Novalis, *General Draft of an Encyclopedia*, no. 45.
2. This is a point well underscored in Pinkard's biography, which views Hegel's life in the context of a tension between German local particularity and the universal ideals of the revolutionary age. See Chapter 4 below.
3. "Of the I as Principle of Philosophy", p. 82 in *The Unconditional in Human Knowledge: Four Early Essays (1794–1796)*, Fritz Marti (trans.) (Lewisburg, PA: Bucknell University Press, 1980), 63–128.
4. This fragment remained unpublished by Hölderlin during his lifetime; it was rediscovered in 1930 at an auction and only published in the Stuttgart edition of Hölderlin's works in 1961. See an account of its origin and imporance in Dieter Henrich, "Hölderlin on Judgment and Being: A Study in the History of the Origins of Idealism", in *The Course of Remembrance and Other Essays on Hölderlin*, Eckart Förster (ed.).
5. Hegel, Letter to Schelling, 2 November 1800, in *Briefe von und an Hegel*, Johannes Hoffmeister (ed.) (Hamburg: Meiner, 1952), vol. I, 59–60. With this should be compared Hegel's own *Systemfragment* of 1800 in *Early Theological Writings*, 309–19.
6. The thorough two-volume study of *Hegel's Development* by H. S. Harris, *Towards the Sunlight 1770–1801* (Oxford: Clarendon Press, 1972) and *Night Thoughts (Jena 1801–1806)* (Oxford: Oxford University Press, 1983) is the most complete resource for students interested in further research on Hegel's earliest years. Besides Harris, studies helpful for sorting out the developing Hegelian system in the Jena period include: Robert Pippin, "The Jena Formulations", ch. 4, *Hegel's Idealism: The Satisfactions of Self-Consciousness* (Cambridge: Cambridge University Press, 1989); Klaus Düsing,

"Spekulation und Reflexion. Zur Zusammenarbeit Schellings und Hegels in Jena", *Hegel-Studien* 5: 95–128 and *Das Problem der Subjektivität in Hegels Logik* (Bonn: Bouvier, 1976); H. Kimmerle, "Zur Entwicklung des Hegelschen Denkens in Jena", *Hegel-Studien* 4: 33–47 and *Das Problem der Abgeschlossenheit des Denkens. Hegels System der Philosophie in den Jahren 1800–1804* (Bonn: Bouvier, 1970); Rolf-Peter Horstmann, "Probleme der Wandlung in Hegels Jenaer Systemkonzeption", *Philosophischer Rundschau* 19: 87–118; "Jenaer Systemkonzeption", in Otto Pöggeler, *Hegel* (Freiburg/Munich: Alber, 1977), 43–58; "Über das Verhältnis von Metaphysik der Subjektivität und Philosophie der Subjektivität in Hegels Jenaer Schriften", *Hegel-Studien* 20: 181–95 and the "Preface" to G. W. F. Hegel, *Jenaer Systementwürfe* (Hamburg: Meiner, 1982); Otto Pöggeler, "Hegels Jenaer Systemkonzeption" and "Hegels Phänonmenologie des Selbstbewusstseins", both in *Hegels Idee einer Phänomenologie des Geistes* (Freiburg/Munich: Alber, 1973); and Michael Forster, *Hegel and Skepticism* (Cambridge, MA: Harvard University Press, 1989).

7. Hegel's first publication is actually the 1798 translation of a political pamphlet about Swiss politics (*Vertrauliche Briefe über das vormalige staatsrechtliche Verhältnis des Waatlandes zur Stadt Bern*), which was published anonymously.
8. In addition to these four works, which represent the longest of Hegel's published writings during the Jena period, there are also several short reviews which Hegel had published in the *Erlanger Literatur-Zeitung* and the shorter pieces in the *Critical Journal* itself: "How the Ordinary Human Understanding Takes Philosophy (as Displayed in the Works of Mr. Krug)" and the introduction to the *Critical Journal*, "On the Essence of Philosophical Criticism Generally, and its Relationship to the Present State of Philosophy". Hegel's *unpublished* manuscripts during the Jena period bear witness to other important moves towards the *Phenomenology*: on the one hand, there are elements of his emerging social and political philosophy that can be discerned here ("The Constitution of Germany", although this was abandoned by 1802; and perhaps even more strikingly "The System of Ethical Life", which should be compared with the *Natural Law* essay). On the other hand, it is especially Hegel's ongoing methodological interests that can best be seen in the several systematic outlines he produced in these years. His methodological advances can particularly be traced by connecting the "First Jena System Draft" (1803–4), "Second Jena System Draft: Logic, Metaphysics and Philosophy of Nature" (1804–5) and "Third Jena System Draft: Philosophy of Nature and Philosophy of Spirit" (1805–6) to the ultimate shape of the *Phenomenology*. I return to some of the concerns of these unpublished drafts at the end of the chapter.
9. *The Difference between Fichte's and Schelling's System of Philosophy*, H. S. Harris & Walter Cerf (trans.) (Albany, NY: SUNY Press, 1977), 89.
10. *Difference*, 90–91.
11. The review, which appeared in the Stuttgart *Allgemeine Zeitung*, was repudiated by Hegel in a signed footnote in the first issue of the *Critical Journal*: see Harris's discussion in *Difference*, 67, n. 10.
12. There are some other important, if subtle, differences between Hegel and Schelling visible in the essay: Schelling at this point, for example, is still focusing on intellectual intuition rather than, as Hegel, on the unity of reflection and intuition; Schelling also gives art, rather than Hegel's combination of art, religion and philosophy the ultimate unificatory role.
13. For a discussion of the importance of scepticism – particularly its ancient forms – for Hegel at Jena and in the *Phenomenology*, see Forster, *Hegel and Skepticism*.
14. *Relationship of Skepticism to Philosophy*, in *Between Kant and Hegel: Texts in the Development of Post-Kantian Idealism*, George di Giovanni & H. S. Harris (trans.) (Albany, NY: SUNY Press, 1985), 323.

15. *Faith and Knowledge*, Walter Cerf & H. S. Harris (eds) (trans.) (Albany, NY: SUNY Press, 1977), 69, *Critique of Pure Reason*, Transcendental Aesthetic, B 150–53, 160–61.
16. Hegel is at particular pains in this essay to link two things that Kant distinguishes: the supersensible, which is an idea of reason, and our sensible intuition of beauty, which is an aesthetic idea: "The aesthetic Idea is a representation of the imagination for which no [conceptual] exposition can be given; the Idea of Reason is a concept of Reason for which no demonstration can be given – demonstration in the Kantian sense being the presentation of a concept in intuition. As if the aesthetic Idea did not have its exposition [*Exposition*] in the Idea of Reason, and the Idea of Reason did not have its demontration [*Darstellung*] in beauty" (*Faith and Knowledge*, 87).
17. *Faith and Knowledge*, 190–91.
18. "We must completely reject that view of freedom whereby freedom is supposedly a choice between opposed entities, so that if +A and –A are given, freedom consists in selecting *either* +A or –A and is absolutely bound to this *either–or* . . . Freedom is rather the negation or ideality of the opposites, as much of +A as of –A . . ." (*Natural Law: The Scientific Ways of Treating Natural Law, Its Place in Moral Philosophy, and Its Relation to the Positive Sciences of Law*, T. M. Knox (trans.) (Philadelphia, PA: University of Pennsylvania Press), 89).
19. Pinkard, *Hegel*, 171.

Chapter 2: The *Phenomenology of Spirit*

1. On what became of the *Phenomenology* in view of the development of Hegel's later system, see below, Chapter 3.
2. For an account of the change in title, see Wolfgang Bonsiepen's discussion in the critical edition of the *Phenomenology* (*Phänomenologie des Geistes* (Hamburg: Meiner, 1988), 547–48; and Friedhelm Nicolin, "Zum Titelproblem der Phänomenologie des Geistes", *Hegel-Studien* 4 (1967), 113–23).
3. Ludwig Siep, *Der Weg der "Phänomenologie des Geistes": Ein einführender Kommentar zu Hegels "Differenzschrift" und zur "Phänomenologie des Geistes"* (Frankfurt: Suhrkamp, 2000), 63. Although Hegel uses the two notions of *phenomenology* and *experience* in new and distinctive ways, neither was a term original to him. As Wolfgang Bonsiepen has pointed out, both Fichte and Reinhold had used the term "phenomenology" (although it is not clear that Hegel was influenced by either). J. H. Lambert referred to "phenomenology" in his *Neues Organon* of 1764 as the name for the general science of how things appear to be but are not; a letter of Kant's from 1770 to Lambert describes Kant's own project in the first critique as a *phaenomenologia generalis*, the "purely negative science" that has to precede the actual reconstruction of metaphysics; in the *Metaphysical Foundations of Natural Science*, Kant insists that such a phenomenology moves not from "mere appearance" (*Schein*) to truth but rather from appearance (*Erscheinung*) to experience (*Erfahrung*). The notion of experience implicit in *Erfahrung* involves both a sense of what is *gone through* (in experiment or trial-and-error) and what *results*.
4. For a longer discussion of Hegel and the use of transcendental arguments, see Robert Stern, *Transcendental Arguments and Scepticism: Answering the Question of Justification* (Oxford: Clarendon Press, 2000), 164–75. For a criticism of transcendental readings (especially Taylor's), see Michael Forster, *Hegel's Idea of a Phenomenology of Spirit* (Chicago, IL: University of Chicago Press, 1998), 161–3.
5. Taylor, "The Opening Arguments of the *Phenomenology*", in MacIntyre, *Hegel: A Collection of Critical Essays*, 157–87.

6. On this point see Brady Bowman, *Sinnliche Gewissheit. Zur systematischen Vorgeschichte eines Problems des deutschen Idealismus* (Belin: Akademie Verlag, 2003).
7. Rolf-Peter Horstmann, "Hegel's *Phenomenology of Spirit* as an Argument for a Monistic Ontology", *Inquiry* **49**(1), February 2006: 114.
8. The German terms are *Herr* and *Knecht*. Miller's translation has the advantage of alluding not only to the feudal relationship implicit in "bondsman" but also to the significant religious connotations of *Herr* (as in Hegel's play on the language of the book of Proverbs that "the fear of the Lord is the beginning of wisdom" – see the discussion of *PhS*: §194 below). Because of the greater familiarity of the translation "master–slave", I have used those terms more prominently in this section.
9. Alexandre Kojève, *Introduction to the Reading of Hegel: Lectures on the "Phenomenology of Spirit"*, Allan Bloom (trans.) (Ithaca, NY: Cornell University Press, 1969), 6.
10. See George Armstrong Kelly, "Notes on Lordship and Bondage" in MacIntyre, *Hegel: A Collection of Critical Essays*, 189–218.
11. See John McDowell, "The Apperceptive I and the Empirical Self: Towards a Heterodox Reading of 'Lordship and Bondage' in Hegel's *Phenomenology*", in *Hegel: New Directions*, Katerina Deligiorgi (ed.) (Chesham: Acumen, 2006), 33–48; and Pirmin Stekeler-Weithofer, "Wer ist der Herr, wer ist der Knecht? Zum Kampf zwischen Denken und Handeln als Grundform jeden Selbstbewußtsein", forthcoming.
12. Cf. Myles Burnyeat, "Can the Skeptic Live His Skepticism?" in *The Skeptical Tradition*, Myles Burnyeat (ed.) (Berkeley, CA: University of California Press, 1983), 117–48.
13. Robert Brandom, *Tales of the Mighty Dead: Historical Essays in the Metaphysics of Intentionality* (Cambridge, MA: Harvard University Press, 2002), 222.

Chapter 3: The *Logic* and Hegel's system

1. There are a number of interesting differences between the two logics, but, along with many scholars, I think those differences can mostly be ignored when trying to get a sense of Hegel's larger project.
2. On the criticism by Schelling, Feuerbach and others of Hegel's presupposed end in the *Logic*, see Houlgate, *The Opening of Hegel's "Logic": From Being to Infinity* (West Lafeyette, IN: Purdue University Press, 2006), 54–9. On more recent engagements with Hegel's claims about presuppositionlessness, see, in addition to Houlgate's book, John Burbidge, *On Hegel's Logic: Fragments of a Commentary* (Atlantic Highlands, NJ: Humanities Press, 1981); Richard Winfield, *Reason and Justice* (Albany, NY: SUNY Press, 1988) and Alan White, *Absolute Knowledge: Hegel and the Problem of Metaphysics* (Athens, OH: Ohio University Press, 1983).
3. Houlgate, *Opening of Hegel's "Logic"*, 67ff.
4. *SL*, 49. But there is a difficulty in this prefatory passage in that Hegel also claims at the same time (in fact, in the same sentence as he insists on the justification that the *Phenomenology* provides) that the notion "emerges *within logic itself*" (*SL*: 48, italics mine).
5. *SL*: 28–9; in an 1831 footnote he indicates further that he will drop that title when the revised edition of the *Phenomenology* is published.
6. The curtailed "phenomenology" is now the second part of "subjective spirit", positioned between longer sections devoted respectively to anthropology (which on Hegel's view means the study of the human soul (*Seele*) from natural characteristics and feeling to habituation) and psychology (for Hegel this means the treatment of theoretical and practical spirit); in its curtailed form within this new context, the "phenomenology" recapitulates only the first three chapter headings of the 1807 *Phenomenology* ("consciousness" and "self-consciousness" and "reason"); and "three attitudes to objectivity" at the start of the *Encyclopedia* likewise involve some kind of

introduction, one that Hegel explicitly compares to the earlier introduction provided by the *Phenomenology*.

7. As Pinkard puts it, Hegel retains from this point forward in the development of his system a certain ambivalence about the status of the *Phenomenology* in relation to the system as a whole (see *Hegel*, 332–8).
8. Some Hegel scholars have suggested that the relationship between *Phenomenology* and the *Logic* is much like Wittgenstein's famous ladder, which can be tossed away once it has been used for ascent.
9. Hartmann, "Hegel: A Non-Metaphysical View", 101–2.
10. A version of this approach can be seen in Béatrice Longuenesse, *Hegel's Critique of Metaphysics*, Nicole Simek (trans.) (Cambridge: Cambridge University Press, 2007).
11. On Houlgate's differences with Pippin, see his *Opening of Hegel's "Logic"*, 137–43.
12. The difficulties here are discussed by Dieter Henrich, "Anfang und Methode der Logik", in Dieter Henrich, *Hegel in Kontext* (Frankfurt: Suhrkamp, 1971), 73–94.
13. *SL*: 83.
14. A sharp contrast can be seen, for example, between the readings of Pippin and Houlgate on this score. On Pippin's non-metaphysical reading, Hegel's concern is with the conditions for objects of thought and thus the *Science of Logic* begins with a claim – that thought can directly or intuitively think being itself, with no specific determination – whose insufficiency will be shown (*Hegel's Idealism*, 183). On Houlgate's reading, "Hegel does not implicitly reject the very idea of immediacy or pure being from the start but rather sets out to establish what pure being is" (*Opening of Hegel's "Logic"*, 280); being is not revealed to be mere illusion but is shown rather to be a "radical underdetermination of being's true character" (281).
15. Hegel himself in the short discussion he gives of the term *Aufhebung* at the end of the first triadic movement in the *Logic* (*SL*: 106–8), suggests a parallel to the Latin verb *tollere*, which inspired an English translation cognate with *sublatio*.
16. Bertrand Russell, *Our Knowledge of the External World as a Field for Scientific Method in Philosophy* (London: Allen & Unwin, 1914), 48–9.
17. For further discussion of the issue of contradiction in Hegel's *Logic*, see the essays by Robert Pippin ("Hegel's Metaphysics and the Problem of Contradiction") and Robert Hanna ("From an Ontological Point of View: Hegel's Critique of the Common Logic") in Stewart, *Hegel Myths and Legends*, 239–52 and 253–84; Richard Aquila, "Predication and Hegel's Metaphysics", *Kant-Studien* **64** (1973): 231–45; Katharina Dulckeit, "Hegel's Revenge on Russell: The 'Is' of Identity versus the 'Is' of Predication", in *Hegel and His Critics: Philosophy in the Aftermath of Hegel*, William Desmond (ed.) (Albany, NY: SUNY Press, 1989), 111–34; and ch. 2 of Longuenesse, *Hegel's Critique of Metaphysics*, 39–84.
18. "Wer denkt abstrakt?" in *G. W. F. Hegel: Jenaer Schriften 1801–1807*, vol. 2, *Werke* (Frankfurt: Suhrkamp, 1986), 575–81.
19. Two recent studies are helpful in exploring the difficulties in this middle section of Hegel's *Logic*: Longuenesse, *Hegel's Critique of Metaphysics* and Franco Cirulli, *Hegel's Critique of Essence: A Reading of Wesenslogik* (New York: Routledge, 2006).
20. In what follows, I discuss these moments according to the ordering in the *Logic*, which initially sets them forth in terms of essence's "showing", appearing and manifesting itself (*SL*: 391). The *Encyclopedia Logic* has a somewhat different way of presenting the moments of essence (the large divisions of which are "essence as ground", appearance and actuality). For a helpful comparison of the differences between the two accounts, see Taylor, *Hegel*, 258–96.
21. Although many Hegel scholars likewise translate *Begriff* as Concept, there is a significant counter-tradition that has preferred the term Notion (as does A. V. Miller in his English translation of the *Logic*).

22. On Hegel's famous dissertation "On the Orbits of the Planets", see Bertrand Beaumont, "Hegel and the Seven Planets", *Mind* **63** (1954): 246–8, reprinted in Stewart, *Hegel Myths and Legends*, 285–8, and Pinkard, *Hegel*, 107–8.
23. See Stephen Houlgate, *An Introduction to Hegel: Freedom, Truth and History*, 2nd edn (Oxford: Blackwell, 2005), 106–60.
24. This is a tricky passage for many reasons, not the least of which is that Hegel's comment here is preceded by the claim that "*for us*, Spirit has nature as its presupposition": how can spirit both have nature as a presupposition *and* be the *truth* of nature? For a discussion of this passage in general, see Michael Quante ("Die Natur: Setzung und Voraussetzung des Geistes. Eine Analyse des §381 der Enzyklopädie", in B. Merker *et al.* (eds) *Subjektivität und Anerkennung* (Paderborn: Mentis, 2004), 81–101), who takes the "us" to be the standpoint of common sense. On the importance of this passage in the context of McDowell's recent ascription of some form of "relaxed naturalism" to Hegel, see Christoph Halbig, "Varieties of Nature in Hegel and McDowell", *European Journal of Philosophy* **14**(2), (2006): 222–41.
25. For a discussion of this paragraph in connection with both ancient and contemporary philosophies of mind, see Michael Wolff, *Das Körper-Seele Problem: Kommentar zu Hegel, Enzyklopädie (1830) §389* (Frankfurt: Klostermann, 1992). Hegel's important appeal to Aristotle in connection with this question – he calls the "books of Aristotle on the soul . . . the most superb or the only work of speculative interest on this topic" – is discussed ably by Alfredo Ferrarin, *Hegel and Aristotle* (Cambridge: Cambridge University Press, 2001).

Chapter 4: Ethics and politics

1. Karl Marx, *Critique of Hegel's Philosophy of Right*, A. Jolin and J. O'Malley (trans.) (Cambridge: Cambridge University Press, 1970); Rudolf Haym, *Hegel und seine Zeit: Vorlesungen über Entstehung und Entwicklung Wesen und Werth der hegelschen Philosophie* (Berlin: Rudolf Gaertner, 1857).
2. "Hegel, who owed much to Rousseau, adopted his misuse of the word 'freedom,' and defined it as the right to obey the police, or something not very different" (Bertrand Russell, *A History of Western Philosophy* (New York: Simon & Schuster, 1945), 697; Karl Popper, *The Open Society and Its Enemies* (London: Routledge & Kegan Paul, 1945).
3. Herbert Marcuse, *Reason and Revolution: Hegel and the Rise of Social Theory* (London: Oxford University Press, 1941); Shlomo Avineri, *Hegel's Theory of the Modern State* (Cambridge: Cambridge University Press, 1972); see also Walter Kaufmann, "The Hegel Myth and its Method", *Philosophical Review* **60** (1951): 459–86 and T. M. Knox, "Hegel and Prussianism", *Philosophy* **15** (1940): 51–63.
4. I mention Wood and Pippin as the most prominent of a number of recent English-language commentators on Hegel's ethics and philosophy of agency. Other notable recent work specifically on Hegelian ethics in English includes that by Neuhouser, Williams and Hardimon and in the German tradition by Siep and Quante.
5. When Hegel arrived at Berlin in the autumn of 1818, there was under way a reform movement headed by Karl vom Stein, and later Karl August von Hardenberg: serfdom was abolished, the army and government were reorganized, and there was a stress on freeing the capitalist economy from feudalistic claims of the guilds. Plans were drawn up for a constitutional regime much like that described in the "State" section of the *Philosophy of Right*. But a reactionary counterwave suddenly began. In March 1819, a nationalistic student by the name of Karl Sand assassinated the playwright August Kotzebue, whom Sand claimed was an agent of the Russian tsar. In the wake of that

event, a set of regulations called the Carlsbad Decrees was put into effect, which meant a much stricter censorship of all publications with political content and the creation of special commissions with power to investigate and prosecute members of the university communities. (One of Hegel's great rivals, J. J. Fries, who was a teacher of the student Sand and whose ethics of conviction he linked directly to the assassination, lost his job as a result.) The result for Hegel was that he wrote a new preface, among other things, for the *Philosophy of Right* (which was finally published in autumn 1820).

6. *Lectures on Natural Right and Political Science: The First Philosophy of Right, Heidelberg 1817–1818 with Additions from the Lectures of 1818–1819*, Peter Wannenmann (transcr.), the staff of the Hegel Archives (eds) and Michael Stewart and Peter C. Hodgson (trans.) (Berkeley, CA: University of California Press, 1995).
7. See the two collections *G. W. F. Hegel: Political Writings*, Laurence Dickey and H. B. Nisbet (eds) (Cambridge: Cambridge University Press, 1999) and *Hegel's Political Writings*, T. M. Knox (trans.) (Oxford: Clarendon Press, 1964), as well as the forthcoming translation of Hegel's Heidelberg essay on the Württemberg constitution in *Hegel: Heidelberg Writings*, Brady Bowman & Allen Speight (trans.) (Cambridge: Cambridge University Press).
8. See Wood on Hegel's ethics as a theory of self-actualization: *Hegel's Ethical Thought*, 17–35.
9. See J. G. Fichte, *Foundations of Natural Right*, Frederick Neuhouser (ed.) and Michael Baur (trans.) (Cambridge: Cambridge University Press, 2000) and F. W. J. Schelling, "New Deduction of Natural Right", in *The Unconditional in Human Knowledge: Four Early Essays (1794–1796)*, Fritz Marti (trans.) (Lewisburg, PA: Bucknell University Press, 1980), 221–46. For a discussion of the treatment of this issue before the appearance of Kant's own *Rechtslehre* in 1797, see Wolfgang Kersting, "Sittengesetz und Rechtsgesetz – Die Begründung des Rechts bei Kant und den frühen Kantianern", in *Rechtsphilosophie der Aufklärung*, Reinhard Brandt (ed.) (Berlin: Walter de Gruyter, 1982), 148–77 and my "The *Metaphysics of Morals* and Hegel's Critique of Kantian Ethics", *History of Philosophy Quarterly* **14**(4), October 1997: 379–402.
10. Robert Pippin, "Hegel, Ethical Reasons, Kantian Rejoinders", in *Idealism as Modernism: Hegelian Variations* (Cambridge: Cambridge University Press, 1997), 92–128.
11. See, for example, Beiser, *Hegel*, 202–5, who makes clear why Hegel's distinction differs from Berlin's.
12. A point stressed by Alan Patten, *Hegel's Idea of Freedom* (Oxford: Oxford University Press, 1999).
13. Pippin, "Hegel, Ethical Reasons, Kantian Rejoinders".
14. John Locke, *The Second Treatise of Government*, Thomas P. Peardon (ed.) (New York: Macmillan, 1952), 27.
15. On the relation between Fichte and Hegel on the concept of right, see Frederick Neuhouser, "Fichte and the Relationship between Right and Morality", in *Fichte: Historical Contexts/Contemporary Controversies*, Daniel Breazeale & Tom Rockmore (eds) (Atlantic Highlands, NJ: Humanities Press, 1994), 158–80.
16. A primary difference between Kantian and Hegelian retributivism is that Hegel's insistence on punishment being something that the agent *wills* is at odds with Kant's claim that "it is impossible to *will* to be punished" (*Metaphysics of Morals* **6**: 335). The difference between their two positions thus rests on Hegel's development of a notion of the "rational will" or the "will in itself", to which the criminal is committed as a participant in the recognitively supported system of right.
17. Hegel's argument about punishment has received a fair amount of recent philosophical attention. Wood (*Hegel's Ethical Thought*, ch. 6) insists that any satisfactory theory of punishment must distinguish between two questions: (a) by *what right* the state punishes the criminal and (b) for what *positive reason* ought the state *actually inflict*

punishment? Wood claims that Hegel has an argument for the first but not the second, and raises yet a further difficulty about whether Hegel's argument can address the problem of legitimate punishment for people who are in a perpetual underclass. Robert Williams (*Hegel's Ethics of Recognition* (Berkeley, CA: University of California Press, 1997)) has suggested a counter to Wood's argument concerning the *positive reason* to punish based on Hegel's claim that a failure to punish amounts to positing transgression as right (see *PR*: §218, where Hegel insists that crime is an injury to a *universal* cause). Mark Tunick in *Hegel's Political Philosophy: Interpreting the Practice of Legal Punishment* (Princeton, NJ: Princeton University Press, 1992) suggests how Hegelians might wrestle with the difficulty of agents in an underclass environment.

18. On the significance of moral luck for Hegel, see Wood, *Hegel's Ethical Thought*, 142–3.
19. There is a long literature on Hegel's critique of Kantian ethics, but see particularly Wood's discussion of the emptiness charge, *Hegel's Ethical Thought*, 154–73; and Pippin's discussion in "Hegel, Ethical Reasons, Kantian Rejoinders".
20. Ludwig Siep, "The *Aufhebung* of Morality in Ethical Life", in *Hegel's Philosophy of Action*, Lawrence Stepelevich & David Lamb (eds) (Atlantic Highlands, NJ: Humanities Press, 1983). See also Frederick Neuhouser, *Foundations of Hegel's Social Theory: Actualizing Freedom* (Cambridge, MA: Harvard University Press, 2000), 232–5; and Daniel Dahlstrom, "The Dialectic of Conscience and the Necessity of Morality in Hegel's *Philosophy of Right*", *Owl of Minerva* **24**(2), Spring 1993: 181–9.
21. See the essays collected in *Feminist Interpretations of G. W. F. Hegel*, Patricia Jagentowicz Mills (ed.) (University Park, PA: Pennsylvania State University Press, 1996) and Neuhouser, *Foundations of Hegel's Social Theory*, 276–7.
22. Whether Hegel is ultimately successful in his treatment of the ethical side of civil society depends in large part on the possibility of some form of "Hegelian" resolution of issues which Hegel himself left to some extent hanging, such as the poverty question. Hegel is clear that poverty prevents adequate participation in ethical life for what he calls "the rabble" (*PR*: §244). But, although he insists that helping the poor is – for all that individuals *can* do – ultimately a matter of *universal* (and hence governmental, not individual philanthropic) concern, it is less clear what he thinks government *should* do, since the solution to poverty, on his view, cannot involve the mere transference of resources to the poor or make-work projects.
23. Hegel's German here is "*Der Gang Gottes durch die Welt, daß der Staat ist* . . ." Shlomo Avineri, one of the first serious scholars in the last two generations to re-examine the charges against Hegel's supposedly statist views, offered the alternative (and probably more correct) translation: "it is the way of God in the world, *that there is* [or should be] the state" – in other words, the claim is not that whatever the state does is divinely authorized, but rather that the existence of the state is something that is not merely a matter of (arbitrary human) caprice or choice. Or, as Hegel says at *PR*: §75A: "it is the *rational destiny of human beings* to live within a state, and even if no state is yet present, reason requires that one be established" (italics mine).
24. On Hegel and the reform period in Berlin, see especially Pinkard, *Hegel*, 418–68.
25. Fries to L. Rödiger, 6 January 1821. (Nicolin (ed.) *Hegel in Berichten seiner Zeitgenossen*, 221).

Chapter 5: Hegel and the narrative task of history

1. This trend in Anglo-American philosophy of history arose in the 1970s with the publication of Hayden White's *Metahistory: The Historical Imagination in Nineteenth-century Europe* (Baltimore, MD: Johns Hopkins University Press, 1973). Influenced by

postmodernism, hermeneutics and literary theory, its adherents (including White, Louis Mink and Frank Ankersmit) emphasized the rhetoric of historical narrative and the inseparability of historical "facts" from the (historically constructed) narrative in which they are embedded. See Daniel Little, "Philosophy of History", *Stanford Encyclopedia of Philosophy*, 18 February 2007 (http://plato.stanford.edu/entries/history/).

2. There has been a long and involved series of scholarly disputes about the status of the manuscript and notes tradition that has come down to us for these lectures. In this chapter, as in Chapter 6 on aesthetics, I have tried to indicate where someone with an interest in pursuing the scholarly issues might find resources but have kept a focus on what philosophically is most important to discern from the texts as we have them.
3. Duncan Forbes, in his introduction to the Nisbet translation of the *Lectures*, notes the dialectical structure of this section but does not bring out how that structure leads to Hegel's own narrative concept of the philosophical approach to history.
4. "Hegel on Faces and Skulls", in MacIntyre (ed.) *Hegel*, 229–30.
5. *PR*: §349; also *Vorlesungen über die Philosophie der Geschichte*, *Werke* (Frankfurt: Suhrkamp, 1986), XII.56: "In der Weltgeschichte kann nur von Völkern die Rede sein, welche einen Staat bilden." ["In world history, we can only speak of peoples when they form a state."]
6. Hannah Arendt, *Lectures on Kant's Political Philosophy*, Ronald Beiner (ed.) (Chicago, IL: University of Chicago Press), 5.
7. Francis Fukuyama, "The End of History?", *The National Interest* (Summer 1989): 3–18.
8. "The state that emerges at the end of history is liberal insofar as it recognizes and protects through a system of law man's universal right to freedom, and democratic insofar as it exists only with the consent of the governed. For Kojève, this so-called 'universal homogenous state' found real-life embodiment in the countries of postwar Western Europe – precisely those flabby, prosperous, self-satisfied, inward-looking, weak-willed states whose grandest project was nothing more heroic than the creation of the Common Market." Fukuyama, "End of History?", 5.
9. On this point, see Philip T. Grier, "The End of History and the Return of History", in Stewart, *Hegel Myths and Legends*, 183–98.
10. This is also a point made in Grier's discussion (*ibid.*).
11. "Aphorismen aus Hegels Wastebook [1803–1806]", *Jenaer Schriften 1801–1807*, 540.

Chapter 6: Art, aesthetics and literary theory

1. Henrich, *Between Kant and Hegel*, 74.
2. The most aesthetically charged text associated with Hegel in his earliest period is no doubt the so-called "Oldest Systematic Program of German Idealism" (a text written in his hand but whose authorship has been variously claimed for Schelling and Hölderlin as well). The development of Hegel's early concern with the Greek "religion of beauty" can be seen in the fragments he wrote during his Frankfurt period (1797–1800) collected under the title "The Spirit of Christianity and its Fate". For important continuities between the aesthetics of Hegel's emerging system at Jena and the ultimate lectures at Heidelberg and Berlin, see Otto Pöggeler, "Die Entstehung von Hegels Ästhetik in Jena", in *Hegel in Jena: Die Entwicklung des Systems und die Zusammenarbeit mit Schelling*, D. Henrich & K. Düsing (eds), *Hegel-Studien* **20** (Bonn: Bouvier, 1980).
3. Editions of the 1820–21, 1823 and 1826 versions of the lectures have been published separately: *G. W. F. Hegel: Philosophie der Kunst oder Ästhetik (1826)*, A. Gethmann-Siefert and B. Collenberg-Plotnikov (eds) (Munich: Wilhelm Fink, 2003);

G. W. F. Hegel: Vorlesungen über die Philosophie der Kunst. Berlin 1823. Nachgeschrieben von Heinrich Gustav Hotho, A. Gethmann-Siefert (ed.) (Hamburg: Meiner, 1998) and *Vorlesung über Ästhetik: Berlin 1820/1*, Helmut Schneider (ed.) (Frankfurt: Peter Lang, 1995). Hotho's text forms the basis of the widely available English translation of the lectures by Knox published under the title: *Aesthetics: Lectures on Fine Art.*

4. *Aesthetics* I: 101; *Vorlesungen* XIII: 139.
5. *Aesthetics* I: 7; *Vorlesungen* XIII: 21.
6. Kant, *Critique of Judgment* I. §42.
7. *Aesthetics* I: 427; *Vorlesungen* XIV: 13.
8. *Aesthetics* I: 79; *Vorlesungen* XIII: 111.
9. On this point, see Pöggeler, "Die Entstehung von Hegels Ästhetik in Jena".
10. Hans-Georg Gadamer, "Hegel und die Heidelberger Romantik", in Gadamer, *Hegels Dialektik. Sechs hermeneutische Studien* (Tübingen: Mohr, 1980), 87–97.
11. On Hegel's sources here, see Paul Oskar Kristeller, "The Modern System of the Arts", *Journal of the History of Ideas* **12** (1951): 496–527 and **13** (1952): 17–46.
12. *G. W. F. Hegel: Vorlesungen über die Philosophie der Kunst*, v–xiv.
13. *Aesthetics* I: 517; *Vorlesungen* XIV: 127–8.
14. See Robert Pippin, "What Was Abstract Art? (From the Point of View of Hegel)", *Critical Inquiry* **29** (Autumn 2002); Dieter Henrich, "Art and Philosophy of Art Today: Reflections with Reference to Hegel", David Henry Wilson *et al.* (trans.), in *New Perspectives in German Literary Criticism: A Collection of Essays*, Richard E. Amacher & Victor Lange (eds) (Princeton, NJ: Princeton University Press, 1979), 107–33, a translation of Henrich's original essay in *Poetik und Hermeneutik*, R. Koselleck & W. D. Stempel (eds) (Munich: 1972); Stephen Houlgate, *An Introduction to Hegel: Freedom, Truth and History*, 2nd edn, ch. 9. For a comparative discussion of Pippin and Houlgate, see Jason Gaiger, "Catching up with History: Hegel and Abstract Painting", in *Hegel: New Directions*, Katerina Deligiorgi (ed.), 159–76.
15. On Hegel's engagement with Romanticism, see Otto Pöggeler, *Hegels Kritik der Romantik* (Bonn: Bouvier, 1956; reprint, München: Fink, 1999).

Chapter 7: Religion and philosophy

1. The claim is that of Carl Ludwig Michelet, *Vorlesungen über die Persönlichkeit Gottes und die Unsterblichkeit der Seele* (Berlin, 1841).
2. On the relatively late emergence of Hegel's mature speculative philosophy of religion, see Walter Jaeschke, *Reason in Religion: The Foundations of Hegel's Philosophy of Religion*, J. Michael Stewart & Peter C. Hodgson (trans.) (Berkeley, CA: University of California Press, 1990).
3. Hegel's use of this phrase is in the context not of an iconoclastic atheism but rather of his attempt to underscore an element within Christianity itself that recognizes the place of the negative and the human within the notion of the divine: "'God himself is dead,' it says in a Lutheran hymn, expressing an awareness that the human, the finite, the fragile, the weak, the negative are themselves a moment of the divine . . ." *LPR* III: 326; see also *PhS*: §785.
4. Mark Lilla, *The Stillborn God: Religion, Politics and the Modern West* (New York: Knopf, 2007).
5. Hegel, *Lectures on the Philosophy of Religion: The Lectures of 1827*, Introduction.
6. Schleiermacher, *On Religion: Speeches to its Cultured Despisers*, Richard Crouter (trans.) (Cambridge: Cambridge University Press, 1988), 116 (italics mine).
7. *Berliner Schriften*, 123; quoted in Quentin Lauer, *Hegel's Concept of God* (Albany, NY: SUNY Press, 1982), 134.

8. *LPR* I: 40, quoted in Lauer, Hegel's Concept, 139.
9. "Positivity" essay, in *Early Theological Writings*, 71.
10. Hegel's preface to H. W. F. Hinrichs, *Die Religion im inneren Verhältnisse zur Wissenschaft* (Heidelberg, 1822), xviii–xix. For discussion of Hegel's remarks in the context of his relation to Schleiermacher, see Richard Crouter, "Hegel and Schleiermacher at Berlin: A Many-sided Debate", *Journal of the American Academy of Religion* **48** (March 1980): 19–43 and Walter Jaeschke, "Paralipomena Hegeliana zur Wirkungsgeschichte Schleiermachers", in *Internationaler Schleiermacher-Kongress Berlin 1984*, Kurt-Victor Selge (ed.), Schleiermacher-Archiv, vol. 1 (Berlin & New York: de Gruyter, 1985), 1157–69.
11. Pinkard, *Hegel*, 292–3.
12. Jaeschke, *Reason in Religion*, 257.
13. At least this is how he saw it in the 1824 version of the lectures; there is some variation in Hegel's treatments of these (in 1831, for example, he linked the teleological proof to Greek religion).
14. Hodgson *et al.*, *Lectures on the Philosophy of Religion*, Editorial Introduction, 76.
15. On the issues of this last section, see the treatment of Hans Friedrich Fulda, *Das Recht der Philosophie in Hegel's Philosophie des Rechts* (Frankfurt: Klostermann, 1967); a shortened version of this work can be found in Robert Pippin & Otfried Höffe (eds), *Hegel on Ethics and Politics*, Nicholas Walker (trans.) (Cambridge: Cambridge University Press, 2004) as "The Rights of Philosophy", 21–48.

Guide to further reading

Below are some suggestions for further reading on Hegel offered particularly with first-time readers in mind. More detailed suggestions about specific issues and texts are made in the notes; a wider research bibliography follows this section.

General books on Hegel (Introduction)

For the general reader who wants to get a sense of Hegel's work in the context of his life and the surrounding intellectual, cultural and political developments of his time, perhaps the best place to begin is with Terry Pinkard's acclaimed *Hegel: A Biography*. Pinkard's larger historical study of the intellectual developments in German philosophy, *German Philosophy: 1760–1860*, stretches that narrative back to the generation before Hegel and forward to the generation that follows him. Hegel's letters are a useful and surprisingly accessible resource for those beginning a study of his work, and the well-edited collection of his letters translated into English (*Hegel: The Letters*, Clark Butler and Christine Seiler (trans.)) frames important issues in the light of Hegel's philosophical development as a whole. For readers with at least some German, Walter Jaeschke's encyclopaedic *Hegel Handbuch: Leben–Werk–Wirkung* is a superb resource that gives a concise account of each phase of Hegel's life and work, with an unusually helpful compendium of the essential secondary literature in each case. Michael Inwood's *A Hegel Dictionary* is also a helpful reference work.

One-volume general introductory books on Hegel's philosophy that a first-time reader may especially want to consult include Frederick Beiser's *Hegel*, which links Hegel closely to the Romantics, and Stephen Houlgate's *An Introduction to Hegel: Freedom, Truth and History*, whose second edition includes one of the most approachable discussions of Hegel's philosophy of nature available. Of somewhat greater length but still approachable for first-time readers are Charles Taylor's *Hegel*, which gives the important historical context for Hegel's philosophical project, especially in its connections to the expressivist tradition, and the more analytic account of Hegel's project in Michael Inwood's *Hegel*. See also the essays in Frederick Beiser (ed.), *The Cambridge Companion to Hegel* and Jon Stewart's *The Hegel Myths and Legends*.

Much recent work has been done on Hegel and German Idealism. A good place to begin for someone with an interest in situating Hegel in the light of his philosophical predecessors might be with the essays in Karl Ameriks (ed.), *The Cambridge Companion to German Idealism*; Frederick Beiser's classic work, *The Fate of Reason: German Philosophy from Kant to Fichte* and more recent *German Idealism: The Struggle Against Subjectivism, 1781–1801* are both important resources offering a narrative of the development, as is the recent translation of Dieter Henrich's famous Harvard lectures, *Between Kant and Hegel: Lectures on German Idealism*, David S. Pacini (ed.), and the suggestive recent work of Paul W. Franks, *All or Nothing: Systematicity, Transcendental Arguments and Skepticism in German Idealism*. On Hegel's connection to German Romanticism, see again Frederick Beiser's recent work (*The Romantic Imperative: The Concept of Early German Romanticism* and *The Early Political Writings of the German Romantics*). Manfred Frank's *Unendliche Annäherung* (which has been translated in part as *The Philosophical Foundations of Early German Romanticism*) and Dieter Henrich's *The Course of Remembrance and Other Essays on Hölderlin* are among the most important sources for participants in the recent discussion of German Romanticism's connections with German Idealism. Important recent work on Romanticism's significance for philosophy can be found in Andrew Bowie's *From Romanticism to Critical Theory: The Philosophy of German Literary Theory* and the collection of essays in Nikolas Kompridis, *Philosophical Romanticism*.

Concerning Hegel's school and influence, the most important English-language intellectual history of the generation that immediately followed Hegel is John Edward Toews, *Hegelianism: The Path toward Dialectical Humanism, 1805–1841*; Karl Löwith's earlier *From Hegel to Nietzsche* is also especially useful. For a selection of representative texts from this period, see Lawrence Stepelevich (ed.), *The Young Hegelians: An Anthology*. Bruce Baugh's *French Hegel: From Surrealism to Postmodernism* examines Hegel's importance for twentieth-century French thought. Noteworthy recent comparative discussions of Hegel and other philosophers include Alfredo Ferrarin, *Hegel and Aristotle*; Will Dudley, *Hegel, Nietzsche and Philosophy: Thinking Freedom*; and Jon Stewart, *Kierkegaard's Relations to Hegel Reconsidered.*

Works mentioned in the text concerning Hegel's importance for Sellars, McDowell and Brandom: Wilfrid Sellars, *Empiricism and the Philosophy of Mind*; John McDowell, *Mind and World* and "The Apperceptive I and the Empirical Self: Towards a Heterodox Reading of 'Lordship and Bondage' in the *Phenomenology of Spirit*"; and Robert Brandom, *Making It Explicit: Reasoning, Representing and Discursive Commitment* and *Tales of the Mighty Dead*, especially chapter 6, "Holism and Idealism in Hegel's *Phenomenology*"; and chapter 7, "Some Pragmatist Themes in Hegel's Idealism".

The young Hegel (Chapter 1)

The thorough two-volume study of *Hegel's Development* by H. S. Harris, *Towards the Sunlight 1770–1801* and *Night Thoughts (Jena 1801–1806)* is the most complete resource for students interested in further research on Hegel's earliest years; see also the important studies by Laurence Dickey, *Hegel: Religion, Economics and Politics of Spirit, 1770–1807* and Georg Lukàcs, *The Young Hegel: Studies in the Relations between Dialectics and Economics*. Philosophically important English-language accounts of the Jena essays in their context include Robert Pippin, "The Jena Formulations", chapter 4, *Hegel's Idealism: The Satisfactions of Self-Consciousness* and Béatrice Longuenesse, "Point of View of Man or Knowledge of God. Kant and Hegel on Concept, Judgment and Reason" and "Hegel and Kant on Judgment", in her *Hegel's Critique of Metaphysics*.

The Phenomenology of Spirit (Chapter 2)

The current standard translation of the *Phenomenology of Spirit* is that of A. V. Miller; a new translation by Terry Pinkard for Cambridge University Press is forthcoming. There are a number of important English-language commentaries to the work as a whole which can guide a reader into the centre of the philosophical issues raised by the *Phenomenology*. For concision, a good place to begin is with Robert Stern, *Hegel and the "Phenomenology of Spirit"*; John Findlay's paragraph-by-paragraph précis of the *Phenomenology* in A. V. Miller's translation can also often be helpful for first-time reading. Especially helpful philosophical commentaries on the *Phenomenology* project as a whole include those of Terry Pinkard, *Hegel's Phenomenology: The Sociality of Reason*; Robert Pippin, *Hegel's Idealism: The Satisfactions of Self-Consciousness*, particularly chapters 5–7; Michael Forster, *Hegel's Idea of a Phenomenology of Spirit*; and Jean Hyppolite, *Genesis and Structure of Hegel's Phenomenology of Spirit*. For readers with German, Ludwig Siep, *Der Weg der "Phänomenologie des Geistes": Ein einführender Kommentar zu Hegels "Differenzschrift" und zur "Phänomenologie des Geistes"* is exemplary. For a learned resource for passage-by-passage work, consult H. S. Harris, *Hegel's Ladder*; Harris's shorter *Hegel: Phenomenology and System* may prove more accessible for first-time readers.

Specific studies of sections of the *Phenomenology* worth noting for initial readers include Yirmiahu Yovel, *Hegel's Preface to the "Phenomenology of Spirit"*; and, for those with German, Brady Bowman, *Sinnliche Gewissheit*; and the contrasting interpretations of the "Master and Slave" section in Alexandre Kojève, *Introduction to the Reading of Hegel: Lectures on the "Phenomenology of Spirit"* and George Armstrong Kelly, "Notes on Lordship and Bondage". See also the essays in Jon Stewart, *The Phenomenology of Spirit Reader: Critical and Interpretive Essays.*

Logic and system (Chapter 3)

Hegel's *Science of Logic* has been translated by A. V. Miller; there are two existing translations of Hegel's *Encyclopedia Logic*, the now-classic (but not always line-for-line accurate) version of William Wallace, a reprint of the original 1873 translation; and the new, more careful translation by T. F. Geraets, W. A. Suchting and H. S. Harris. (New translations from Cambridge University Press by George di Giovanni of the *Science of Logic* and by Klaus Brinkmann and Daniel Dahlstrom of the *Encyclopaedia Logic* are forthcoming.) Oxford University Press has recently re-issued William Wallace and A. V. Miller's translation of *Hegel's Philosophy of Mind* with a new commentary by Michael Inwood. For those with scholarly interest in the development of the concrete parts of Hegel's system, there are multi-volume sets of both his philosophy of nature and his philosophy of subjective spirit edited by Michael John Petry (*Hegel's Philosophy of Nature* and *Hegel's Philosophy of Subjective Spirit*). Robert Williams has also recently translated the *Lectures on the Philosophy of Subjective Spirit, 1827–8.*

Useful commentaries include those by John Burbidge, *On Hegel's Logic: Fragments of a Commentary*; Stephen Houlgate, *The Opening of Hegel's Logic: From Being to Infinity*; Errol E. Harris, *An Interpretation of the Logic of Hegel*; J. M. E. McTaggart, *A Commentary on Hegel's Logic*; Paul Owen Johnson, *The Critique of Thought: A Re-Examination of Hegel's Science of Logic*; Giacomo Rinaldi, *A History and Interpretation of the Logic of Hegel*; Robert Stern, *Hegel, Kant and the Structure of the Object*; Michael Rosen, *Hegel's Dialectic and its Criticism*; and Clark Butler, *Hegel's Logic: Between Dialectic and History.*

Recent work of interest on Hegel's philosophy of mind includes Willem A. deVries, *Hegel's Theory of Mental Activity*, and Michael Wolff, *Das Körper–Seele Problem.* On Hegel's philosophy of nature, see Stephen Houlgate, *Hegel and the Philosophy of Nature*; Alison Stone, *Petrified Intelligence: Nature in Hegel's Philosophy*; John Burbidge, *Real Process: How Logic and Chemistry Combine in Hegel's Philosophy of Nature*; Dieter Wandschneider, *Raum, Zeit, Relativität: Grundbestimmungen der Physik in der Perspektive der Hegelschen Naturphilosophie*; Robert Cohen and Marx Wartofsky (eds), *Hegel and the Sciences*, and M. J. Petry, *Hegel and Newtonianism.*

Ethics and politics (Chapter 4)

H. B. Nisbet's translation of the *Elements of the Philosophy of Right*, edited by Allen Wood, with substantial annotation, is essential for study of Hegel's ethics and politics. Nisbet and Laurence Dickey's collection of Hegel's *Political Writings* brings together in a single volume most of Hegel's journalistic writing on political matters, with the exception of his Heidelberg essay, *Proceedings of the Estates Assembly of the Kingdom of Württemberg*, which is translated in Brady Bowman and Allen Speight, *Hegel's Heidelberg Writings* (forthcoming, Cambridge University Press).

Helpful commentaries on the *Philosophy of Right* can be found in Dudley Knowles, *Hegel and the Philosophy of Right* and in Adriaan Peperzak, *Modern Freedom: Hegel's Legal, Moral and Political Philosophy* and *Philosophy and Politics: A Commentary on the Preface to Hegel's "Philosophy of Right"*.

Important recent discussions of Hegel's ethical and political works include: Allen Wood, *Hegel's Ethical Thought*; Frederick Neuhouser, *Foundations of Hegel's Social Theory: Actualizing Freedom*; Robert Pippin, *Idealism as Modernism*; Alan Patten, *Hegel's Idea of Freedom*; Paul Franco, *Hegel's Philosophy of Freedom*; Steven B. Smith, *Hegel's Critique of Liberalism: Rights in Context*; Shlomo Avineri, *Hegel's Theory of the Modern State*; Michael Hardimon, *Hegel's Social Philosophy: The Project of Reconciliation*; Mark Tunick, *Hegel's Political Philosophy: Interpreting the Practice of Legal Punishment*; Robert R. Williams, *Hegel's Ethics of Recognition*; Norbert Waszek, *The Scottish Enlightenment and Hegel's Account of Civil Society*; Z. A. Pelczynski (ed.), *Hegel's Political Philo-sophy: Problems and Perspectives* and *The State and Civil Society: Studies in Hegel's Political Philosophy*; Lawrence Stepelevich and David Lamb (eds), *Hegel's Philosophy of Action*; Michael Quante, *Hegel's Concept of Action*; and Gillian Rose, *Hegel Contra Sociology*. See also the recent essays in Robert Pippin and Otfried Höffe (eds), *Hegel on Ethics and Politics* and Ludwig Siep's classic article "The *Aufhebung* of Morality in Ethical Life".

History (Chapter 5)

Hegel's Introduction to his *Lectures on the Philosophy of World History* is translated by H. B. Nisbet and has a helpful introduction by Duncan Forbes; see also George Dennis O'Brien, *Hegel on Reason and History*; Joseph McCarney, *Hegel on History*; Jon Stewart's *The Hegel Myths and Legends* has essays by Philip Grier, Reinhart Klemens Maurer and H. S. Harris on the topic of the "end of history"; on Hegel and the question of the future, with particular connection to Heidegger, see Catherine Malabou, *The Future of Hegel*.

Aesthetics and philosophy of literature (Chapter 6)

T. M. Knox's two-volume translation of *Hegel's Aesthetics: Lectures on Fine Art* is the best existing English translation of the Hotho version of the lecture series, but those with German who are interested in getting a closer sense of Hegel's own texts should consult the critical editions which have recently emerged.

For discussions of particular issues relating to Hegel's view of aesthetics, see Pöggeler's reissued *Hegels Kritik der Romantik*; Stephen Houlgate, *Hegel and the Arts*; Anne and Henry Paolucci (eds), *Hegel on Tragedy*; Mark William Roche, *Tragedy and Comedy*; Michael Schulte's *Die "Tragödie im Sittlichen"*; Paul Redding, *Hegel's Hermeneutics*; Allen Speight, *Hegel, Literature and the Problem of Agency*; Stephen Bungay, *Beauty and Truth: A Study of Hegel's Aesthetics*; William Maker (ed.), *Hegel and Aesthetics*; Dieter Henrich, "Art and Philosophy of Art Today: Reflections with Reference to Hegel" (a translation of Henrich's original essay in *Poetik und Hermeneutik*, R. Koselleck and W. D. Stempel (eds)); Martin Donougho, "Hegel on the Historicity of Art"; and Robert Pippin, "What Was Abstract Art? (From the Point of View of Hegel)".

Religion and philosophy (Chapter 7)

The multi-volume English translation of the *Lectures on the Philosophy of Religion*, translated by R. F. Brown, P. C. Hodgson, and J. M. Stewart with the assistance of H. S. Harris and based on the German edition of Walter Jaeschke, is currently being republished by Oxford University Press (those interested in a more quickly readable version can consult within that series the single volume that gives all of the material from the 1827 lectures). Peter Hodgson has also recently published a new translation of Hegel's *Lectures on the Proofs of the Existence of God.*

Specific works of note on Hegel's philosophy of religion include those by Emil L. Fackenheim, *The Religious Dimension in Hegel's Thought*; Quentin Lauer, *Hegel's Concept of God*; Peter Hodgson, *Hegel and Christian Theology: A Reading of the Lectures on the Philosophy of Religion*; James Yerkes, *The Christology of Hegel*; Stephen Crites, *Dialectic and Gospel in the Development of Hegel's Thinking*; Thomas A. Lewis, *Freedom and Tradition in Hegel: Reconsidering Anthropology, Ethics and Religion*; Walter Jaeschke, *Reason in Religion: The Foundations of Hegel's Philosophy of Religion*, J. Michael Stewart and Peter C. Hodgson (trans.); Alan Olson, *Hegel and the Spirit*; Cyril O'Regan, *The Heterodox Hegel*; Robert Wallace, *Hegel's Philosophy of Reality, Freedom and God*; and William Desmond, *Hegel's God: A Counterfeit Double?*

An abbreviated version of Hans Friedrich Fulda's classic *Das Recht der Philosophie in Hegels Philosophie des Rechts* is translated in Pippin and Höffe, *Hegel on Ethics and Politics*, as "The Rights of Philosophy".

Bibliography

Works by Hegel

Aesthetics: Lectures on Fine Art, 2 vols. Translated by T. M. Knox. Oxford: Clarendon Press, 1988.

Briefe von und an Hegel. Edited by Johannes Hoffmeister. Hamburg: Meiner, 1952.

The Difference between Fichte's and Schelling's System of Philosophy. Translated by H. S. Harris & Walter Cerf. Albany, NY: SUNY Press, 1977.

Early Theological Writings. Translated by T. M. Knox. Chicago, IL: University of Chicago Press, 1948.

Elements of the Philosophy of Right. Edited by Allen Wood and translated by H. B. Nisbet. Cambridge: Cambridge University Press, 1991.

The Encyclopedia Logic: Part I of the Encyclopedia of Philosophical Sciences with the Zuzätze. Edited and translated by T. F. Geraets, W. A. Suchting and H. S. Harris. Indianapolis, IN: Hackett, 1991.

Faith and Knowledge. Edited and translated by Walter Cerf & H. S. Harris. Albany, NY: SUNY Press, 1977.

Hegel: Heidelberg Writings. Translated by Brady Bowman & Allen Speight. Cambridge: Cambridge University Press, forthcoming.

G. W. F. Hegel: Political Writings. Edited by Laurence Dickey & H. B. Nisbet. Translated by H. B. Nisbet. Cambridge: Cambridge University Press, 1999.

Hegel: The Letters. Translated by Clark Butler & Christine Seiler. Bloomington, IN: Indiana University Press, 1984.

G. W. F. Hegel: Philosophie der Kunst oder Ästhetik (1826). Edited by A. Gethmann-Siefert and B. Collenberg-Plotnikov. Munich: Wilhelm Fink, 2003.

Hegel on Tragedy. Edited with introduction by Anne & Henry Paolucci. Garden City, NY: Anchor Books, 1962.

G. W. F. Hegel: Vorlesungen über die Philosophie der Kunst. Berlin 1823. Nachgeschrieben von Heinrich Gustav Hotho. Edited by A. Gethmann-Siefert. Hamburg: Meiner, 1998.

Hegel's Philosophy of Mind. Translated by William Wallace & A. V. Miller. Includes commentary by Michael Inwood. Oxford: Clarendon Press, 2007.

Hegel's Philosophy of Nature. Edited by Michael John Petry. London: Allen & Unwin, 1970.

Hegel's Philosophy of Subjective Spirit. Edited by Michael John Petry. Dordrecht: Reidel, 1978.

Hegel's Political Writings. Translated by T. M. Knox. Oxford: Clarendon Press, 1964.

Hegel's Preface to the "Phenomenology of Spirit". Translation and commentary by Yirmiahu Yovel. Princeton, NJ: Princeton University Press, 2005.

Hegel's Science of Logic. Translated by A. V. Miller. Atlantic Highlands, NJ: Humanities Press, 1969.

Introduction to H. W. F. Hinrichs, *Die Religion im inneren Verhältnisse zur Wissenschaft*. Heidelberg, 1822, xviii–xix.

Jenaer Systementwürfe. Hamburg: Meiner, 1982.

Lectures on Natural Right and Political Science: The First Philosophy of Right, Heidelberg 1917–1818 with Additions from the Lectures of 1818–1819. Transcribed by Peter Wannenmann. Edited by the staff of the Hegel Archives. Translated by J. Michael Stewart & Peter C. Hodgson. Berkeley, CA: University of California Press, 1995.

Lectures on the Philosophy of Religion. Edited by Peter C. Hodgson. Translated by R. F. Brown, P. C. Hodgson, J. M. Stewart & H. S. Harris. Berkeley, CA: University of California Press, 1988.

Lectures on the Philosophy of Subjective Spirit, 1827–8. Translated by Robert Williams. Oxford: Oxford University Press, 2007.

Lectures on the Philosophy of World History: Introduction, Reason in History. Translated by H. B. Nisbet, with an introduction by Duncan Forbes. Cambridge: Cambridge University Press, 1975.

Lectures on the Proofs of the Existence of God. Translated by Peter Hodgson. Oxford: Clarendon Press, 2007.

Natural Law: The Scientific Ways of Treating Natural Law, Its Place in Moral Philosophy, and Its Relation to the Positive Sciences of Law. Translated by T. M. Knox. Philadelphia, PA: University of Pennsylvania Press, 1975.

Phenomenology of Spirit. Translated by A. V. Miller. Includes analysis by J. N. Findlay. Oxford: Oxford University Press, 1977.

The Relationship of Skepticism to Philosophy. In *Between Kant and Hegel: Texts in the Development of Post-Kantian Idealism*, translated by George di Giovanni & H. S. Harris. Albany, NY: SUNY Press, 1985.

Three Essays, 1793–1795: The Tübingen Essay, Berne Fragments, The Life of Jesus. Edited and translated by Peter Fuss & John Dobbins. Notre Dame, IL: University of Notre Dame Press, 1984.

Vorlesung über Ästhetik: Berlin 1820/1. Edited by Helmut Schneider. Frankfurt: Peter Lang, 1995.

Vorlesungen über die Philosophie der Geshichte, Werke. Frankfurt: Suhrkamp, 1986. "Wer denkt abstrakt?". In *G. W. F. Hegel: Jenaer Schriften 1801–1807*, vol. 2, *Werke*. Frankfurt: Suhrkamp, 1986, 575–81.

Other works

Ameriks, Karl (ed.) 2000. *The Cambridge Companion to German Idealism*. Cambridge: Cambridge University Press.

Aquila, Richard 1973. "Predication and Hegel's Metaphysics". *Kant-Studien* **64**: 231–45.

Arendt, Hannah 1992. *Lectures on Kant's Political Philosophy*, Ronald Beiner (ed.). Chicago, IL: University of Chicago Press.

Avineri, Shlomo 1972. *Hegel's Theory of the Modern State*. Cambridge: Cambridge University Press.

Baugh, Bruce 2003. *French Hegel: From Surrealism to Postmodernism*. New York: Routledge.

Beaumont, Bertrand 1954. "Hegel and the Seven Planets". *Mind* **63**: 246–8. Reprinted in *The Hegel Myths and Legends*, Jon Stewart (ed.), 285–8. Evanston, IL: Northwestern University Press, 1996.

Behler, Ernst 1993. *German Romantic Literary Theory*. Cambridge: Cambridge University Press.

Beiser, Frederick C. 1987. *The Fate of Reason: German Philosophy from Kant to Fichte*. Cambridge, MA: Harvard University Press.

Beiser, Frederick C. (ed.) 1993. *The Cambridge Companion to Hegel*. Cambridge: Cambridge University Press.

Beiser, Frederick C. (ed. and trans.) 1996. *The Early Political Writings of the German Romantics*. Cambridge: Cambridge University Press.

Beiser, Frederick C. 2002. *German Idealism: The Struggle Against Subjectivism, 1781–1801*. Cambridge, MA: Harvard University Press.

Beiser, Frederick C. 2003. *The Romantic Imperative: The Concept of Early German Romanticism*. Cambridge, MA: Harvard University Press.

Beiser, Frederick C. 2005. *Hegel*. London: Routledge.

Bernstein, Richard J. 2002. "McDowell's Domesticated Hegelianism". In *Reading McDowell: On "Mind and World"*, Nicholas H. Smith (ed.), 9–24. London: Routledge.

Bowie, Andrew 1997. *From Romanticism to Critical Theory: The Philosophy of German Literary Theory*. London: Routledge.

Bowman, Brady 2003. *Sinnliche Gewissheit. Zur systematischen Vorgeschichte eines Problems des deutschen Idealismus*. Berlin: Akademie Verlag.

Brandom, Robert 1994. *Making It Explicit: Reasoning, Representing and Discursive Commitment*. Cambridge, MA: Harvard University Press.

Brandom, Robert 2002. *Tales of the Mighty Dead: Historical Essays in the Metaphysics of Intentionality*. Cambridge, MA: Harvard University Press.

Bungay, Stephen 1984. *Beauty and Truth: A Study of Hegel's Aesthetics*. Oxford: Oxford University Press.

Burbidge, John 1981. *On Hegel's Logic: Fragments of a Commentary*. Atlantic Highlands, NJ: Humanities Press.

Burbidge, John 1992. *Hegel on Logic and Religion: The Reasonableness of Christianity*. Albany, NY: SUNY Press.

Burbidge, John 1996. *Real Process: How Logic and Chemistry Combine in Hegel's Philosophy of Nature*. Toronto: University of Toronto Press.

Burnyeat, Myles 1983. "Can the Skeptic Live His Skepticism?" In *The Skeptical Tradition*, Myles Burnyeat (ed.), 117–48. Berkeley, CA: University of California Press.

Butler, Clark 1996. *Hegel's Logic: Between Dialectic and History*. Evanston, IL: Northwestern University Press.

Cirulli, Franco 2006. *Hegel's Critique of Essence: A Reading of the Wesenslogik*. New York: Routledge.

Cohen, Robert S. & Marx W. Wartofsky (eds) 1984. *Hegel and the Sciences*. Dordrecht: Reidel.

Crites, Stephen 1998. *Dialectic and Gospel in the Development of Hegel's Thinking*. University Park, PA: Pennsylvania State University Press.

Crouter, Richard 1980. "Hegel and Schleiermacher at Berlin: A Many-sided Debate". *Journal of the American Academy of Religion* **48** (March): 19–43.

Dahlstrom, Daniel 1993. "The Dialectic of Conscience and the Necessity of Morality in Hegel's *Philosophy of Right*". *Owl of Minerva* **24**(2), Spring: 181–9.

Desmond, William 2003. *Hegel's God: A Counterfeit Double?* Aldershot: Ashgate.

DeVries, Willem A. 1988. *Hegel's Theory of Mental Activity: An Introduction to Theoretical Spirit*. Ithaca, NY: Cornell University Press.

Dickey, Laurence 1987. *Hegel: Religion, Economics and Politics of Spirit, 1770–1807*. Cambridge: Cambridge University Press.

Donougho, Martin 1998. "Hegel on the Historicity of Art". In *Encyclopedia of Aesthetics*, Vol. 3, Michael Kelly (ed.), 365–9. Oxford: Oxford University Press.

Dudley, Will 2002. *Hegel, Nietzsche and Philosophy: Thinking Freedom*. Cambridge: Cambridge University Press.

Dulckeit, Katharina 1989. "Hegel's Revenge on Russell: The 'Is' of Identity versus the 'Is' of Predication". In *Hegel and His Critics: Philosophy in the Aftermath of Hegel*, William Desmond (ed.), 111–34. Albany, NY: SUNY Press.

Düsing, Klaus 1969. "Spekulation und Reflexion. Zur Zusammenarbeit Schellings und Hegels in Jena". *Hegel-Studien* 5: 95–128.

Düsing, Klaus 1976. *Das Problem der Subjektivität in Hegels Logik*. Bonn: Bouvier.

Fackenheim, Emil L. 1967. *The Religious Dimension in Hegel's Thought*. Bloomington, IN: Indiana University Press.

Ferrarin, Alfredo 2001. *Hegel and Aristotle*. Cambridge: Cambridge University Press.

Fichte, J. G. 2000. *Foundations of Natural Right*, Frederick Neuhouser (ed.), Michael Baur (trans.). Cambridge: Cambridge University Press.

Flay, Joseph 1984. *Hegel's Quest for Certainty*. Albany, NY: SUNY Press.

Forster, Michael N. 1989. *Hegel and Skepticism*. Cambridge, MA: Harvard University Press.

Forster, Michael N. 1998. *Hegel's Idea of a Phenomenology of Spirit*. Chicago, IL: University of Chicago Press.

Förster, Eckart 2002. "The Importance of §§76, 77 of the *Critique of Judgment* for the Development of Post-Kantian Philosophy". *Zeitschrift für philosophische Forschung* **56**(2): 169–90.

Franco, Paul 1999. *Hegel's Philosophy of Freedom*. New Haven, CT: Yale University Press.

Frank, Manfred 2004. *The Philosophical Foundations of Early German Romanticism*, Elizabeth Millán-Zaubert (trans.). Albany, NY: SUNY Press.

Franks, Paul W. 2005. *All or Nothing: Systematicity, Transcendental Arguments and Skepticism in German Idealism*. Cambridge, MA: Harvard University Press.

Fukuyama, Francis 1989. "The End of History?" *The National Interest*, Summer: 3–18.

Fulda, Hans Friedrich [1967] 2004. *Das Recht der Philosophie in Hegels Philosophie des Rechts*. Frankfurt: Klostermann. In *Hegel on Ethics and Politics* as "The Rights of Philosophy", Robert Pippin & Otfried Höffe (eds), 21–48. Cambridge: Cambridge University Press.

Gadamer, Hans-Georg 1980. *Die Heidelberger Romantik*. In his *Hegels Dialektik. Sechs hermeneutische Studien*, 87–97. Tübingen: Mohr.

Gaiger, Jason 2006. "Catching up with History: Hegel and Abstract Painting". In *Hegel: New Directions*, Katerina Deligiorgi (ed.), 159–76. Chesham: Acumen.

Grier, Philip T. 1996. "The End of History and the Return of History". In *The Hegel Myths and Legends*, Jon Stewart (ed.). Evanston, IL: Northwestern University Press.

Habermas, Jürgen 1987. *The Philosophical Discourse of Modernity: Twelve Lectures*, Frederick G. Lawrence (trans.). Cambridge, MA: MIT Press.

Halbig, Christoph 2006. "Varieties of Nature in Hegel and McDowell". *European Journal of Philosophy* **14**(2): 222–41.

Hanna, Robert 1996. "From an Ontological Point of View. Hegel's Critique of the Common Logic". In *The Hegel Myths and Legends*, Jon Stewart (ed.), 253–84. Evanston, IL: Northwestern University Press.

Hardimon, Michael O. 1994. *Hegel's Social Philosophy: The Project of Reconciliation*. Cambridge: Cambridge University Press.

Harris, Errol E. 1983. *An Interpretation of the Logic of Hegel*. Lanham, MD: University Press of America.

Harris, H. S. 1972. *Hegel's Development: Toward the Sunlight, 1770–1801*. Oxford: Clarendon Press.

Harris, H. S. 1983. *Hegel's Development, Night Thoughts (Jena 1801–1806)*. Oxford: Oxford University Press.

Harris, H. S. 1995. *Hegel: Phenomenology and System*. Indianapolis, IN: Hackett.

Harris, H. S. 1997. *Hegel's Ladder*. Indianapolis, IN: Hackett.

Hartmann, Klaus 1972. "Hegel: A Non-Metaphysical View". In *Hegel: A Collection of Critical Essays*, Alasdair MacIntyre (ed.), 101–24. New York: Anchor Books.

Haym, Rudolf 1857. *Hegel und seine Zeit: Vorlesungen über Entstehung und Entwicklung Wesen und Werth der hegelschen Philosophie*. Berlin: Rudolf Gaertner.

Haym, Rudolf 1870. *Die romanistische Schule. Ein Beitrag zur Geschichte des deutschen Geistes*. Berlin: Gaertner.

Heidegger, Martin 1988. *Hegel's Phenomenology of Spirit*, Parvis Emad & Kenneth Maly (trans.). Bloomington, IN: Indiana University Press.

Henrich, Dieter 1971. "Anfang und Methode der Logik". In *Hegel im Kontext*, Dieter Henrich, 73–94. Frankfurt: Suhrkamp.

Henrich, Dieter 1972. "Kunst und Kunstphilosophie der Gegenwart: Überlegungen mit Rücksicht auf Hegel". In *Poetik und Hermeneutik*, 2, R. Koselleck & W. D. Stempel (eds), 11–32. Fink: Munich.

Henrich, Dieter 1979. "Art and Philosophy of Art Today: Reflections with Reference to Hegel", David Henry Wilson *et al.* (trans.). In *New Perspectives in German Literary Criticism: A Collection of Essays*, Richard E. Amacher & Victor Lange (eds), 107–33. Princeton, NJ: Princeton University Press.

Henrich, Dieter 1997. *The Course of Remembrance and Other Essays on Hölderlin*. Edited by Eckart Förster. Stanford, CA: Stanford University Press.

Henrich, Dieter 1997. "Hölderlin on Judgment and Being: A Study in the History of the Origins of Idealism". In The *Course of Remembrance and Other Essays on Hölderlin*, Eckart Förster (ed.). Stanford, CA: Stanford University Press.

Henrich, Dieter 2003. *Between Kant and Hegel: Lectures on German Idealism*, David S. Pacini (ed.). Cambridge, MA: Harvard University Press.

Hodgson, Peter C. 2005. *Hegel and Christian Theology: A Reading of the Lectures on the Philosophy of Religion*. Oxford: Oxford University Press.

Horstmann, Rolf-Peter 1972. "Probleme der Wandlung in Hegels Jenaer Systemkonzeption". *Philosophischer Rundschau* **19**: 87–118.

Horstmann, Rolf-Peter 1977. "Jenaer Systemkonzeption". In *Hegel: Einf. in Seine Philosophie*, Otto Pöggeler (ed.), 43–58. Freiburg: Alber.

Horstmann, Rolf-Peter 1980. "Über das Verhältnis von Metaphysik der Subjektivität und Philosophie der Subjektivität in Hegels Jenaer Schriften". *Hegel-Studien* **20**: 181–95.

Horstmann, Rolf-Peter 2006. "Hegel's *Phenomenology of Spirit* as an Argument for a Monistic Ontology". *Inquiry* **49**(1), February: 103–18.

Houlgate, Stephen (ed.) 1998. *Hegel and the Philosophy of Nature*. Albany, NY: SUNY Press.

Houlgate, Stephen 2005. *An Introduction to Hegel: Freedom, Truth and History*, 2nd edn. Oxford: Blackwell.

Houlgate, Stephen 2006. *The Opening of Hegel's "Logic": From Being to Infinity*. West Lafayette, IN: Purdue University Press.

Houlgate, Stephen (ed.) 2007. *Hegel and the Arts*. Evanston, IL: Northwestern University Press.

Hyppolite, Jean 1974. *Genesis and Structure of Hegel's Phenomenology of Spirit*, Samuel Cherniak & John Heckman (trans.). Evanston, IL: Northwestern University Press.

Inwood, Michael 1983. *Hegel*. London: Routledge.

Inwood, Michael 1992. *A Hegel Dictionary*. Oxford: Blackwell.

Jaeschke, Walter 1985. "Paralipomena Hegeliana zur Wirkungsgeschichte Schleiermachers". In *Internationaler Schleiermacher-Kongreß Berlin 1984*, Kurt-Victor Selge (ed.), Schleiermacher-Archiv, vol. 1, 1157–69. Berlin: Walter de Gruyter.

Jaeschke, Walter 1990. *Reason in Religion: The Foundations of Hegel's Philosophy of*

Religion, J. Michael Stewart & Peter C. Hodgson (trans.). Berkeley, CA: University of California Press.

Jaeschke, Walter 2003. *Hegel Handbuch: Leben–Werk–Wirkung*. Stuttgart: Metzler.

Johnson, Paul Owen 1988. *The Critique of Thought: A Re-Examination of Hegel's Science of Logic*. Aldershot: Avebury.

Kainz, Howard P. 1976–83. *Hegel's Phenomenology*. 2 vols. Athens, OH: Ohio University Press.

Kaufmann, Walter 1951. "The Hegel Myth and its Method". *Philosophical Review* **60**: 459–86.

Kelly, George Armstrong 1972. "Notes on Lordship and Bondage". In *Hegel: A Collection of Critical Essays*, Alasdair MacIntyre (ed.), 189–218. New York: Anchor Books.

Kersting, Wolfgang 1982. "Sittengesetzt und Rechtsgesetz – Die Begründung des Rechts bei Kant und den frühen Kantianern". In *Rechtsphilosophie der Aufklärung*, Reinhard Brandt (ed.), 148–77. Berlin: Walter de Gruyter.

Kimmerle, Heinz 1965. "Zur Entwicklung des Hegelschen Denkens in Jena". *Hegel-Studien* **4**: 33–47.

Kimmerle, Heinz 1970. *Das Problem der Abgeschlossenheit des Denkens. Hegels System der Philosophie in den Jahren 1800–1804*. Bonn: Bouvier.

Knowles, Dudley 2002. *Hegel and the Philosophy of Right*. London: Routledge.

Knox, T. M. 1940. "Hegel and Prussianism". *Philosophy* **15**: 51–63.

Kojève, Alexandre 1969. *Introduction to the Reading of Hegel: Lectures on the "Phenomenology of Spirit"*. Lectures assembled by Raymond Queneau, Allan Bloom (ed.), James H. Nichols, Jr. (trans.). Ithaca, NY: Cornell University Press.

Kompridis, Nikolas (ed.) 2006. *Philosophical Romanticism*. London: Routledge.

Kreines, Jim 2006. "Hegel's Metaphysics: Changing the Debate". *Philosophy Compass* **1**(5), September: 466–80.

Kristeller, Paul Oskar 1951/1952. "The Modern System of the Arts". *Journal of the History of Ideas* **12**: 496–527 and **13**: 17–46.

Lacoue-Labarthe, Philippe & Jean-Luc Nancy 1988. *The Literary Absolute: The Theory of Literature in German Romanticism*, Philip Bernard & Cheryl Lester (trans.). Albany, NY: SUNY Press.

Lauer, Quentin 1976. *A Reading of Hegel's Phenomenology of Spirit*. New York: Fordham University Press.

Lauer, Quentin 1982. *Hegel's Concept of God*. Albany, NY: SUNY Press.

Lewis, Thomas A. 2005. *Freedom and Tradition in Hegel: Reconsidering Anthropology, Ethics and Religion*. Notre Dame, IL: University of Notre Dame Press.

Lilla, Mark 2007. *The Stillborn God: Religion, Politics and the Modern West*. New York: Knopf.

Little, Daniel 2007. "Philosophy of History". *Stanford Encyclopedia of Philosophy*, accessed 18 February 2007 (http://plato.stanford.edu/entries/history/).

Locke, John 1952. *The Second Treatise of Government*, Thomas P. Peardon (ed.). New York: Macmillan.

Longuenesse, Béatrice 2007. *Hegel's Critique of Metaphysics*, Nicole Simek (trans.). Cambridge: Cambridge University Press.

Löwith, Karl [1964] 1991. *From Hegel to Nietzsche: The Revolution in Nineteenth-Century Thought*, David E. Green (trans.). New York: Holt, Rinehart & Winston. Reprint, New York: Columbia University Press.

Lukács, Georg 1975. *The Young Hegel: Studies in the Relations between Dialectics and Economics*, Rodney Livingstone (trans.). Cambridge, MA: MIT Press.

MacIntyre, Alasdair (ed.) 1972. *Hegel: A Collection of Critical Essays*, Garden City, NY: Anchor Books.

Maker, William (ed.) 2000. *Hegel and Aesthetics*. Albany, NY: SUNY Press.

Malabou, Catherine 2004. *The Future of Hegel: Plasticity, Temporality, and Dialectic*, Lisabeth During (trans.). London: Routledge.
Marcuse, Herbert 1941. *Reason and Revolution: Hegel and the Rise of Social Theory*. London: Oxford University Press.
Marx, Karl 1970. *Critique of Hegel's Philosophy of Right*, A. Jolin and J. O'Malley (trans.). Cambridge: Cambridge University Press.
McCarney, Joseph 2000. *Hegel on History*. London: Routledge.
McDowell, John 1994. *Mind and World*. Cambridge, MA: Harvard University Press.
McDowell, John 2006. "The Apperceptive I and the Empirical Self: Towards a Heterodox Reading of 'Lordship and Bondage' in Hegel's *Phenomenology*". In *Hegel: New Directions*, Katerina Deligiorgi (ed.), 33–48. Chesham: Acumen.
McDowell, John 2007. "Real colour", Review of Willem A. deVries, *Wilfrid Sellars* (Chesham: Acumen, 2006). *Times Literary Supplement*, 27 April: 7.
McTaggart, J. M. E. 1910. *A Commentary on Hegel's Logic*. Cambridge: Cambridge University Press.
Michelet, Carl Ludwig 1941. *Vorlesungen über die Persönlichkeit Gottes und die Unsterblichkeit der Seele*. Berlin.
Mills, Patricia Jagentowicz 1996. *Feminist Interpretations of G. W. F. Hegel*. University Park, PA: Pennsylvania State University Press.
Mueller, Gustav E. 1958. "The Hegel Legend of 'Thesis–Antithesis–Synthesis'". *The Journal of the History of Ideas* X, June: 412–14.
Mure, G. R. G. 1965. *The Philosophy of Hegel*. London: Oxford University Press.
Neuhouser, Frederick 1994. "Fichte and the Reationship between Right and Morality". In *Fichte: Historical Contexts/Contemporary Controversies*, Daniel Breazeale & Tom Rockmore (eds), 158–80. Atlantic Highlands, NJ: Humanities Press.
Neuhouser, Frederick 2000. *Foundations of Hegel's Social Theory: Actualizing Freedom*. Cambridge, MA: Harvard University Press.
Nicolin, Friedhelm 1967. "Zum Titelproblem der Phänomenologie des Geistes". *Hegel-Studien* 4: 113–23.
Nicolin, Günther 1970. *Hegel in Berichten seiner Zeitgenossen*. Hamburg: Meiner.
O'Brien, George Dennis 1975. *Hegel on Reason and History: A Contemporary Interpretation*. Chicago, IL: University of Chicago Press.
Olson, Alan M. 1992. *Hegel and the Spirit: Philosophy as Pneumatology*. Princeton, NJ: Princeton University Press.
O'Regan, Cyril 1994. *The Heterodox Hegel*. Albany, NY: SUNY Press.
Patten, Alan 1999. *Hegel's Idea of Freedom*. Oxford: Oxford University Press.
Pelczynski, Z. A. (ed.) 1971. *Hegel's Political Philosophy, Problems and Perspectives: A Collection of New Essays*. Cambridge: Cambridge University Press.
Pelczynski, Z. A. (ed.) 1984. *The State and Civil Society: Studies in Hegel's Political Philosophy*. Cambridge: Cambridge University Press.
Peperzak, Adriaan T. 1987. *Philosophy and Politics: A Commentary on the Preface to Hegel's "Philosophy of Right"*. Dordrecht: Nijhoff.
Peperzak, Adriaan T. 2001. *Modern Freedom: Hegel's Legal, Moral and Political Philosophy*. Dordrecht: Kluwer.
Petry, Michael John (ed.) 1993. *Hegel and Newtonianism*. Dordrecht: Kluwer.
Pinkard, Terry 1994. *Hegel's Phenomenology: The Sociality of Reason*. Cambridge: Cambridge University Press.
Pinkard, Terry 1999. "Virtues, Morality and *Sittlichkeit*: From Maxims to Practices". *European Journal of Philosophy* 7(2), August: 217–39.
Pinkard, Terry 2000. *Hegel: A Biography*. Cambridge: Cambridge University Press.
Pinkard, Terry 2002. *German Philosophy, 1760–1860: The Legacy of Idealism*. Cambridge: Cambridge University Press.

Pippin, Robert 1989. *Hegel's Idealism: The Satisfactions of Self-Consciousness*. Cambridge: Cambridge University Press.

Pippin, Robert 1996. "Hegel's Metaphysics and the Problem of Contradiction". In *The Hegel Myths and Legends*, Jon Stewart (ed.), 239–52. Evanston, IL: Northwestern University Press.

Pippin, Robert 1997. *Idealism as Modernism: Hegelian Variations*. Cambridge: Cambridge University Press.

Pippin, Robert 1997. "Hegel, Ethical Reasons, Kantian Rejoinders". In *Idealism as Modernism: Hegelian Variations*, 92–128. Cambridge: Cambridge University Press.

Pippin, Robert. "The Jena Formulations". Ch. 4 in *Hegel's Idealism: The Satisfactions of Self-Consciousness*.

Pippin, Robert 2002. "What Was Abstract Art? (From the Point of View of Hegel)". *Critical Inquiry* **29**(1) Autumn: 1–24.

Pippin, Robert & Otfried Höffe (eds) 2004. *Hegel on Ethics and Politics*, Nicholas Walker (trans.). Cambridge: Cambridge University Press.

Plant, Raymond 1973. *Hegel*. Bloomington, IN: Indiana University Press.

Pöggeler, Otto 1973. "Hegels Jenaer Systemkonzeption". In *Hegels Idee einer Phänomenologie des Geistes*. Freiburg: Alber.

Pöggeler, Otto 1973. "Hegels Phänomenologie des Selbstbewusstseins". In *Hegels Idee einer Phänomenologie des Geistes*. Freiburg: Alber.

Pöggeler, Otto 1980. "Die Entstehung von Hegels Ästhetik in Jena". In *Hegel in Jena: Die Entwicklung des Systems und die Zusammenarbeit mit Schelling*, D. Henrich & K. Düsing (eds), *Hegel-Studien* **20**. Bonn: Bouvier.

Pöggeler, Otto [1956] 1999. *Hegels Kritik der Romantik*. Bonn: Bouvier. Reprint, München: Fink.

Popper, Karl 1945. *The Open Society and Its Enemies*. London: Routledge & Kegan Paul.

Quante, Michael 2004. *Hegel's Concept of Action*, Dean Moyer (trans.). Cambridge: Cambridge University Press.

Quante, Michael 2004. "Die Natur: Setzung und Voraussetzung des Geistes. Eine Analyse des §381 der Enzyklopädie". In *Subjektivität und Anerkennung*, B. Merker *et al.* (eds). Paderborn: Mentis.

Redding, Paul 1996. *Hegel's Hermeneutics*. Ithaca, NY: Cornell University Press.

Rinaldi, Giacomo 1992. *A History and Interpretation of the Logic of Hegel*. Lewiston, NY: Edwin Mellen Press.

Ritter, Joachim 1982. *Hegel and the French Revolution: Essays on the "Philosophy of Right"*, Richard Dien Winfield (trans.). Cambridge, MA: MIT Press.

Roche, Mark William 1998. *Tragedy and Comedy: A Systematic Study and a Critique of Hegel*. Albany, NY: SUNY Press.

Rockmore, Tom 2005. *Hegel, Idealism and Analytic Philosophy*. New Haven, CT: Yale University Press.

Rose, Gillian 1981. *Hegel Contra Sociology*. London: Athlone.

Rosen, Stanley 1974. *G. W. F. Hegel: An Introduction to the Science of Wisdom*. New Haven, CT: Yale University Press.

Rosen, Michael 1982. *Hegel's Dialectic and its Criticism*. Cambridge: Cambridge University Press.

Russell, Bertrand 1914. *Our Knowledge of the External World as a Field for Scientific Method in Philosophy*. London: Allen & Unwin.

Russell, Bertrand 1945. *A History of Western Philosophy*. New York: Simon & Schuster.

Schelling, F. W. J. 1980. "New Deduction of Natural Right". In *The Unconditional in Human Knowledge: Four Early Essays (1794–1796)*, Fritz Marti (trans.), 221–46. Lewisburg, PA: Bucknell University Press.

Schelling, F. W. J. 1980. "Of the I as Principle of Philosophy". In *The Unconditional in Human Knowledge: Four Early Essays (1794–1796)*, Fritz Marti (trans.), 63–128. Lewisburg, PA: Bucknell University Press.

Schleiermacher, Friedrich 1988. *On Religion: Speeches to its Cultural Despisers*, Richard Crouter (trans.). Cambridge: Cambridge University Press.

Schulte, Michael 1992. *Die "Tragödie im Sittlichen": Zur Dramentheorie Hegels*. München: Fink.

Sellars, Wilfrid 1997. *Empiricism and the Philosophy of Mind*. Cambridge, MA: Harvard University Press.

Siep, Ludwig 1983. "The *Aufhebung* of Morality in Ethical Life", Thomas Nenon (trans.). In *Hegel's Philosophy of Action*, Lawrence Stepelevich & David Lamb (eds), 137–153. Atlantic Highlands, NJ: Humanities Press.

Siep, Ludwig 2000. *Der Weg der "Phänomenologie des Geistes": Ein einführender Kommentar zu Hegels "Differenzschrift" und zur "Phänomenologie des Geistes"*. Frankfurt: Suhrkamp.

Singer, Peter 1983. *Hegel*. Oxford: Oxford University Press.

Smith, Steven B. 1989. *Hegel's Critique of Liberalism: Rights in Context*. Chicago, IL: University of Chicago Press.

Solomon, Robert C. 1983. *In the Spirit of Hegel: A Study of G. W. F. Hegel's Phenomenology of Spirit*. New York: Oxford University Press.

Speight, Allen 1997. "The *Metaphysics of Morals* and Hegel's Critique of Kantian Ethics". *History of Philosophy Quarterly* **14**(4), October: 379–402.

Speight, Allen 2001. *Hegel, Literature and the Problem of Agency*. Cambridge: Cambridge University Press.

Stace, W. T. 1955. *The Philosophy of Hegel: A Systematic Exposition*. New York: Dover.

Stekeler-Weithofer, Pirmin Forthcoming. "Wer ist der Herr, wer ist der Knecht? Zum Kampf zwischen Denken und Handeln als Grundform jeden Selbstbewußtsein".

Stepelevich, Lawrence S. (ed.) 1983. *The Young Hegelians, an Anthology*. Cambridge: Cambridge University Press.

Stepelevich, Lawrence S. & David Lamb (eds) 1983. *Hegel's Philosophy of Action*. Atlantic Highlands, NJ: Humanities Press.

Stern, Robert 1990. *Hegel, Kant and the Structure of the Object*. London: Routledge.

Stern, Robert 2000. *Transcendental Arguments and Scepticism: Answering the Question of Justification*. Oxford: Clarendon Press.

Stern, Robert 2002. *Hegel and the "Phenomenology of Spirit"*. London: Routledge.

Stewart, Jon (ed.) 1996. *The Hegel Myths and Legends*. Evanston, IL: Northwestern University Press.

Stewart, Jon (ed.) 1998. *The Phenomenology of Spirit Reader: Critical and Interpretive Essays*. Albany, NY: SUNY Press.

Stewart, Jon 2000. *The Unity of Hegel's Phenomenology: A Systematic Interpretation*. Evanston, IL: Northwestern University Press.

Stewart, Jon 2003. *Kierkegaard's Relations to Hegel Reconsidered*. Cambridge: Cambridge University Press.

Stone, Alison 2005. *Petrified Intelligence: Nature in Hegel's Philosophy*. Albany, NY: SUNY Press.

Taylor, Charles 1975. *Hegel*. Cambridge: Cambridge University Press.

Toews, John Edward 1980. *Hegelianism: The Path toward Dialectical Humanism, 1805–1841*. Cambridge: Cambridge University Press.

Tunick, Mark 1992. *Hegel's Political Philosophy: Interpreting the Practice of Legal Punishment*. Princeton, NJ: Princeton University Press.

Wallace, Robert M. 2005. *Hegel's Philosophy of Reality, Freedom and God*. Cambridge: Cambridge University Press.

Wandschneider, Dieter 1982. *Raum, Zeit, Relativität: Grundbestimmungen der Physik in der Perspektive der Hegelschen Naturphilosophie*. Frankfurt: Klostermann.

Waszek, Norbert 1988. *The Scottish Enlightenment and Hegel's Account of "Civil Society"*. Dordrecht: Kluwer.

Westphal, Kenneth 1989. *Hegel's Epistemological Realism: A Study of the Aim and Method of Hegel's Phenomenology of Spirit*. Dordrecht: Kluwer.

Westphal, Kenneth 2003. *Hegel's Epistemology: A Philosophical Introduction to the Phenomenology of Spirit*. Indianapolis, IN: Hackett.

Westphal, Merold 1978. *History and Truth in Hegel's Phenomenology*. Atlantic Highlands, NJ: Humanities Press.

Williams, Robert R. 1997. *Hegel's Ethics of Recognition*. Berkeley, CA: University of California Press.

Winfield, Richard 1988. *Reason and Justice*. Albany, NY: SUNY Press.

White, Alan 1983. *Absolute Knowledge: Hegel and the Problem of Metaphysics*. Athens, OH: Ohio University Press.

White, Hayden 1973. *Metahistory: The Historical Imagination in Nineteenth-century Europe*. Baltimore, MD: Johns Hopkins University Press.

Wolff, Michael 1992. *Das Körper–Seele-Problem*: *Kommentar zu Hegel, Enzyklopädie (1830) §389*. Frankfurt: Klostermann.

Wood, Allen W. 1990. *Hegel's Ethical Thought*. Cambridge: Cambridge University Press.

Yerkes, James 1983. *The Christology of Hegel*. Albany, NY: SUNY Press.

Index